SHADOWS OF THE PAST IN
CONTEMPORARY BRITISH FICTION

By the same author

TIME AND ENGLISH FICTION

SHADOWS OF THE PAST IN CONTEMPORARY BRITISH FICTION

David Leon Higdon

The University Of Georgia Press
Athens

Published in 1985 in
the United States of America
by the University of
Georgia Press, Athens,
Georgia 30602.

Printed in Hong Kong

ISBN 0-8203-0742-4

To
Andrew and Mary Ann

Contents

Preface

Shadows of the Past, a title incidentally which does not allude to J. R. R. Tolkien's *The Lord of the Rings*, began to shape itself in my mind during the first weeks of July 1977, although I did not realize it at the time. As I toured Wiltshire, visting Old Sarum, Stonehenge, Salisbury Cathedral, Longleat, Stourhead, and Wilton House with my eleven-year-old son, I began to wonder how living in a timescape in which every plot of land, every brook, every hill seems to have a name and a history affects the individuals who constantly see the past impinging on the present in very physical forms. As never before, the English landscape struck me as being a palimpsest in which past, present, and future co exist, sometimes comfortably, sometimes uneasily. The idea sank unheeded at the time into my thoughts as I directed my attention to a series of essays on Graham Greene but reasserted itself in 1979 as the result of my reading a number of contemporary novels. Suddenly the outlines for the study appeared fully developed, with the problem being less which novels to include in the discussion than which of the many to exclude.

I have incurred a number of debts during the writing of the book. First I must thank my University for granting me a Faculty Development leave for the 1979 fall semester. Particular thanks go to Professors Bernard Bergonzi and Owen Knowles who arranged lectures at the University of Warwick and the University of Hull which enables me to test some of the readings presented in the study. I also wish to thank the staffs of the McFarlin Library, University of Tulsa, the British Library, the Bodelian Library and the National Library of Scotland who graciously assisted me in the study of manuscripts, notes, letters and other material and who answered numerous questions. Thanks are also due the editors of the *D. H. Lawrence Review* and *Nineteenth-Century Fiction* who granted permission for the reprinting of parts of two earlier essays.

Finally, and most importantly, special thanks go to the various authors who granted interviews either in person or by letter. The warm courtesies extended to me by Richard Adams, Brian Aldiss, Margaret Drabble, John Fowles, Rayner Heppenstall, and Angus Wilson made my months in England, Scotland and the Isle of Man truly memorable. Their frank openness deepened and broadened my understanding of the contemporary literary scene and encouraged me to believe that my idea was worth pursuing. Valuable advice also came from Malcolm Bradbury, Diana Athill and Harvey Joanning.

D.L.H.

Acknowledgements

The author and publishers wish to thank the following who have kindly given permission for the use of copyright material: Random House Inc., and Jonathan Cape Ltd, for the extracts from *Frankenstein Unbound*, copyright 1973 by Brian Aldiss; Alfred A. Knopf, Inc., and Weidenfeld & Nicolson Ltd, for the extracts from *The Realms of Gold*, copyright 1975 by Margaret Drabble; Little, Brown & Co., and Jonathan Cape Ltd, for the extracts from *Daniel Martin*, copyright 1977 by John Fowles; Alfred A. Knopf, Inc. and The New American Library, Inc., for the extracts from *Royal Flash*, copyright 1970 by George Macdonald Fraser; Stein and Day Publishers and Hamish Hamilton Ltd, for the extracts from *The Go-Between*, copyright 1954, 1981 by L. P. Hartley; the Hutchinson Publishing Group Ltd, for the extracts from *The Woodshed*, copyright 1962 by Rayner Heppenstall; Viking Press, Jonathan Cape Ltd, and Curtis Brown Ltd, for the extracts from *I Am Mary Dunne*, copyright 1968 by Brian Moore; W. W. Norton & Co. Inc., and Wallace and Sheil Agency, Inc., for the extracts from *Wide Sargasso Sea*, copyright 1966 by Jean Rhys; Viking Penguin, Inc., Secker & Warburg, and Curtis Brown Ltd, for the extracts from *Anglo-Saxon Attitudes*, copyright 1956 by Angus Wilson; and Viking Penguin, Inc., Secker & Warburg, and Curtis Brown Ltd, for the extracts from *Late Call*, copyright 1964, 1965 by Angus Wilson.

List of Abbreviations

ASA	*Anglo-Saxon Attitudes* Angus Wilson
CD	*The Connecting Door* Rayner Heppenstall
DM	*Daniel Martin* John Fowles
F	*Flashman* George Macdonald Fraser
FC	*Flashman at the Charge* George Macdonald Fraser
FGG	*Flashman in the Great Game* George Macdonald Fraser
FL	*Flashman's Lady* George Macdonald Fraser
FU	*Frankenstein Unbound* Brian Aldiss
G	*Gog* Andrew Sinclair
GB	*The Go-Between* L. P. Hartley
HT	*Hard Times* Charles Dickens
IP	*The Intellectual Part* Rayner Heppenstall
J	*Justine* Lawrence Durrell
JE	*Jane Eyre* Charlotte Brontë
JTLJ	*John Thomas and Lady Jane* D. H. Lawrence
LC	*Late Call* Angus Wilson
MD	*I Am Mary Dunne* Brian Moore
PZ	*The Prisoner of Zenda* Anthony Hope
RF	*Royal Flash* George Macdonald Fraser
RG	*The Realms of Gold* Margaret Drabble
SB	*The Steel Bonnets* George Macdonald Fraser
TD	*Tess of the d'Urbervilles* Thomas Hardy
W	*The Woodshed* Rayner Heppenstall
WC	*A Word Child* Iris Murdoch
WSS	*Wide Sargasso Sea* Jean Rhys

Part I
Future Pasts

1 One Curious and Significant Melody

Half a century ago, the protagonist of Elias Canetti's *Auto-da-Fé* prophesied, 'A time will come when men will beat their senses into recollections, and all time into the past. A time will come when a single past will embrace all men, when there will be nothing except the past, when everyone will have one faith — the past.'[1] A most unlikely programme for the twentieth century this seemed in 1935, not only for England but for most of Western civilization. Henry Ford had already told Americans that 'History is bunk', and Filippo Marinetti, in his usual exclamatory hysteria, had condemned the Italian past as a 'forger', 'our most dangerous enemy', 'a gloomy prevaricator', and an 'execrable tutor'.[2] In philosophy, Friedrich Nietzsche had told the era that history must be 'seriously hated as a costly and superfluous luxury of the understanding' inducing a false morality through the memory, and Paul Valéry had called history 'the most dangerous product evolved from the chemistry of the intellect'.[3] In England, James Joyce's Stephen Dedalus had labelled history 'a nightmare'; and with considerable misgivings, Aldous Huxley envisioned a society in which knowledge of the past was at best a social blunder and at worst a crime against the state, and soon George Orwell's Winston Graham would be speaking of 'an endless present', in which the past had been 'scraped clean', 'erased', and 'actually abolished'.[4] Yet within 25 years, this prophecy had begun to be realized in English fiction as the past reasserted itself, marking one of those crucial boundaries which loosely divide one period from another. No longer a nightmare to be fled, no longer an irrelevancy to be ignored, at some point following World War II, the concept of and the attitude towards the past changed, and this change has manifested itself fully in the literature and the culture, requiring as new a metaphorical map as the one boldly offered by Virginia Woolf when she declared 'on or about December, 1910, human character changed'.[5]

Consider but one incident which suggests how dramatically the attitude towards the past has changed. In 1977, when John Percival, a BBC producer and archaeology buff, quietly advertised for individuals

3

willing to spend a year living in an Iron Age settlement, dressing, eating, working, and surviving as Iron Age man had, he received over one thousand applications. Percival, who believes that 'the only way to see what life was like in the past is to see people living in the past',[6] established a village site at Berwick St. John near Shaftesbury in Wiltshire, gave the selected 'villagers' crash courses in Iron Age crafts, and then planned, twice a week, to film the activities of this anachronistic village. On a brisk day in March 1977, 'three school-teachers, a hairdresser, a nurse, a doctor, a social worker, a builder, a mathematician, a National Farmers Union official, two students and three children . . . two dogs, three cows, four pigs, nine goats, 25 sheep, 40 chickens and some bees' shed the twentieth century and stepped back in time to cope through trial and error with a totally foreign way of life.[7] The villagers built a communal hut, fired pottery, grew crops, wove cloth, practised animal husbandry, and adjusted with general success to a slower paced life and to an emerging matriarchy, though as John Rockcliff, one of the volunteers, said, ' "It takes more than a year to leave this century." '[8] They emerged a year later with a new appreciation of the bath tub and the Wellington boot, but with a new awareness of self-sufficiency. Jill Grainger commented that 'above all I've enjoyed living in a community and seeing myself and others in terms of a group of people', and Kate Rossetti, one of the three teachers, agreed that 'Here you have a sense of belonging − of who you are and what you do.'[9] Perhaps, as Katherine Whitehouse objected in the *Observer*, they were only enacting a myth, 'a dream of simple communal living', but theirs was more than yet another communal experiment trailing in the wake of B. F. Skinner's *Walden Two*.[10]

This experiment could not have happened during the first half of the century, because the attitude towards the past would have precluded it.

As early as the 1890s, hostility towards the past had begun to define a new temper. When Thomas Hardy's Tess Durbyfield explains what the narrator labels 'the ache of modernism' to Angel Clare, she underlines a fear of the future and a hostility towards the past.[11] In her 'horrid fancies', she tells Clare, she sees 'numbers of to-morrows just all in a line, the first of them the biggest and the clearest, the others getting smaller and smaller as they stand farther away; but they all seem very fierce and cruel and as if they said, "I'm coming! Beware of me! Beware of me!" ' (*TD*, 105). When Angel probes her melancholy further, asking if she would like his assistance in studying history or reading, she abruptly rejects his offer, telling him

What's the use of learning that I am one of a long row only — finding out that there is set down in some old book somebody just like me, and to know that I shall only act her part; making me sad, that's all. The best is not to remember that your nature and your past doings have been just like thousands' and thousands', and that your coming life and doings'll be like thousands' and thousands'. (*TD*, 107)

The morbidly guilty, destructively proud, and disturbingly passive Tess is no anomaly in feeling isolated in a world of collapsing values yet fearful of groping towards new values in a new world. H. G. Wells' Time Traveller, never once entertaining thoughts of travelling back in time, flings himself into futurity only to be driven into despair and eventual nausea by the failure of the future to embody the scientific and social advances he had expected. Joseph Conrad's Jim believes the past is something to flee but finds that it destructively pursues him, rendering him unable 'to lay the ghost of a fact'.[12] Perhaps Kirylo Sidorovitch Razumov, the protagonist of Conrad's *Under Western Eyes*, captures the malaise best when he says, after breaking his watch but before re-enacting in minute detail the crucial events in his life, ' "To-morrow would be like yesterday." '[13] Marcel Proust, the pathologist of the past, added that the personal past, memory, was 'a kind of pharmacy or chemical laboratory in which chance guides our hand now to a calming drug and now to a dangerous poison'.[14] To many novelists, memory far more often selected the dangerous poison; indeed, the past itself reeked of such dangers that it was better avoided or destroyed — an idea far more prevalent among novelists than among poets and dramatists whose genres have always enjoyed a quite different relationship with the past.

Novelists thus joined forces with philosophers, revolutionaries, and other artists in seeing the necessity for a sharp break, a moment of absolute discontinuity, between the past and the present even though the moment may only have existed in the modernist mythology of the period.[15] The overthrow of tradition and the expulsion of history, became key ideas in modernist art, and they found companions in discontinuity within the sciences as well, which, within a decade, rediscovered Mendel's genetic experiments, heard Planck's quantum theory revealing a discontinuity in matter and energy, saw Einstein point his special theory of relativity, and ultimately confronted Heisenberg's indeterminacy principle.[16] The substitution of discontinuity, sequence, and cycle, for continuity, process, and line constitutes a major reinterpretation of the relationship the culture perceived between past, present, and future. Hayden White has thoughtfully and carefully documented the expulsion of history, the historian, and the historical consciousness from 'the first rank of the sciences', placing this expulsion in the decade preceding World War I when 'this hostility towards the historical consciousness and the historian gained wide currency among intellectuals in every country of Western Europe' and seeing it then expanding through later works by authors convinced that 'the historical consciousness must be obliterated if the writer is to examine with proper seriousness those strata of human experience which it is *modern* art's peculiar purpose to disclose'.[17] In *The Death of the Past*, J. H. Plumb has carried the melancholy note to the logical conclusion that an industrial and technological society may simply no longer need the past since its orientation towards change instead of conservation finds 'no sanction in the past and no roots in it'.[18]

In post-war art, however, the past in its three major manifestations of memory, tradition, and history, has reasserted itself, demanding attention, allegiance, and even homage from the present. By 1950, Western culture had begun to question seriously its break with the past, especially since the pastless present has given the world concentration camps, totalitarian governments, cold war, atomic bombs, and industrial pollution. Carl Jung analysed the new awareness and identified at least some of its causes:

We have plunged down a cataract of progress which sweeps us on into the future with even wilder violence the further it takes us from our roots. Once the past has been breached . . . there is no stopping the forward motion. But it is precisely the loss of connection with our past, our uprootedness, which has given rise to the 'discontents' of civilisation; and to such a flurry and haste that we live more in the future and its chimerical promises of a golden age than in the present, with which our whole evolutionary background has not yet caught up.[19]

Many dates offer themselves as boundaries for the new sensibility. Was it 1951 with the Festival of Britain? 1952 with the accession of Elizabeth II? 1953 with the coronation? Or some crucial date whose importance has yet to be recognized, such as the publication of Orwell's *Nineteen Eighy-Four* in 1949, a novel which makes a strong plea for the uses of the past? No date by itself will satisfactorily account for the shift, but the new attitude towards the past had begun to take definite form in the popular mind by the mid-1950s and the June 1953 coronation encouraged it by giving people the feeling not only that something was beginning but also that this something new was at the same time something very old. Lord Altrincham, now John Grigg, one of the most outspoken critics of the monarchy, penned an attack on the institution which also contains one of its more trenchant defences. 'The basic virtue of Monarchy', he wrote in 1957.

> is that it appeals to the imagination. It emphasizes the unity of the living with the living, of the living with the dead, and of the living with those yet unborn; for tradition reaches forwards as well as backwards. Thus, when we cheer the calm, dignified, serious and self-improving young woman who is now the Head of the Commonwealth . . . all citizens of the Commonwealth can share the excitement of creating a common tradition for the future; and in that process of creation Elizabeth of Windsor is the central figure.[20]

The seven thousand individuals crowded into Westminster for a ceremony little changed for a millenium and the millions throughout the world who heard or saw the procession and coronation would probably have agreed in principle with Lord Altrincham, though they might not have shared the excesses of the Brtish press which forecast a new Elizabethan Age. In a 30 May 1953 *New Statesman and Nation* advertisement, the reader sees the sixth volume of *A New History of Britain* opened to chapter XII, 'The New Renaissance 1953–2003', whose opening lines read, 'Just fifty years ago – in June, 1953 – Elizabeth II was crowned Queen at Westminster. From this, the year of her coronation, date the first steps towards Britain's recovery. At long last the nation's pride, the nation's will to leadership, re-asserted themselves. The second Elizabethan age was to witness, like the first, a far-reaching renaissance of the spirit'.[21] Lord Altrincham more pointedly emphasized the concept of continuity, an important reversal from the earlier discontinuity, the recognition that the future is vitally related to the past, and an awareness that tradition was not in and of itself a reactionary concept. With the accelerating changes confronting the average man daily, tradition did give him something to cling to, a point George V, who had been tutored by the constitutional historian, J. R. Tanner, voiced when he wrote 'the existence of the Crown serves to *disguise* change & therefore to deprive it of the evil consequences of revolution'.[22]

None of the authors discussed in this study was a monarchist in 1953, (and only one has become so since), but each felt the appeal of the coronation even when he or she attempted to resist it. Angus Wilson, for

example, 'urged perhaps by some innate Republicanism', spent the day
in Essex, planning to avoid the whole affair, but found himself drawn
to a television in a Trust Hotel bar. He later described the ambiguous
response of himself and the crowd in a short essay:

> It was fascinating to see them fight the strange beauty, the formal
> Byzantinism of the ceremony that appeared upon the screen. They
> were prepared, of course, for an occasional catch in the throat, a
> moment of lowered head, but the elaborate grace before them
> demanded less prefunctory reverence.... It was a people, then,
> dazed with ritual that poured out at the afternoon's end into the
> Essex countryside.[23]

Rayner Heppenstall, too, attempted to avoid that 'portentous ceremony'
by spending his day at a local London pub, but now looks back to the
moment with some feeling.[24]

By one of the coincidences history is given to, the accession and
coronation of Elizabeth II came as the logical conclusion to an earlier
public statement about the past, the Festival of Britain, planned as early
as 1947 but not staged until 1951. As chauvinistic and as insular as the
great exhibition of 1851 was international and imperial, the Festival, as
its official guide informed visitors, told 'the story of British contributions
to world civilization in the arts of peace. That story has a beginning, a
middle, and an end — even if that end consists of nothing more final
than finger posts into the future'. 'This story', the guide reminded its
readers, 'begins with the past, continues with the present, and ends with
a preview of the continuing future',[25] a somewhat hopeful note on which
to end even though the logic of the statement does not bear close
scrutiny. The links between past and present were to increase faith in
the future. The Exhibition of Industrial Power, Glasgow's contribution
to the Festival, even more didactically stressed the relationship. Its Hall
of the Future was arranged almost along Dantean lines: 'On entering,
the visitor walks in the present...' its catalogue read, 'looks down on
the past, and looks up to the future. In a series of pits below floor level
the great pioneers of the past are seen at work. Above is a shining cone
rising from the floor, its tip pulsating and throwing off great flashes
of lightning to a night sky which curves above it in a twinkling
hemisphere — the limitless future.'[26] For Brian Aldiss, who
apostrophized the Festival as 'a memorial to the future', the early 1950s
came as 'rather a hopeful punctuation ... new things were beginning'.[27]
Margaret Drabble recalls the Festival itself as an exciting time because

'suddenly you had Fun Fair, and space age, and neon lighting, and it was more of a change from the war than the coronation was'.[28]

Throughout its history, the English novel has offered variety, and the English novelists have responded to the new awareness of the past with a still reassuring variety, reassuring in that it suggests a new vitality and imaginativeness.[29] Specifically, the novel began to take three recognizable directions. Whereas Victorian fiction focused on the process of experience and modernist fiction concentrated on the moment of epiphany, much contemporary fiction turns to the retrospective dialogue created when an individual confronts his past. Brian Moore, author of three important retrospective novels, told an interviewer: 'I feel that when ordinary people are forced to examine themselves and when they're lucky enough to have that moment of insight — of seeing themselves — it's astonishing how they manage to get up and go on'.[30] He could have been speaking for Angus Wilson, William Golding, Rayner Heppenstall, Iris Murdoch, Doris Lessing, Lawrence Durrell, or a number of other novelists who believe that unexamined lives are not worth living and hence have turned their talents to retrospective narratives in which the act of looking backwards transforms the individual who becomes both subject and object. These narratives reflect the necessity of the historical consciousness called for in the 1950s by Wolfhart Pannenberg in *Basic Questions in Theology*: 'Only a conception of the actual course of history linking the past with the present situation and its horizon of the future can form the comprehensive horizon within which the interpreter's limited horizon of the present and the historical horizon of the text fuse together.'[31]

From the complexities of space–time continuums in Lawrence Durrell's *Alexandria Quartet* to the complexities of personality and web-like plot in Iris Murdoch's *A Word Child*, characters return to their individual pasts in attempts to understand. Pursewarden of *Justine*, in his attempt to achieve a 'sort of prism-sightedness' (*J*, 27),[32] wishes for psychic health and in the opening pages specifically says, 'I have come here to heal myself, if you like to put it that way . . .' (*J*, 12). He returns 'link by link along the iron chains of memory to the city . . . [he has] come so far away from . . . in order to understand it all' (*J*, 13). Murdoch's Hilary Burde, the 'word child' who has overcome the difficulties of hereditary and environment to rise from being an illegitimate orphan to being a Fellow at Oxford only to sink 'near to the bottom of the power structure' (*WC*, 28)[33] in a minor Whitehall office, finds that he too must return 'along the iron chains of memory' which have dominated his life before he can comfortably authorize a new self.

A second direction, equally marked, involves fiction imitating past fiction in a very self-conscious fashion. Recently, novelists such as Alain Robbe-Grillet and B. S. Johnson have polemically denounced authors who attempt any commerce with the fiction of the past. In *Aren't You Rather Young to be Writing Your Memoirs?*, Johnson wondered testily: 'Imagine the reception of someone producing a nineteenth century symphony or a Pre-Raphaelite painting today', and Robbe-Grillet has argued that 'repetition of the forms of the past is not only absurd and futile, but that it can even become harmful: by blinding us to our real situation in the world today, it keeps us, ultimately from constructing the world and man of tomorrow'.[34] There is indeed much to be said against art that immerses itself in a sentimental, nostalgic, or escapist involvement with the past; however, fewer and fewer novelists are meditating, as did Virginia Woolf, on how they can 're-form the novel' and instead tend more to echo Margaret Drabble's remark: 'I don't want to write an experimental novel to be read by people in fifty years, who will say, well, yes, she foresaw what was coming . . . I'd rather be at the end of a dying tradition, which I admire, than at the beginning of a tradition which I deplore.'[35] Some years back, Jacques Barzun mercilessly satirized novels at the end of such dying traditions for their self-conscious imitativeness:

> Hardy country. A Jamesian young man, whose father is a Dickens' character, steps out of a Galsworthy house just as a Jane Austen girl goes by. Thackeray suspicions are in order. Alas, the Meredith ahead! But no, the girl's father is a Trollope clergyman. Early a widower, he brought up his baby Austen as a Charlotte Yonge lady . . . Flaubert! Flaubert![36]

A novelist can be too conscious of past literature and, like the Angus Wilson protagonist, shout 'Oh damn Eng. Lit. that brought to one's mind always metaphors, symbols, and characters from books'[37] — perhaps the penalty a culture pays when it makes available a university education and fully acquaints a generation of potential writers with the major works, traditions, and conventions of the genre. Faced with the prospect of creating within the shadows of earlier works, contemporary writers have turned to at least three alternatives. They have adapted the tradition and even the form of earlier fiction, thus continuing the tradition in transformed shapes. They have engaged in a dialogue with earlier fiction, thus complementing and often completing its silences. Finally, they have rebelled against the assumptions and techniques of earlier writers and parodied them. In each instance, however, the newly created works stand inextricably tied to the earlier works.

In discussing the situation of today's young writers so keenly aware of earlier fiction, David Lodge spoke of the difficulties of writing burdened by the knowledge. The young writer, he feels, grows 'somewhat intimidated, fascinated and occasionally infuriated by the sense that it's all been done better than you'll ever be able to do it. You could see, I suppose, the parody techniques in that novel . . . [*The British Museum Is Falling Down*] . . . as a way of meeting ironically that particular problem'.[38] Parody is not the only answer, but it has been a frequently given one in post-war fiction. William Golding, for example, discarded three highly imitative novels before publishing *Lord of the Flies*, a twentieth century response to Robert Michael Ballantyne's *The Coral Island*. As Golding explained to an American campus audience, he adapted the story line, the characters, the setting, and the themes of Ballantyne's moralistically comfortable treatment of the Victorian ethos and inverted its 'truths' to twentieth-century readings, creating an essentially ironic rebuttal of earlier assumptions:

> Ballantyne's island was a nineteenth-century island inhabited by English boys; mine was to be a twentieth-century island inhabited by English boys .... One of our faults is to believe that evil is somewhere else and inherent in another nation. My book was to say: you think that now the war is over and an evil thing destroyed, you are safe because you are naturally kind and decent. But I know that the thing rose in Germany. I know it could happen in any country. It could happen here.[39]

Susan Sontag has suggested that parodies, even the very sophisticated parodies written by Golding, are a valid albeit decadent response but not an answer: 'The ghost of cultural goods', she has written, 'creates a kind of fatigue – having too many models, too many stimuli. And parody is one way of handling the problem and copping out at the same time.'[40] Parody meets a need but ultimately should also free the artist for his own independent style and vision. The 'imitations' of George Macdonald Fraser, Jean Rhys, Brian Aldiss, and John Fowles have moved into this area of answers in which the work frees itself from the Victorian sibling while still maintaining valuable links with the past, sometimes by simply consuming the earlier artifact.

A third and very significant development in post-war fiction has been the interest shown in a new group of protagonists–biographers, bibliographers, historians, geologists, anthropologists, archaeologists, and even paleontologists – whose lives are caught up with the past. These protagonists define the spirit of the age as did the artist protagonists in the fiction of the 1910s and 1920s. Their restorations, excavations, journeys, and research into a culture's past parallel their search for individual identities and utilize the culture's artifacts as complex metaphors for complex inner processes. Significantly, several historians, perhaps most obviously Angus Wilson and Andrew Sinclair, have turned to fiction, bringing to it the professionally trained historian's perceptions of scope and scale and an understanding of the relationship between the individual and those forces which gradually transform the geographical, economic, and intellectual boundaries of individuals, countries, and eras.

When a historian holding a double first from Cambridge and a doctorate in American history and known for such studies as *Prohibition: the Era of Excess*, *The Available Man: the Life Behind the Masks of Warren Gamaliel Harding*, *The Better Half: the Emancipation of the American Woman*, and *A Concise History of the United States* turns his talents to the writing of fiction, his readers might expect the conventional historical novel replete with famous battles, peopled by well-known figures, and grounded in descriptions of period customs, dress, and architecture. Instead, Andrew Sinclair gave his audience *Gog,* a fantastic, grotesque picaresque tale crammed with a millenium of English history, kaleidoscopic dreams, characters who wander freely in and out of identities, linguistic pyrotechnics, private and public myths, and a totally eclectic and idiosyncratic talent drawing freely on fiction, history, film, and comic strips. For psychological motivation, Sinclair has substituted 'an incredibly rich evocation of the past'.[41] *Gog* details the wanderings of Mr George Griffin, a university historian and British Army Intelligence Officer, a gigantic seven-foot tall man, stripped of identity at the end of World War II when his ship sinks and he washes up on a Scottish beach near Edinburgh, knowing only what the tattoos on his hands tell him – that he is Gog or Magog. The 36 chapters detail Gog's wanderings from Edinburgh to London and his quest for personal and national identity since his search for his name and his past becomes a nation's act of self-discovery. 'Within Gog,' writes Peter Wolfe, 'pulse the energies of the British folk. Whereas history records event, myth captures the essence of event, digging under a heap of adventure and misadventure to find the underlying pattern. *Gog* involves these patterns, or archetypes in different ways. They objectify images and situations that constitute the British spirit; they cohere as paradigms of British conduct.'[42]

Gog's journey reads like a travelogue — a film re-enacting the Battle of Hastings, Hermitage Castle, Hadrian's Wall, Durham Cathedral, Rievaulx Abbey, Marston Moor, Byland Abbey, York Minster, Glastonbury Abbey, Winchester, Stonehenge, Brighton Pavilion, Hampstead Heath — and in the hands of less a daring, less adventurous talent could easily have become nothing more than a sentimental wandering from site to site. Sinclair prepared himself for writing the novel by exploring the multi-layered timescape of the English and Scottish countryside on foot. He told his BBC audience:

> If you sleep out on Hadrian's Wall in a gale, looking towards Scotland, your actual physical experience compared with the Roman sentries' two thousand years ago is exactly the same. The weather has not changed, the view has not changed, the experience of cold and wind has not changed. At two in the morning all men are equal; it's equally blank and equally hard. And it was a pilgrimage, like for Gog.[43]

He then stressed his concern for personal and national identity, using the one as a metaphor for the other:

> I think as we lose one place in the world we're forced in on ourselves far more, and there's a lot to be said for losing that power and that one might discover Britain at the end of it instead of diffusing it over an imperial tradition. But the question of national identity is certainly on, and Gog is certainly to do with it, as a man seeks for his own identity from some mythological tradition.[44]

Sinclair has reiterated these thoughts in other interviews, which outline the keys to his themes and styles, and stress his 'obsession with mythology as the only root to keep a man hoping in this mean mechanized world'.[45]

Gog brawls his epic and mythic way to London and selfhood accompanied by characters who at one moment are his wife, brother, and a displaced evangelist named Weyland Merlin Blake Smith, and at the next are supernatural shape-shifters, the Wandering Jew, and Magog himself. Remembering that 'each man carries his own past within his own skull' (*G*, 175)[46], Gog 'the Baedeker of the English byways' (*G*, 407), wonders if his adventures are a game or history. Cluckitt, one of his various companions, tells him:

> "Theer's no difference at all between t' two. History plays wi' us half t' time, 'cos we must do just wha' she tells us. An' we play wi' history

t'other half, 'cos we never learn from t' mistakes o' others, so we go
on doing just as bad an' just t' same as ever. Thoo'rt history, owld
Goggie . . ." (*G*, 67)

By the end of his adventures in the phantasmogoria of his mind, the
palimpsest of the countryside, and the labyrinth of history, Gog arrives
at a new sense of identity and a new consciousness, knowing now that
'Memory is all, memory is all, a man is his memory . . .' (*G*, 485) and
understanding that a choice must be made to use the past as a force to
shape the future or to forget it in a debauch of Magog materialism and
mechanization, insights also glimpsed by the protagonists of *The Realms
of Gold, Anglo-Saxon Attitudes,* and *Daniel Martin.*

In 1931, Aldous Huxley stepped back for a moment from the bustling
activity, the multifarious babel, and the tensions of his age to ask himself
if he could find any common point of agreement. Yes, he wrote in *The
New Romanticism,* 'in the midst of this general confusion, it is possible to
recognize one curious and significant melody, repeated in different keys
and by different instruments in every one of the subsidiary babels. It is
the tune of our modern Romanticism'.[47] Today's 'curious and significant
melody' echoed in a variety of styles by a variety of talents is the
renewed interest in the pasts of characters, of fictional types, and of
cultures. As the individual character and the individual artists enter
into dialogue with the past, they become able to confront an unknown
future with a new awareness. The past, to these authors, is not a
nightmare from which one strives to awaken but rather is a 'mode of
playing with the total contents and values of our culture. It plays with
these as, say, in the great age of the arts a painter might have played
with the colors on his palette'.[48] In surveying the 'current almost
obsessional desire to preserve the past in a physical form', E. R.
Chamberlain met a Frenchman who felt he had an explanation.
' "World War II was the watershed," ' he told Chamberlain, ' "the
breakup of the European empire left scores of fragments looking for
centres and they found the centres of gravity in their own past." '[49]

Shadows of the Past chronicles, then, both a game played with the past
and a compellingly serious search through the past. The pages that
follow discuss this new attitude towards and concept of the past from
several angles, using as evidence novels drawn from creative and critical
strata, both popular and serious, since it is more important to locate
the 'significant melody' than to concentrate more narrowly on the works
of one author if we are to understand directions in contemporary fiction.
Offered as examples are works of older novelists who had begun to

publish before the war and younger novelists whose works have sold thousands of copies and novelists who have reached only very small audiences, 'popular' novelists and 'serious' novelists, and works from science fiction, the anti-novel, the anti-anti-novel, the traditional novel, experimental novels, parodies, and pastiches. The 'God's plenty' Dryden saw in Chaucer's *Canterbury Tales* still obtains in the English novel, even when one is tracing but one thematic melody.

Part II
Waves of Memory

Retrospection, the art of looking backwards and reviewing past events, structures much fiction, but at times goes out of fashion only to return with renewed vigour later. Retrospective fiction experienced one such eclipse during the nineteenth century. Little Victorian fiction is retrospective in nature, with the notable exception of Charles Dicken's *David Copperfield* and of Charlotte Brontë's *Jane Eyre* , which seldom exploit their retrospective framework and virtually no modernist fiction, except Ford Madox Ford's *The Good Soldier*, utilizes the retrospective structure. After World War II, however, retrospective art suddenly began to be exploited fully again. In 1937, the Catalonian surrealist, Juan Miro, using a magnifying mirror to help him render 'everything [he] saw in it, in the tiniest detail and on a very large scale', drew a self-portrait.[1] When he sold the drawing to James T. Soby, an American collector, 20 years later, he had it photographed, then enlarged the photograph to the drawing's original size, and finally superimposed a second self-portrait over it. The self-portraits juxtapose a painstaking though poetic realism with a deflatingly ironic image comprised of 'heavy black lines, a pair of ghoulish eyes and a head that sprouted three tufts of hair' embodying what Miro called 'a change of focus'.[2] Separated by contrasting styles, differing attitudes, a cataclysmic war, and a personal change in focus the two selves confront one another, manifesting discontinuous states of being. Juan Miro of the 1960s realized he simply no longer was the Juan Miro of 1937.

The English essayist, critic, and writer of short stories, V.S. Pritchett, addressed the same problems of the discontinuous self in his memoir, *Midnight Oil*. He opens his memoir with a description of himself staring at two photographs:

One is, I regret, instantly recognizable: A bald man, sitting before a pastry board propped on a table, and writing. He does little else besides sit and write. His fattish face is supported by a valance of chins; the head is held together by glasses that slip down a bridgeless nose that spreads its nostrils over a mustache. He is trying to find some connection with the figure in the other picture taken fifty years ago. He knows that the young fellow sitting on the table of a photographer's in Paris, a thin youth of twenty with thick fairish hair, exclaiming eyebrows, loosely grinning mouth and the eyes raised to the ceiling with a look of passing schoolboy saintliness, is himself. The young one is shy, careless, very pleased with himself, putting on some impromptu act; the older one is perplexed. The two, if they could meet in the flesh, would be stupefied, and the older one would certainly be embarrassed.[3]

Across the intervening 50 years, two very different V.S. Pritchetts stare at one another. The language of the paragraph underlines the dualities: bald, fattish, meditative, formal versus thickly haired, thin, active, careless. The older self is puzzled, perplexed, even disconcerted; the younger self is pleased, perhaps even confident. They are virtual strangers who happen to have shared the same name. Like William Golding's Sammy Mountjoy, the older Pritchett could exclaim 'he is not I. He is another person' and would probably agree that he is not a man who once sat on a photographer's table but rather is a man who remembers a young man once sitting on the table, posing and playing a role.[4]

More and more frequently, novelists of the 1960s and 1970s have turned to retrospective narratives in which protagonists suddenly, often quite unexpectedly, confront a past they have buried, fled, or repressed in some way, only to discover that the meeting of past and present brings healing, freeing, or releasing. These protagonists have discovered what Walter Benjamin long ago concluded in his discussion of Marcel Proust: 'a remembered event is infinite, a possible key to everything that preceded it and to everything that will follow it'.[5] The past functions as a key unlocking secrets about the present which needed to be unlocked so the promise of the future can be realized. It is as though Aristotelian reversal and recognition have been separated in time with the younger self experiencing the reversal and the older self achieving the moment of insight and understanding. Looking backwards may be a reconstitutive act in a number of contemporary novels, but looking backwards involves neither nostalgia nor sentimentality, because confrontation, not escapism, serves as the pivotal action in the novel. Two stories occur simultaneously – the story of the earlier self, and the story which results through the recapitulation of the earlier action by the older self. Neither Jane Eyre nor David Copperfield nor John Dowell is transformed by looking backwards, but L.P. Hartley's Leo Colston, Angus Wilson's

Sylvia Calvert, Rayner Heppenstall's Harold Atha, and Brian Moore's Mary Dunne are.

A cluster of conventions has begun to evolve in retrospective novels. In them, characters sit down with a box of photographs, letters, books, or other mementos collected or created by the earlier, discontinuous self and a meeting of the two selves evolves from the remembering. Photographs have been particularly favored by a number of authors, appropriately, since, as Lewis Hine has said, they are 'ever – the Human Document to keep the present and the future in touch with the past'.[6] Sometimes a death sparks the confrontation; occasionally, the present self meets an individual from his past, not a literal but rather a figurative ghost from the past, whom he can no longer avoid. In each instance, however, the character comes to see that he can get to the future only by going through the past, and sometimes the narratives are guided by metaphorical psychiatrists helping the protagonist heal himself by coming to terms with his past. In a complex way, the two selves re-fashion one another across the years. Because of certain crucial events or decisions, the earlier self largely made the later self what it is, but in turn the later self, in looking back, refashions the earier self through a new and often more mature perspective. Christopher Isherwood, one of the century's most autobiographical writers, has commented on this relationship quite perceptively in *Christopher and His Kind*:

> Christopher's declared reason for burning his Berlin diary was unconvincing. He used to tell his friends that he had destroyed his real past because he preferred the simplified, more creditable, more exciting fictitious past which he had created to take its place. This fictitious past, he said, was the past he wanted to 'remember.' Now that I am writing about Christopher's real past, I sadly miss the help of the lost diary and have no patience with this arty talk.[7]

Elsewhere, he explained even more candidly that, 'I write because I am trying to study my life in retrospect and find out what it is, what it is made of, what it is all about. The attempt to do this is ultimately frustrating, of course, but nevertheless the most fascinating occupation I can imagine.'[8]

Saying that looking backwards heals and frees implies a Freudian ethos in retrospective fiction, and, undoubtedly, the influence is there, but the novels are rarely case studies in neurotic personalities. Rather, they partake of the same world view pinpointed by Rudolf Bultmann in his Gifford Lectures:

Man who complains: 'I cannot see meaning in history, and therefore my life, interwoven in history, is meaningless', is to be admonished: do not look around yourself into universal history, you must look into your own personal history. Always in your present lies the meaning in history, and you cannot see it as a spectator, but only in your responsible decisions. In every moment slumbers the possibility of being the eschatological moment. You must awaken it.[9]

2 L. P. Hartley, *The Go-Between*, 'the past is a foreign country'

In August 1962, L. P. Hartley recalled his feelings when, at age four-and-a-half in 1900, he moved from Whittlesey in the Cambridgeshire fens to the cathedral city of Petersborough. 'It was the first time', he recalled,

> I was consciously aware of the weather–at least it was the first time the weather made a mark òn my memory. From then on, for many years, I always hoped that the long succession of hot days would be repeated, but unless my memory betrays me it never was, in England at any rate, until 1959. It became for me a kind of Golden Age – almost literally, for I think of it as being the colour of gold. I didn't want to go back to it but I wanted it to come to me, and I still do.[1]

Elsewhere, in *Promise of Greatness*, a collection of retrospective essays dealing with the experience of World War I, Hartley and others looked fondly back to the late Victorian and the Edwardian years as a time of almost prelapsarian innocence. The past was different, genuinely different, in mood and outlook, Hartley writes,

> the difference between feeling that life was then a boor, but is now a menace, does partly describe it; in those days hope took for granted what in these days fear takes for granted.... The First World War shook one's belief in the essential goodness of humanity–the belief that all's for the best in the best of all possible worlds that, with many conspicuous exceptions, had dominated Victorian thought.[2]

Thus, the opening line of Hartley's *The Go-Between* – 'The past is a foreign country: they do things differently there'[3] – is no casual generalization by the author but rather records an intense feeling on his part and hints a great sense of loss for the present at some point in

the past. The past may be a Golden Age for Hartley, but he also views
it as an age inevitably doomed since its dominant characteristics – its
innocence, its naïveté, its trust – are paradoxically both its major
weaknesses and attractions and also are as ephemeral as the English
weather. Hartley's interest in the past, however, is neither sentimental
nor nostalgic nor escapist. He wishes not to return to the past but rather
to have the past return to him. Once man enjoyed a golden relationship,
now lost because of the alienation, the destruction, and the disillusionment man has forced on man during the twentieth century. Change
and anxiety now go hand in hand, obliterating the slower pace of life
before World War I.

The Go-Between's epigraph, taken from one of Emily Brontë's four 'boy
of sorrow' poems, suggests the depths of Hartley's interest in the
relationship between the past and the present.[4] In the poem, whose
fourth stanza serves as the epigraph, the narrator observes a child leave
his 'cheerful play' one summer day to lie in the grass, sighing mournfully.
The narrator explains that these sighs come from a frustrated desire to
know what the 'portals of futurity' will bring:

> I knew the wish that waked that wail;
> I knew the source whence sprung those tears;
> You longed for fate to raise the veil
> That darkened over coming years. (ll. 5–8)

The narrator, who may be fate or time but in either case has the ability
to grant such visions, waits, watching his time, until summer and
autumn pass, and then on a 'doleful winter night' appears 'this evening
fell' 'To banish joy and welcome care' (ll. 19,24). But now the knowledge
is unwelcome, even feared:

> Those tiny hands in vain essay
> To thwart the shadowy fiend away;
> There is a horror on his brow,
> An anguish in his bosom now;–
> ...
> A fearful anguish in his eyes
> Fixed strainedly on the vacant air;
> Heavily bursts in long-drawn sighs
> His panting breath, enchained by fear. (ll. 33–40)

The narrator pictures the child who sees 'the sunshine disappear' but the process, very reminiscent of similar Wordsworthian experiences, cannot be escaped:

> But it is doomed, and mornings light
> Must image forth the scowl of night,
> And childhood's flower must waste its bloom
> Beneath the shadow of the tomb. (ll. 50–3)1

This poem prefigures and very well may have been a formative source for the novel. The parallels between the novel and the poem are many and striking, underlinng the relationship between innocent boy and knowing narrator, the opposition between cheerful summer days and doleful winter nights, the frightful disillusionment the future brings especially in terms of one's mortality, and the dialogue between past, present, and future. Missing, however, is the qualified victory over the future Leo Colston achieves in *The Go-Between*, for his hands manage 'to thrust the shadowy fiend away' but only at great expense to himself.

Samuel Taylor Coleridge wrote that 'the sense of Before and After becomes both intelligible and intellectual when, and *only* when, we contemplate the succession in its relations of Cause and Effect, which, like the two poles of the magnet manifest the being and unity of the one power by relative opposition...'.5 A century later, Leo Colston and a number of other characters have taken just such a programme as the route to resurrecting a partially dead being into full life again. The contrast between the foreign past and the menacing present structures the novel as the 12-year-old Leo Colston of 1900 and the 64-year-old Leo Colston of 1952 confront one another over a long forgotten diary in which the young Leo recorded the 18 most crucial days of his life. The events of 9–23 July 1900 changed the direction of his life, separated his older self sharply from his younger self, and will unexpectedly return to change his life a second time after he has reread the diary entries.6 The confrontation between past and present begins one winter evening, as in the poem, in 1952 between the hours of ten and twelve when Leo starts sorting through some boxes. In a 'rather battered red cardboard collar-box' (*GB*, 11), he finds a magnet, a lock, and the diary, objects which call him back to the past. They are 'children of the past' (*GB*, 11) announcing their names, and, 'for the first time for over fifty years, a recollection of what each had meant to me came back, faint as the magnets' power to draw, but as perceptible' (*GB*, 11). In addition to these, he also finds a photograph, score cards from the cricket match, several letters from his mother and to his mother, and a letter which has lain unopened for over half a century, detritus from his past which suddenly forces him to confront memories he has repressed all these years. He knows they contribute to his current condition:

> had it not been for the diary, or what the diary stood for, everything would be different. I should not be sitting in this drab, flowerless room, where the curtains were not even drawn to hide the cold rain beating on the windows, or contemplating the accumulation of the past and the duty it imposed on me to sort it out. I should be sitting in another room, rainbow-hued, looking not into the past but into the future; and I should not be sitting alone. (*GB*, 13)

Leo realizes that the diary explains his being and that he can only understand himself by 'unlocking' the diary. He can, after all, only unlock the combination by using his own name–L–E–O–the letters which form the combination. His realization that 'my secret – the explanation of me – lay there' (*GB*, 24) and his courage in confronting the facts in the diary enlarge his Proustian quest simply to recall. In *My Sister's Keeper*, published 18 years after *The Go-Between* Hartley again pointed the function of such objects as those Leo finds: 'we are part of you,' the objects say to the character, 'however humble or however valuable, . . . as long as you can see *us*, that person, and that place will still be vivid to you, and you won't have lost touch with your past life, which will be all the more precious to you, the older you grow'.[7] The art of recalling becomes therapeutic in that it matures and frees him to accept the adulthood he has refused. Hartley may perhaps have been oversubtle on this crucial point, because he only mentions once that the narrator writes the central chapters of rediscovery between the winter evening and mid-May, moving from dead winter to reviving spring. The past finally demands that Leo re-enter experience in an attempt to join the two facets of himself into one vital being. Only by confronting the naïvely recorded facts and the mature interpretation of these facts can Leo find himself and escape his burden of guilt. His search leads him to the conclusion that

> The facts that I had brought to light had been sufficient for my purpose. They were incomplete, of course. If I wanted to know more precisely how I stood *vis-à-vis* life – success and failure, happiness and unhappiness, integration, and disintegration, and so on – I should have to examine other facts, facts beyond the reach of memory and gleaned from outside, from living sources. (*GB*, 305)

The narrator and the character are two distinct personalities. The elder Leo is a fastidiously prim man of facts who has withdrawn almost entirely from the world of experience. Precise bedtime hours regulate his Prufrockian world. When 'called upon to exchange the immunities of childhood for the responsibilities of the grown-up world' (*GB*, 169), something in him died. Now a self-admitted 'dull dog' (*GB*, 25), :he has become a bibliographer cataloguing others' books rather than becoming the writer he once wished to be. He has come to terms with life and has insulated himself in facts, facts which have saved him physically but not spiritually: 'the life of facts proved no bad substitute for the facts of life. It did not let me down; on the contrary it upheld me and probably saved my life; for when the First World War came, my skill in marshalling facts was held to be more important than any service I was likely to perform on the field. So I missed that experience, along with many others, spooning among them' (*GB*, 303). He senses that a promise, though, has been blighted. He admires his younger self who was imaginative, open to experience, totally naive, but also romantically adventurous. Looking through the diary, he feels 'a certain envy of the self of those days, who would not take things lying down, who had no notion of appeasement, and who was prepared to put all he had into making himself respected in society' (*GB*, 19).

These lines succinctly but none too accurately describe the twelve-year-old Leo, a dabbler in magic spells, as he approaches his fateful thirteenth birthday while visiting a school friend at his home in the Norfolk broads. More accurate is Marian Maudsley's description of him as 'green', for Leo is a naïve, unsophisticated, unsexual being, caught in the midst of an adult love triangle he does not recognize until too late and cannot understand even then. Passion, especially sexual passions and jealous passions, lies beyond his twelve-year-old ken, and he candidly admits: 'I did not understand the nature of the bond that drew the two together' (*GB*, 268). Quite simply, Leo is a foreigner in realms of class, sexuality, and adult relationships, dangerous realms which use him as a go-between.

In many ways a prelapsarian being, Leo is entirely unsophisticated and blunderingly innocent, partly because of the isolation encouraged by his now dead father and furthered by his mother. Leo, however, is a promising boy, confidently expecting a golden age of the gods to be ushered in concurrently with the new century. He longs to become as herioc as Hercules and looks forward to the tests life will bring to assay his courage, his initiative, and his resources. His visit to the Maudsleys at Brandham Hall translates him into a new realm, and he thinks 'My dream had become my reality; my old life was a discarded husk' (*GB*, 89). He sees himself as being 'free from all my imperfections and limitations; I belonged to another world, the celestial world. I was one with my dream life' (*GB*, 177).

Not unlike Hamlet before his mother's remarriage, Leo Colston is most immediately vulnerable because he lacks a sense of evil, however rudimentary. He emphatically resists his culture's awareness of sin. His snobbish class sensibility resists 'the levelling aspect of this sinnerdom' (*GB*, 81) thinking that 'life has its own laws, and it is for me to defend myself against whatever comes along, without going snivelling to God about sin, my own or other people's' (*GB*, 81). Like the other boys in his school and probably in his generation, he has little sense of abstract right and wrong, though he understands rules and punishments, but he cannot 'find a flaw in the universe and was impatient with Christianity for bringing imperfection to my notice' (*GB*, 182). Because 'the idea of Right and Wrong as two gigantic eavesdroppers spying on my movements was most distasteful' (*GB*,240), he resents the spire of the church near the cricket field which ruins the symmetry of his vision:

> There were two arches: the arch of the sky beyond the cricket field, and the arch of the sky above; and each repeated the other's curve. This delighted my sense of symmetry; what disturbed it was the spire of the church. The church itself was almost invisible among the trees, which grew over the mound it stood on in the shape of a protractor, an almost perfect semicircle. But the spire, instead of dividing the protractor into two equal segments, raised its pencil-point to the left of the center–about eight degrees, I calculated. Why didn't the church conform to nature's plan? (*GB*, 153–4).

He wants to keep a concept of sin absent from his world since 'sin was undiscriminating and reduced to a uniform shade of grey many fine actions that might otherwise have been called Golden Deeds' (*GB*, 266), and it fails to occur to Leo that if he is unhappy or if he suffers that 'there was something wrong with the system, or with the human heart' (*GB*, 20).

Between these two beings stands an event which clouds the young Leo's world with evil and blights the old Leo's world. In a preface to his novel, written in 1962, Hartley notes that he originally meant *The Go-Between* to be a study of innocence betrayed, and not only betrayed but corrupted. I was and still am irritated by the way the bad boys and girls of modern fiction are allowed to get away with the most deplorable behaviour, receiving not reproof, but compassion, almost congratulations, from the author. My story, I thought, shall be of a quite different kind. There shall be a proper segregation of sheep and goats and the reader shall be left in no doubt as to which of the characters I, at any rate, feel sorry for. I didn't know what was to become of Marian and Ted, but through their agency Leo was to be utterly demoralized.[8]

Hartley, however, 'softened towards them' as the work progressed, and it is quite difficult now to perceive just who constitutes the sheep and the goats in his novel. Not unlike the works of Hawthorne and James, *The Go-Between* becomes both a critique of modern ways of explaining evil and an investigation of the extent to which an individual must bear responsibility for his own loss of innocence.

Hartley was for many years an outspoken critic of contemporary absolution of the individual from such responsibility. He recalled once that he was reared 'on the theories of John Stuart Mill to believe that the state is the great enemy because it takes man's moral reponsibility out of his own hands and imposes its decisions on him, which have come to be accepted as fatalistically as if they were laws of God.... In the material and to some extent in the moral sphere, the state can make you what it likes, whereas God cannot'.[9] In words that resemble Hartley's own attack on Sigmund Freud and Karl Marx in 'The Novelist's Responsibility', Stephen Hilliard writes Eustace in the final volume of the *Eustace and Hilda* trilogy:

> I feel constrained to write, if only to allay the sense of guilt which (so you told me) was aggravating your natural terrors at the prospect of such a portentous journey – I wish you would not worry yourself about the Moral Law: Marx undermined it and Freud has exploded it. You cannot have any personal responsibility for your actions if your whole thought is conditioned by the class of society in which you were brought up, still less if your mind was infected by an Oedipus Complex before it had attained to self-consciousness.[10]

The Go-Between seems a sustained attack on both the sociological and the psychological explanations of guilt and evil, which offers an alternative which, when finally perceived, allows Leo to salvage the few remainng years of his life by taking responsibility out of the hands of class and sex.

In his desire to preserve his vision of an idealized social order in which Marian will 'reign at Brandham' (*GB*, 209), Leo decides to falsify the messages he is carrying in hopes of creating a quarrel between Marian and Ted which will break off the affair. Such a break-up, Leo feels, will restore order: 'social order, universal order; and Puck or whoever he is who has produced this miracle will vanish gracefully from the scene' (*GB*, 270).

Little wonder, then, that Leo idealizes the Viscount, after having corrected his initial error in dismissing him as only a Mister. He comes to identify him with the Archer, one of the three zodiac figures who fascinate him. Hugh is 'nine times as glorious as the first' viscount (*GB*, 83) to Leo; he is a god, and his language is 'star-talk' (*GB*, 107). In a most revealing admission, Leo confides that 'I didn't seriously regard Lord Trimingham as a rival: he was on a higher plane, the plane of imagination. I sincerely wanted Marian's happiness, both for her sake and for mine; my happiness would be crowned by hers' (*GB*, 181) – revealing because Leo wants to create an ideal social unit free of all the qualities he objects to in Ted. He literally wants to save Hugh from possible death, knowing as he does that one of the viscounts was killed in a duel over questions of honor involving his wife's fidelity. Hugh's actions vindicate Leo's perceptions of him; Marian tells him that 'Hugh was as true as steel. He wouldn't hear a word against me. We held our heads very high' (*GB*, 315). Why then, a reader must ask, if Leo succeeds as he does in protecting the stratified, static social order, does his success lead directly to his emotional collapse and his withdrawal from life? In Hartley's view, a sociological explanation fails to account adequately for the breakdown.

Nor, Hartley suggests, does the Freudian explanation most evident in the conflict between Leo and Ted. The novel insists on Ted's sexual dimensions and presents him as a powerfully phallic personality associated with guns, bats, procreation, spooning, harvests, and births. Seeing Ted first as a half-naked swimmer, Leo spies on him through the rushes on the bank, and 'retreated almost in fear of something I did not know.... I, whose only acquaintance was with bodies and minds developing, was suddenly confronted by maturity in its most undeniable form; and I wondered: 'What must it feel like to be him, master of those limbs...' (*GB*, 68). No gentleman, Ted only interests Leo when in his farms clothes; when dressed 'Ted's fine feathers made him look a yokel' (*GB*, 164). Drawn to but also repelled by Ted, Leo becomes extremely jealous of Ted; only in his prepubscent state he does not fully understand why:

The novel invites its readers to entertain Freudian and Marxist readings concurrently while simultaneously suggesting their inadequacy. Like the conflicts in George Eliot's *Adam Bede* and D. H. Lawrence's *Lady Chatterley's Lover*, the conflict within the triangle of characters involves class, status, wealth, and position. Ted Burgess, whom the Maudsleys 'don't know . . . socially of course' (*GB*, 66) is a farmer, while Hugh Winlove, whose courtship of Marian her parents encourage, is the ninth Viscount Trimingham, an aristocrat whose ancestors' tombs dominate the village church and whose heroic qualities have been tested and proven in war. Leo's social values, with all their snobbish underpinings, are laid bare in a brief exchange with Marian:

> "Leo, if you go that way [towards Ted's farm], will you do something for me?"
> "Of course. What is it?" But I knew before she spoke.
> "Give him a letter."
> "I was hoping that you'd say that!" I exclaimed. . .
> "Why? Because you like him?"
> "Ye–es. Not so much as Hugh, of course."
> "Why do you like Hugh better? Because he's a Viscount?"
> "Well, that's one reason," I admitted, without any false shame.
> Respect for degree was in my blood and I didn't think of it as snobbery. (*GB*, 114)

A highly developed 'respect for degree' possesses Leo's outlook on the love affair and life in general, partly because his mother's highly sensitive reponses to social nuance have shaped his life and partly because of his own adolescent ideas developed at boarding school. Leo knows that he 'carried [his] hierarchical principles into [his] notions of morality' (*GB*, 93), and he is keenly aware of the social gap between himself and Ted, betwen Ted and Marian, and, most of all, between Ted and Hugh. The cricket match becomes for him a collision of social and philosophical principles, at a personal level between 'Landlord and tenant, peer and commoner, Hall and village' (*GB*, 16), and at a more abstract level as well:

> Dimly I felt that the contest represented something more than the conflict betwen Hall and village. It was that, but it was also a struggle between order and lawlessness, between obedience to tradition and defiance of it, between social stability and revolution, between one attitude to life and another. (*GB*, 156)

I liked Ted Burgess in a reluctant, half-admiring, half-hating way. When I was away from him I could think of him objectively as a working farmer whom no one at the Hall thought much of. But when I was with him his mere physical presence cast a spell on me; it established an ascendency that I could not break. He was, I felt, what a man ought to be, what I should like to be when I grew up. At the same time I was jealous of him, jealous of his power over Marian, little as I understood its nature, jealous of whatever it was he had that I had not. He came between me and my image of her. (*GB*, 178)

To protect Marian from the passion, physicality, and sexuality he only partly recognizes and in no way understands, Leo 'kills' Ted several times, first by catching him out at the cricket match, then by eclipsing his song at the dinner, then by pointing a gun at him, When Ted sings his sentimental Balfe love song ('this resigned and mellifluous passage of infidelities to come' [GB, 167]), Leo responds with the emotional and dramatic climax to the first act of Handel's *Theodora*: "Angels! Ever bright and fair, / Take, oh take me to your care. / Speed to your own courts my flight / Clad in robes of virgin white" (*GB*, 172). 'If the Cricket Concert of 1900 was remembered,' Leo thinks years later, 'it would be remembered for my songs – my songs of death, not his songs of love. I had killed him, he was dead, and that was why I no longer felt him as a discordant element in my orchestra' (*GB*, 179). Later, while helping Ted clean his gun, Leo points it straight at Ted 'feeling almost a murderer' (*GB*, 199). From these passages, it should be evident that *The Go-Between* joins D. H. Lawrence's *Sons and Lovers* and Yukio Mishima's *The Sailor Who Fell from Grace with the Sea* as a major treatment of the Oedipus complex and as a revaluation of Freud's interpretation of the complex, first proposed in 1897 and later expanded in 1910. His comments in *The Interpretation of Dreams* concerning it more adequately gloss Leo's problems than does the sociological reading: 'His destiny moves us only becuse it might have been ours.... It is the fate of all of us, perhaps, to direct our first sexual impulses towards our mother and our first hatred and our first murderous wish against our father.... Here is one in whom these primeval wishes of our childhood have been fulfilled.'[11]

Hartley deftly exposes the inadequacy of both sociological and psychological explanations in that the sociological does not appropriately account for Leo's overwhelming sense of guilt and the psychological does not fully gloss Leo's consciousness of guilt. Leo seems to take too incidents, recalled from his earlier past, demonstrate that the young Leo felt that he possessed magical powers. While at school, Leo strives for 'a high standard of literary attainment' (*GB*, 61) in his diary, a habit which leads him to write pretentious sentences. Two schoolmates, Jenkins and Strode, read his diary and set upon him every day until he is 'vanquished', one of the offending words he used. Leo retaliates by concocting 'out of figures and algebraical symbols and what I remembered of some Sanskrit characters' (*GB*, 19) three curses which he writes in blood in his diary. When both Jenkins and Strode fall from the roof of the school and are taken to their homes with brain concussions, Leo suddenly finds himself respected as a sorcerer and fears what will be done to him 'in case I was a murderer' (*GB*, 21). Leo is 'secretly terrified' with his success and admits that he 'might easily have got into a morbid state about it' (*GB*, 22). The following term, Leo again succeeds in the black arts, believing that his psychic forces are responsible for the outbreak of measles which ends the term abruptly. 'Modestly' Leo takes 'some credit for it' (*GB*, 35). The spell he casts on Marian and Ted, however, recoils on him.

Why Leo casts a third spell has been suggested. Leo's father, somewhat an eccentric, is dead, and his mother is ineffectual. Marian and Hugh become idealized surrogate parents to Leo, while the possible union of Marian and Ted threatens the sexual union he directly fears. Hugh and Ted, more significantly, are the two sides of a fully integrated, mature personality Leo does not wish to accept. Just as the Archer and the Water-carrier in his zodiac both attract and repel him, Leo is drawn to both men at Brandham. Even though he is jealous of Ted, he 'also identified with him, so that I could not think of his discomfiture without pain; I could not hurt him without hurting myself' (*GB*, 178). When he decides to sacrifice Ted to keep his vision of order, harmony, and the golden age intact, Leo realizes later that he also sacrificed a major part of himself:

> I did not realize that this attempt to discard my dual or multiple vision and achieve a single self was the greatest pretence that I had yet embarked on. It was indeed a self-denying ordinance to cut out of my consciousness the half I most enjoyed. (*GB*, 287)

Hartley traces Leo's sacrifice of himself in terms of an ever increasingly complex and ambivalent symbol – a deadly nightshade bush flourishing unknown in a deserted shed at Brandham Hall, which has dual ancestry in Nathaniel Hawthorne's 'Rappaccini's Daughter' and Hartley's own experience. Like Leo, Hartley visited a school friend's home, and many

things from that visit found their way into Leo's story. Hartley admitted
that 'certain features of my visit have always stuck in my memory: the
double staircase stemming from the hall, the cedar on the lawn, the
cricket match against the villagers, and most vividly of all, the deadly
nightshade growing in the outhouse. I can still see it, it was enormous
like a tree, and I remember wondering if I ought to warn my hostess
about it'.[12]

Leo finds the *atropa belladonna* on 11 July 1900 while poking through
the outhouses of the Hall: 'it was a shrub, almost a tree, and as tall as
I was. It looked the picture of evil and also the picture of health, it was
so glossy and strong and juicy-looking' (*GB*, 46). Poisonous in itself,
the shrub quickly acquires sexual connotations, hinted by Hartley's
preference for the 'beautiful lady' rather than the 'deadly nightshade'
name. It beckons enticingly to Leo: 'Its beauty, of which I was well
aware,' Leo recalls, 'was too bold for me, too uncompromising in every
particular. The sullen, heavy purple bells wanted something of me that
I could not give, the bold black burnished berries offered me something
that I did not want.... this plant seemed to be up to something, to be
carrying on a questionable traffic with itself' (*GB*, 220). When Leo
decides to become a magician a third time and cast a spell on Marian
and Ted, he battens quickly on the idea of using the belladonna as the
specific for his magic. His night time uprooting of the shrub simultaneously images his grappling with knowledge of evil in his world and his
attempt to remove evil, his encountering of the principles of sexuality
and passion along with his denial of them, and his own sexual initiation
in that the scene culminates in the language of sexual orgasm, here
masturbatory in its connotations. Leo sees the nightshade, 'like a lady
standing in her doorway looking out for someone' (*GB*, 275), and,
unprepared 'for the tumult of emotions it aroused in me' (*GB*, 275), he
enters 'the unhallowed darkness' to learn its secrets as though entering
a sexual embrace. Tearing madly at the main stem while chanting
'Delenda est belladonna', Leo rips it from the earth:

> it gave, came away in my hands, throwing up with a soft sigh a little
> shower of earth, which rustled on the leaves like rain; and I was
> lying on my back in the open, still clutching the stump, staring up
> at its moplike coronal of roots, from which grains of earth kept
> dropping on my face. (*GB*, 276)

Knowing that his summer is ended and 'a sterner season' (*GB*, 279)
lays ahead, Leo silently takes total responsibility 'in common with other
much responsibility for what happens. This is not unexpected. Two

murders' (*GB*, 286) for the subsequent discovery of Marian and Ted in sexual embrace and for Ted's suicide. He feels he has betrayed them all and breaks down 'like a train going through a series of tunnels; sometimes in the daylight; sometimes in the dark, sometimes knowing who and where I was, sometimes not knowing' (*GB*, 300). He feels he has been presumptuous in involving supernatural powers, and in retaliation they have punished him.

At this point, the motion picture adaptation ended, truncating the novel which continues for one more chapter, an epilogue, for which Hartley has been criticized, quite unjustly in my view, since it is crucial to the encounter between the two Leos and essential to Hartley's vision of the relationship between past and present.[13] Underlining his moral intentions in the 1962 Preface, Hartley commented:

> I am not altogether a pessimist, and another reason for the Epilogue was that it gave a slightly more hopeful ending to the story than it would have had if it had finished with Ted's death. At last Leo gets a glimpse of the South-West prospect of Brandham Hall – the good side of it, so to speak – which had always been hidden from his memory. To his memory the whole episode had been an unrelieved disaster, so unrelieved as to turn him into a misanthrope and virtually to cut him off from human fellowship. With the recognition that there had always been a silver lining to the cloud we are to suppose that his attitude relaxes and that by acting as go-between for Marian and her grandson he re-enters the world of feelings.[14]

Hartley's modest and somewhat ingenuous statement marks the direction sketched in the prologue. *The Go-Between* is not the story of the destruction of an individual but rather is the story of the initial destruction and the much later resurrection of this individual. The voice he hears from the past early in the novel leaves Leo thinking:

> it had done its work. I *was* thinking of them. The cerements, the coffins, the vaults, all that had confined them was bursting open, and I should have to face it.... If it isn't too late, I thought confusedly, neither is it too early: I haven't much life left to spoil ... But they should witness my resurrection. (*GB*, 27)

Leo completes this quest in the epilogue when he returns to Brandham Hall to meet Marian and ultimately to free the eleventh Viscount Trimingham from the burden of the past. Though he still claims to be a 'foreigner in the world of the emotions, ignorant of their language but compelled to listen to it' (*GB*, 319), Leo has begun his entry back into this land simply by driving to Brandham after exploring in his own mind 'the fateful Friday' of 27 July 1900. Perhaps Aristotle would not have approved of this 52 year separation of reversal and recognition, but it provides a powerful, moving conclusion to Hartley's novel. The conclusion has largely been made possible by use of the retrospective frame.

At second glance, the novel's title is ambiguous. Leo is *the* go-between; his experience is *a* go-between separating the two states of being. Time is Leo's antagonist in that his struggles for wholeness must overcome time by virtually fusing past and present. In the novel, life is a test which Leo fails when he retreats into nervous collapse and memory suppression, but passes when he discovers his 'home in the past' (*GB*, 26). Leo undergoes no spiritual conversion such as the one experienced by Sammy Mountjoy in William Golding's *Free Fall*, but he finds that he can understand his being only by juxtaposing the past and the present and by using the past to explain the present. He looks at his diary and the papers piled around him early in the novel and thinks: 'Under those cliffs .... I have been buried.' But they should witness my resurrection, the resurrection that had begun in the red collar-box' (*GB*, 27). By the end of the novel, he has been fully transformed, and his past is no longer a foreign country.

Leo progresses through four stages during the course of the novel which transform him from an innocent youngster eagerly awaiting the future into a 64 year old aware that he has some years left and should not squander them. When Marian takes him to Norwich to buy his summer clothes a 'spiritual transformation took place ... it was there that, like an emerging butterfly, I was first conscious of my wings ... my apotheosis' (*GB*, 59). New clothing provides him a new identity, a new outlook on the world, and a new confidence in the Golden Age and the world of his adult gods. This transformation lasts until he reads one of the notes he carries from Marian to Ted. Her '*Darling, darling, darling*' (*GB*, 127) plunges him immediately into disillusionment and bitter disappointment: 'Not Adam and Eve, after eating the apple, could have been more upset than I was' (*GB*, 128), he recalls, suddenly sensing that he has been used and abused, simply for the ends to which he could be put in the conduct of the affair. The 'scaffolding of [his] life seemed to collapse' (*GB*, 190), especially since logic forces him to blame Ted. Hugh, whom he cannot blame since Hugh is the wronged man, tells him that women are never to blame. This leaves only Ted. He tries to escape by writing his mother, requesting that she wire for him to return, and his letter brings some relief since 'afternoon had put my mental age back and dealt my spirit a shrewd blow...' (*GB*, 207). When his mother refuses, however, Leo enters into his third stage – corruption – as he renounces his own innocence to strive to manipulate the adults. His new personality at this point 'tasted rather flat' (*GB*, 286), and it is in this state that the paralyzing trauma strikes, causing him to retreat from life, to withdraw from the world of feelings, and to exist for half a century, like Prufrock, measuring out his life in minute coffee spoons. If the past can destroy, it can also heal. The recollection of lost time, which begins with the opening of the box, culminates with the opening of the undelivered note which has lain unopened all these years. The search, Leo admits, 'bore fruit, enabling me to lay some unction to my soul *which at the time I had denied myself*' (*GB*, 303, italics added), and he perceives through his reconstruction of the events that 'I was not so guilty as I had believed myself to be in the long months that followed my visit, or so blameless as, in the years that followed them, I had come to think I was' (*GB*, 304). At this point in his search for truth which has already had 'a tranquillizing and reconciling affect' (*GB*, 305), he opens the letter and reads it. It brings tears, 'tears, which I had never shed, I think, since I left Brandham Hall' (*GB*, 306), and the next day he rents a car and drives to Brandham where he finds himself, once again, acting as go-between, this time between Marian and her grandson who feels ashamed of his grandmother and cursed by her actions. Directed by Marian to tell Edward there is 'no spell or curse except an unloving heart' (*GB*, 319), he returns to the Hall and for the first time views the splendid southwest prospect 'long hidden from my memory' (*GB*, 320). Immersion in the past, driving Leo to a confrontation of the climactic day in his young life, has freed and restored Leo, lifting the 'curse' more from him than from Edward. The memories, so painfully and expensively repressed, are reconstituted in a Laingian 're-search. A search constantly reasserted and reconstituted for what we have all lost ....'.[15]

In Hartley's *A Perfect Woman*, one of the characters dismisses the novels of Alexander Goodrich, another character, as chronicles of 'little wails' no longer relevant since 'we've all heard such much louder noises – flying bombs, high-explosive bombs, V-2 bombs, atom bombs, and soon may hear the hydrogen bomb! What we want now, but what he can't or will not give us, is a different sort of report – a good report of humanity in general – not the individual's screech of pain...'.[16] The 'little wail' recorded in *The Go-Between* makes much less noise in and may be less important to the larger world, but the novel asserts firmly that so long as the individual bears responsibility for the self the wail must continue to be recorded and that the whole individual can never be created until past and present authorize a future.

3   Angus Wilson, *Late Call*, 'a strange gale of memories'

Like John Fowles' *The French Lieutenant's Woman* and William Faulkner's *The Sound and the Fury*, Angus Wilson's *Late Call* originated in the provocative image of a woman.[1] The 'moment of vision', Wilson recalled, came from a drive through one of the New Towns, when [I] saw an elderly woman standing in a yard looking out over the landscape'.[2] In the 'moment of vision' are evident the major concerns of the novel — life in a New Town, the condition of the elderly, the look which became a searching for purpose, and perhaps even the limited perspective of the central character. The conflict between the newness of the New Town and the oldness of the elderly woman is a uniquely post-modernist one, too; before Virginia Woolf few aged protagonists appear in English fiction, but since her novels, especially amongst those novelists influenced by her, the problems of the elderly, their retirement, and their perception of pattern or meaning to their lives loom large as viable fictional topics.

Sylvia Carter, the protagonist of *Late Call*, is another example of a wasted life, shards of which are salvaged when the character integrates or connects her present with her past. Technically, Sylvia presented several problems for Wilson: she is a genuinely good character, and she is a totally imperceptive character. Moreover, Sylvia feels worthless and believes that her entire existence has perhaps been a worthless, meaningless sixty-four years. While reading a *Daily Mail* puzzle obviously involving saving a certain number of individuals in a lifeboat, she thinks:

> it is probably easier to answer the question by eliminating those whom you would *not* save. First, sorry for her, the Captain's wife will have to go overboard. She's fifty-five. Her children are all grown up. She's not particularly bright, she doesn't even get on very well with the Captain. In fact their relations if anything rock the boat. In any case she's had her life. (*LC*, 57)[3]

Sylvia projects on this nameless woman all of her own problems. Now retired, Sylvia, too has 'had her life'. Two of her children, Len and Iris,

39

are dead, killed during the war and in a lorry accident respectively; he remaining child, Harold, is the Headmaster of a school and author of successful textbooks. Arthur, her husband, called The Captain, was invalided out of World War I after being gassed, and their relationship has been far less than ideal. His persistent borrowing of money and his gambling debts have led to her forced retirement from the hotel business

Sylvia is surrounded by images of old women everyone, including herself, sees as being useless. Reading the accounts of the Sydney Fox trial involving a young man's murder of his mother for insurance proceeds, she thinks, 'At the very end of his tether, what could the loving son do but sell the old woman for the best money he could get for her? The question she had conjured up from the book presented itself so unexpectedly, so directly to Sylvia that she shivered, lit cigarette and inhaled deeply' (*LC* 157). And when the niece of Miss Priest, an old lady Sylvia knew during her hotel years, is murdered Muriel Bartley unfeelingly tells Sylvia:

> You see, this old girl had got all the lolly. They're bound to go selfish. Look at the facts of the case. I mean, all she'd got to do was to give her niece a bit of dough and tell her to push off on her own But no, money's power with these old girls. Nobody wants them, and they know it, so they take it out on people round them. (*LC*, 180)

During the production of John Osborne's *Look Back in Anger*, a play which echoes throughout the novel, Ray shouts his line '"That old bitch should be dead!"' sparking Sylvia to think 'across her vision there ran and stumbled and fell a line of fat naked old women — some haggard and ancient as witches . . .' (*LC*, 161). Even Mrs. Kragnitz the 76 year old woman she meets near the end of the novel, believes that her niece is gradually poisoning her though Mrs. Kragnitz, Sylvia learns, is 'quite round the bend' (*LC*, 228).

Sylvia feels the plight of these old women deeply. Forced by her husband's actions to retire from a job she liked, she feels displaced and abandoned — even laughable because of her size. The kitchen in her son's home, 'The Sycamores', is almost animistically hostile: 'suddenly the black night outside, the heat, the dark green walls, the white machines, all closed in on her. The washing-up machine, the quick grill the deep freeze, the cooker, the spin dryer, and all the other white monsters stood in line against the green wall like so many marble tombstones. . . . She looked round for some escape from this enveloping whiteness but only a tiny angry red eye glared at her from the smooth hite surface warning her off sacred ground that was not hers . . .' (*LC*, 4). She does master 'the electronic monsters' but she 'still felt herself no real use to the household' (*LC*, 86). Her future now 'stretched out n front of her in empty uselessness' (*LC*, 98). Just how little self-worth ylvia feels is underlined when she takes a ruined sweater as the symbol f her life. She recalls that her daughter had knitted a jumper years go:

> a garment so badly strung together, so loose and shapeless, its two-colour pattern so muddled that even the little girl herself had started at once unpicking the wool in order to knit it all over again. It seemed clear to Sylvia that she was that jumper. Perhaps to weave all the threads together again, she needed to return to the country world of her childhood. (*LC*, 208)

When asked by Sally Bulmer ' "how do you think of yourself?" ' (*LC*, 132), Sylvia first laughs the question away with ' "I'm very fat" ' and then, more seriously, says, ' "I was a manageress, *but I'm nothing now*" ' (*LC* 132, italics added).

Because Sylvia has no one to care for at present, direction and purpose disappear from her life. Sylvia has been 'of use' and 'in service' since childhood and has not developed a keen sense of selfhood. Self has always been sacrificed as she cared for her brothers and sisters, worked as a housemaid, and managed private hotels. The visiting Mrs Longmore looks at Sylvia and thinks, 'old head on young shoulders, poor little thing, everything was left to her. She had to be mother to the whole brood — not more than twelve years old and responsible for heavens knew how many little indistinguishables' (*LC*, 9). Childhood on the Suffolk farm, near Woodbridge, is difficult. Sylvia's family is poor and decidedly unsuccessful, her mother given to chapel excesses, and her brutal father to drunkenness. Intensely conscious of her social class and her own personal failure, Mrs Tuffield, Sylvia's mother sees her children as made for '*All* work', and numbers games, laughter, and even emotions as simply being sins:

> *All* work. That's what the Almighty made for her. That's been the trouble, as I doubted it would — all that crubble and playin' 'em air games. That's all right for the gentry, but that's not for 'er . . . Wicked little thing . . . that'll be lucky if the Devil don't take you' (*LC*, 29)

Mr Tuffield's response is a 'bum bastin' ' (*LC*, 30). Both her parents
believe, as Mrs Tuffield tells Mrs Longmore — a horrifying glimpse of
the stature of children in 1911 rural England —

> There's nothing special about 'her! . . . God put 'er here to work for
> others. That's what she's to do. Special! . . . *You* wanted to be
> different! Well, you're nothin'. Nothin'. And you always will be (*LC*
> 31)

Sylvia escapes farm life within less than two years by going into
service as a housemaid at the Rectory, then, with the outbreak of war
to the officers' convalescent home. Next comes her own guest house at
Paignton, lost in the 1929 depression, and thirty-four years of managing
private hotels where the guests' wishes are always paramount. Never
allowed a self or simply to 'be', Sylvia has insulated herself though work
and through immersion in life as retailed in certain kinds of books and
television shows. She particularly likes 'Down Our Way' (whose Mr
Harber's 'I don't know' tag line she shares), 'Wardress Webb', and
mindless novels, usually historical romancs, whose florid rhetoric Wilson
parodies so skilfully. She immerses herself in *Fotheringay Pilgrimage, A
Winter's Holiday, Queen or Duchess*, and *Within an Ace*, the last freely
parodied thus:

> They called my generation a golden one and I truly think that we
> were in love with life. Even when years later the big break-up came
> between Duncan and me and we knew that we were not really suited
> to one another, we romped through the months of separation and
> finally of divorce as we had through three fortunes and a thousand
> parties. On the night the decree was made absolute we had dinner
> *à deux* (quails with grapes and brown bread ices) at Quaglino's, and
> dear Quaggie (what a terrible waste of human life — but war means
> just that!) thought we looked so happy that he asked if we'd been
> remarried that day! A month later Duncan's rather enchanting old
> father died. I had been "within an ace" again. This time of being a
> duchess. (*LC*, 196)

Little wonder that this type of fiction ultimately fails her. Like the 'tree
without leaves', the title of chapter two, Sylvia has been stripped bare
barer than she dared fear, when retirement brings her and her husband
to Carshall to live with their widowed son.

Carshall is a searching look at the phenomenon of the New Town and the emotional and psychological conditions of the inhabitants. An experiment of the Labour government and 'the first jewel in the Labour Government's crown', the New Towns were created 'primarily to relieve overcrowding in large cities such as London, Birmingham, Liverpool and Glasgow . . . and also to provide growth points for industry. [4] The New Towns Act of 1946 originally established eight such new towns, and under acts of 1965 and 1968 this number expanded to 32 (21 in England, 2 in Wales, 5 in Scotland, and 4 in Northern Ireland). As an experiment desiged to cope with the housing, crowding, and distribution problems of World War II, the New Towns by 1970 had become a potential liability. While calling them 'a noble achievement in positive land use . . . generally recognized as among the most successful postwar experiments . . . and a profitably long-term investment', *Britain 1978: An Official Handbook* noted that 'the policy of population dispersal has been reviewed and the future role and pace of development of the new town are being re-assessed'.[5] During a 1975 conference held at Walton Hall, seven speakers seriously questioned the role of the New Towns in relation to agricultural land, the individual psyche, and the sense of community and James Simmie concluded that 'old towns satisfy more the needs of a greater number of different groups and individuals than do new towns'.[6]

Harold Calvert, Sylvia's son, has firmly committed himself to the social theory behind the new town concepts. Harold and his society have 'given [themselves] up to the false notions that there can be no unhappiness'.[7] Indeed, Wilson perceives an underlying evil in this attitude; evil 'lies in the quality of constant jollity and laughter and good fellowship in the new town which hides loneliness . . . an evil jollity because it is preventing people from really getting close to each other', he confided to one interviewer.[8] Harold, who eschews 'pioneer sentimentality' (*LC*, 43), desires in Carshall a 'mixed society — status wise . . . nothing to do with class' (*LC*, 141) which 'has to be fought for by alertness, by caring' (*LC*, 163). He tells his audience after the performance of John Osborne's *Look Back in Anger*:

We've got a new hopeful young world here of uncrowded leisureful happy living. We've got a cause to fight for — something that Jimmie couldn't find in his squalid cramped surroundings. (*LC*, 163)

Harold has sublimated all his energies into Carshall, especially since his wife's death, because, as he tells his mother, 'the New Town and what it stands for were the centre of all Beth and I believed in, and now she's dead, it's all I have' (*LC*, 44–5).

But the New Town's dream of happiness, or rather of lack of unhappiness, is a dream not shared by either the older or the younger generations. Harold's children have rejected it — Judy through her interest in old forms which her father partly sees as a bad case of adolescent snobbery, Ray through his flight to London, and Mark through his involvement in protest activities such as nuclear disarmament marches. Sylvia, too, senses a forced atmosphere in the New Town, one which can be ascribed to lack of tradition and refusal to allow the individual to be unhappy. The centre of her discontent is the Carshall Church, St. Saviour's, near the Town Centre:

> Yet despite the odd metal steeple more like a piece of children's Meccano and the funny slots in the side of the building, it was rather plain inside — spacious and light enough, but more like a lecture hall with unpolished wooden chairs and little tie-on cushions seats covered in jade green American cloth. Apart from a long thin silver crucifix that stoood on the altar steps you'd hardly know it for a church — not that it was at all like chapel; it was just a big room with everything very simple and quiet, especially the thin slotted glass windows through which the sun poured with a lovely silky-blue light. (*LC,* 144)

Its vicar, Harold tells her, 'is quite an unusual man' whose Easter sermons tend to the eleven pluses but contain none of 'this dry-as-dust theological stuff . . . ' (*LC*, 190). This particular Easter, however, the vicar, disabled by a slipped disc, is replaced by a Scots clergyman, 'a very old man with a very long red nose and a rather dirty-looking beard of the kind old King Edward VII had worn' (*LC*,191). His sermon concerned with works and grace generates in Sylvia 'an entirely unfamiliar urge to action' (*LC*, 193) as the words well might because the sermon is aimed at her:

> Said the one carlinwife to the other, 'Aye, Annie,' says she, 'I've been aye doing so muckle guid. I've noe had time to set me down and mind who I am.' Ah! And she can sit on her buttie to all eternity, for buttie's all she'll have — there'll be no living soul to save. Is there nothing we can do to help us to God's Grace? Indeed there is. The Lord forbid that I should preach to you folks any strait-jacketed

Calvinistic doctrine. There's a great deal you can do. You can be toward. You can go out to meet God's Grace. Go out to mind who you are. Go out, not into the busy clamour of getting and spending, nor even into the soothing clamour of good works. No, go out into the dreadful silence, into the dark nothingness. Maybe ye are no but a wisp of straw, but if you go out to fan the fire, out through the desert and the night, then indeed may the Lord send the light of his face to shine upon you, then indeed may you be visited by that Grace which will save your soul alive. (*LC,* 193)

Like the preacher's Annie, Sylvia has been so busy with good works for others that she has virtually no soul to save. Now without the protective insulation of a hotel to run, guests' whims to cater to, or a family to look after, she is alone on her 'buttie'. Retirement has stripped her of vocation; the electronic monsters of 'The Sycamores' have stripped her of activity; and the New Town has stripped her of being. No one has minded who Sylvia is or what she is.

Sylvia discovers who and what she is through a cathartic reenactment of her past. Unlike Harold who ignores the past and Arthur who fancifully reconstructs it accordingly to his audience, Sylvia at first seems to have no past. A problem in presenting the difficulties faced by Sylvia is Sylvia herself. A simple, often imperceptive character, Sylvia cannot verbalize her difficulties, their causes, or their cures. She can only experience them. Wilson recognized the difficulty of visualizing through such a simple character and, like most novelists who use limited protagonists, enters into a secret commerce with the reader, requiring the reader to make essential connections, to verbalize depths beneath the obvious surface Sylvia hints, and finally to sense a broader salvation in Sylvia's last decision than she does herself.

Sylvia begins the nine months progress of the novel 'just weary and disappointed' (*LC,* 37), feeling that her life suddenly is 'a whole diary of blank pages' (*LC,* 52) and that she and Arthur somehow 'don't belong to the great future' (*LC,* 50). More pointedly, Sylvia simply refuses to think and to confront the 'black desolate thoughts [which] creep in ... [and] make her more hungry for the penned-up safety of "The Sycamores"' (*LC,* 178). Images of a 'murky past' (*LC,* 205) appear until Sylvia finally decides that 'only through the dark nothingness and the dreadful silence . . . could she hope to pass' and to overcome her 'growing sense of futile evasion' (*LC,* 206). Sylvia realizes that 'the long familiar sketchy outlines of her grey life had now suddenly so blurred and dissolved that she had altogether lost herself' (*LC,* 207) and, significantly, that 'all that remained was a pervasive depression or a nagging ache of anxiety — *as from fugitive, forgotten bad dreams*' (*LC*, 208, italics added). Like Clarissa Dalloway, she feels assaulted by 'a savage beast camouflaged amid the sad, grey flora of her melancholy world' (*LC*, 247). The way through this darkness is immersion of self in its own past to rediscover a sense of identity now that the cessation of the public identity granted through work has left the naked private self alone and vulnerable.

Sylvia establishes the necessary connection by design and by accident. Her search, indeed her quest, mirrored in her constant walking abroad to Gorman's Woods, Sugley Manor, and elsewhere mirrors the wanderings of her mind. First, she writes Ivy Priest, recalling 'some of the excursions they had taken together around Ilfracombe' and affirming ' "what pleasure it all gave me" ' (*LC*, 182). Second, she rescues a little girl, Amanda (called Mandy) Egan during a thunderstorm. While walking in the fields near Carshall, Sylvia is unexpectedly trapped by the storm. All her childhood fears of lightning revive and suddenly the storm assaults her both literally and symbolically:

> All the pressed in, tight packed nervous terrors of the past months burst out with the storm's explosion; yet at the same time all wandering fragments of nightmare came together in on sudden overwhelming flash and roar. Whatever it was had found her, driven her from cover, and now would strike her down. (*LC*, 231)

But the lightning brings release and salvation rather than destruction, as with William Golding's Pincher Martin. Sylvia sees a small girl, screaming with fright, clinging closely to a 'tall, crumbling, leafless, ghostly-fingered oak tree' (*LC*, 231), and tears her away from it moments before lightning strikes the tree sending it 'down in a moment's flame and a long plume of funeral smoke' (*LC*, 232).

To understand the significance of this scene, one must return to the oft-criticized Prologue of the novel. Early reviewers, sometimes downright puzzled by the Prologue, complained that there was 'nothing to connect the woman [of the novel] with the girl [of the Prologue]', that the Prologue bore on Sylvia's later life 'in no discernible way', or that it was simply irrelevant.[9] When asked to comment on the Prologue, Wilson explained his intentions:

> The prologue is intentionally written in Edwardian style so as to belong to the old world, the world from which Sylvia came as a girl.

It is intended to relate the whole problem of the book to something deeper simply than the problem of old age or loneliness in old age or the conflict between a new town and the old way of living; it is intended to relate the book to the problem of injustice. The injustice that perhaps is done to some people who from the earliest times are taught somehow that they are not important and that they don't matter. The whole story of Sylvia is about how everybody matters, and she matters because she seems to matter less than anybody. She is for once encouraged in her childhood to feel that she matters and then snubbed when it happens. So this is a beginning of importance in life and it is also the beginning, I think, very often of the lives of people like her, lives built upon work, upon the concept of duty only. So the book leads up to what is really its fundamental theme: Do we have any other part of ourselves, any kind of grace, as you might say, besides work?[10]

In other words, much of the significance of Sylvia's story resides in the blank spaces between the conclusion of the prologue 'The Hot Summer of 1911' and the first chapter 'Leavetaking', because since Sylvia accepted the principle of work she has had no life of any importance until her retirement.

In 'The Hot Summer of 1911', which easily could stand as a short story of a farm girl misunderstood and thus potentially destroyed by a brutal father, a zealous mother, and a 'wonderful dodo' guest, Wilson introduces the oldest Tuffield girl who cares for her younger brother and sisters and also the children of the visiting Mrs Longmore. Encouraged by Mrs Longmore to participate in games, to appreciate the cut of a dress, and to adhere to the values of freedom, the girl and Myra Longmore decided to do 'something different' (*LC*, 30). Wandering through Knapp's meadows and Paddock Wood, they make daisy crowns, float their hats in a stream, and, as the day grows warmer, progressively shed layers of their clothing and their symbolical layers of publicly imposed identities and roles. Brushing aside momentary thoughts of pain, the girls emerge from the woods near the rectory only to be laughed at by Albert Snushnall. Sexuality clouds the innocent scene when Myra tells her mother that the Tuffield girl is 'horrid' and 'nasty' (*LC*, 27). The Tuffield girl, refusing to defend herself, resigns herself to punishment. It is as much the memory of the girl as it is the very real and frightened Amanda Egan that Sylvia rescues from the lightning. In a very real sense, she rescues her younger self. She clasps Amanda so tightly that they seem 'to merge into one sodden mass' (*LC*, 232).

Sylvia early senses the necessity of returning to her past but only vaguely senses how. She decides to shop in Carshall Old Town rather than the New Town and finds much comfort there. One day as she rides on the bus, 'a strange gale of memories blew her back into the past' (*LC*, 204). This leaves her confused, but rescue of Amanda releases a flood of healing memories 'that came from she couldn't really tell where of long, happy summer country days' (*LC*, 248). Mrs Kragnitz, the old lady she meets in the park, tells Sylvia, supposedly quoting Grillparzer, 'the child makes the woman . . . however hard the later years may be' (*LC*, 222), a belief one finds running like a thread through Wilson's critical writing. In *Emile Zola; an Introductory Study of His Novels*, Wilson argued:

> The form in which an artist's creative impulses are ultimately expressed is frequently moulded by the stresses placed upon his emotions in childhood and early adolescence; stresses produced by the gradual realization of the dreadful gulf that lies between his fantasy world . . . and the vast, uncomforting desert of the society in which he must live.[11]

And in *The Wild Garden, Or Speaking of Writing*, Wilson more pointedly directed tha idea at himself: 'I started to write at the age of thirty-six and in unconscious response, I believe, to a definite crises to which my earlier years had steadily moved'.[12] Sylvia is in no sense an artist, but she too re-establishes the vital connection between the child and the adult, embracing in Amanda her free, unselfconscious, innocent self.

Sylvia's life, wasted in large part, had been simplified and repressed. She lacked the ability to 'let go' and express her own emotions as Shirley Egan counsels her to do. Making herself an example, Sylvia tells her children 'that the Calverts didn't go on like that; that making an exhibition of themselves wouldn't help them; that they must be manly like their Dad' (*LC*, 297). Now, though, Amanda's family provides a new pattern for her. Spontaneous in their expressions of sorrow, joy, anger, and love, the Egans give Sylvia a glimpse of a balanced life in which the modern ideals of 'freedom and companionship' and the Edwardian ideals of 'responsibility and manliness' coexist and cohere into a wonderous wholeness. As Arthur Edelstein has pointed out, 'returning across time to the early crisis in the wood, [Sylvia] has re-entered, re-enacted, and reversed it'.[13] The Egan household enables Sylvia to move through the darkness and emerge healed:

She no longer felt the guilt of her unhappiness, the strangeness of her long desperate walks coming between her and her family. She carried the shopping and the roster duties . . . without any sense of strain she sat in the evenings reading or watching tele without any sense of melancholy. The pleasure that came from her afternoons at the farm lasted all that day and into the next. Of course there were tensions still but she was not their cause. (*LC*, 254)

At this point, Sylvia undergoes a serious testing of her new self. In a burst of family crises, Mark quarrels with his father and moves out, one of Ray's homosexual friends commits suicide and Ray, feeling dangerously compromised, flees to London, and Arthur, her husband, rather unexpectedly dies. A year earlier these events would have paralyzed Sylvia, but having re-established a whole personality, she faces them with equanimity and surprising control, unlike her own son whose socially conscious jollity collapses. Sylvia feels grief for her husband, but she feels more deeply for her own wasted life:

She tried deliberately to recall, to cling to, those few happy secret times they had known together; but a desperate grief closed in upon her, grief for all the years and years that had been nothing or worse than nothing, for tenderness dried up and tenderness drained away into indifference. For more than an hour she lay there, pressing her face close into the pillow, stifling her frantic crying that no one must hear, as wave followed wave and knocked her down again, punishing her for shyness, prudery, laziness, selfish bitterness, failures she couldn't name. (*LC*, 307–8)

At this point, Sylvia makes a crucial decision in her life. She can understand Ray's dilemma and continues to love him whereas Harold shreds his letter and renounces him as a son. When Muriel Bartley tells her '"It's easy to see who's going to hold [Harold's] hand from now on"' (*LC*, 315), for a moment, a familiar pattern temptingly offers itself, that of submerging her own life and helping a male family member. Sylvia now has a valuable sense of self restored by her confrontation with the past, however, and she rejects this role.

While Sally Bulmer and Harold busy themselves with plans, charts, and questionnaires strewn on the study floor a few weeks later, Sylvia declares her independence by reverting to the closing symbols of Osborne's *Look Back in Anger*. Looking at them, Sylvia sees that

There(s no room in one house for two big bums.
She watched their heads in close discussion.
Bears and squirrels! (*LC*, 316)

She decides at this moment to leave 'The Sycamores':

Now for her last move but one. She only looked forward to finding a place of her own. Somewhere near Town Centre, if she could get it. That would be a good centre for operations. (*LC*, 316)

Sylvia has finally 'grown up,' a concept explained by a character in *No Laughing Matter* as seeing 'that life's all one thing, that however silly you have been in the past it's all part of you, you can't refuse it . . . suddenly one day I saw that it [childhood] was all part of my life; I couldn't turn my back on any of it. I think that's when I grew up'.[14]

4 Rayner Heppenstall, *The Woodshed*, 'the deep trawl of memory'

In *The Intellectual Part*, an autobiographical volume published in 1963, Rayner Heppenstall, 'one of the few English novelists who have done truly experimental work, one of the very few who can–and wish to–compete with, say, Michel Butor or Nathalie Sarraute on their own difficult ground',[1] sketched both his intentions and his desires for his novels, admitting that he would like to write like Marcel Johandeau:

> What I mean is that I should have liked to write, from day to day, simply about the moment and its consciousness and any past matters which pressed on the memory, the prose being merely careful, transparent, exact, easy on eye and ear, varied only by the variety of the word's approach to what it scrupulously dealt with, utterly shameless, wholly personal. That it was quite impossible is due to the rigid formality of British literary customs. The novel and the diary-without-date cannot flow into each other here, and I had long been sickened by the contrivance expected of a novelist.[2]

A year earlier, however, Heppenstall had published two novels, *The Connecting Door* and *The Woodshed*, in which he achieved this rigorous programme. The reviewers greeted them warmly, but the reading public let them sink quietly into oblivion where scholars have largely let them remain. That Heppenstall has received little mention in studies of contemporary fiction puzzles him as well as those readers who are familiar with his works because they offer a most intriguing record of the evaluation of a man of letters, an assimilation of existential philosophy into fiction less stridently than in John Fowles – a writer, by the way, whom Heppenstall much admires –, and an extraordinarily stylish *nouveau roman* whose prose is translucently exact, whose subject is wholly personal, yet whose technique avoids the gimmicks and trickery of some anti-novels.

Two novels are a tightly related pair (much as are Joseph Conrad's *Almayer's Folly* and *An Outcast of the Islands* or D. H. Lawrence's *The Rainbow* and *Women in Love*) in that they share the same protagonist, Harold Atha, and treat various stages in his life. *The Connecting Door*, written and published first, seems to have confused its publisher somewhat, for its introductory note reads: 'It is 1948. A man in his late thirties arrives on a journalistic assignment at a city in the Rhineland. He is met at the station by two younger men, and his relations with them and with a girl called Annelies are developed.'[3] Not mentioned, however, is the crucial fact that the two young men who meet him are his younger selves who visited the same city in 1931 and 1936 and that the novel probes the relationship between discontinuous versions of the self. Very young Harold, Atha, and the unnamed narrator have shared the same body but not the same attitudes, outlooks, or desires, as indicated by their respective seasons of arrival. Very Young Harold arrives, not inappropriately, on April Fool's Day; 'wintry' Atha, 'disillusioned and suicidal', in dreary February, and the narrator in June. As the narrator revisits locales, especially the Minster which dominates the landscape, and people, he encounters his earlier selves and during the course of the short novel becomes 'ghost-free' (*CD*,157). Harold, his nineteen-year-old self, is open, spontaneous, romantic, given to writing poetry, and flirting a bit more than half-heartedly with Catholicism; he is 'a bit of a fool, but did not mind' (*CD*, 18). The narrator, with whom he enters in league against Atha, tells Harold: 'In the past seventeen years, you've lived in occasional flickers, when I had you in mind. You forget, or, rather, you haven't quite realised, that without me you don't exist' (*CD*, 121). Existing in a world 'always Lent' (*CD*, 129), Atha, who disapproves of the romantic outlook of the younger self and the journalistic career of the elder self, has been disappointed in love and contemplates committing suicide by disappearing, 'whether by way of the great, unswimmable river or from up high the tallest of all Gothic spires known to him' (*CD*, 66). Of him, the narrator finally comes to realize: 'He served his turn. I ought to be grateful to him. It is summer now, outside and, by and large, in. I am not standing here nagged at by any dark thought' (*CD*, 157).

The Connecting Door has a dual ancestry in Heppenstall's own experiences and in the writings of Soren Kierkegaard, especially in his short, autobiographical *Repetition*.[4] In *The Connecting Door*, the narrator knows he is 'more conscious of a quite different type of mystical thought' than Atha's Catholic mysticism, 'the result, no doubt, of reading Kierkegaard' (*CD*, 52) and notes that the 'very sound of Kierkegaard's name makes my eyeballs ache' (*CD*, 52). In *The Intellectual Part*,

Heppenstall recalls reading Kierkegaard in 1944 and starting a novel concerned with 'a certainly doomed return journey, intended to achieve some kind of *redintegratio in pristinum*, which I had made to Strasbourg eight years before'[5] (*IP*, 212).

Repetition, a very short but dense work, appealed to Heppenstall as a novel. In it, Constantine Constantius, the friend of the protagonist, confidant, and putative author, tells of a young man who has fallen deeply in love but whose melancholy introspection frustrates possible union. Encouraged by Constantius, the languishing young man pretends he has a mistress and then disappears, leaving the narrator to recount a journey he made to Berlin in search of a 'repetition' or a 'recollection'. Repetition is, of course, a recurrent theme in Kierkegaard's works, one which enables him to develop the idea that one goes forward in existence mainly by going backwards in consciousness. One of his most quoted aphorisms, 'Life can only be explained after it has been lived' posits the necessity of retrospection, but, as made apparent elsewhere, retrospection is not a static or nostalgic action.[6] Another aphorism reads, 'It is perfectly true, as philosophers say, that life must be understood backwards. But they forget the other proposition, that it must be lived forwards. And if one thinks over that proposition it becomes more and more evident that life can never really be understood in time simply because at no particular moment can I find the necessary resting place for which to understand it – backwards.'[7] Because the self is constantly in the process of becoming, it cannot truly look back and understand fully, but must look back hesitantly and uncertainly as does the narrator in *The Connecting Door*. Looking backwards is thus both an act of remembering and an act of forgetting. In many ways, it is also an act of escape. At one point in *Sickness Unto Death*, Kierkegaard turns to the unspelling motif of fairy tales to explain how the individual goes forward by going backwards in consciousness: 'For here applies what the fairy-tale recounts about a certain enchantment: the piece of music must be played through backwards otherwise the enchantment is not broken.'[8] These divisions between past, present, and future selves are magnified in acts of remembering and forgetting which, we are reminded in *Either/Or*, 'will also insure against standing fast in some relationship of life, and make possible the realization of a complete freedom'.[9] Since Heppenstall wrote in *The Blaze of Noon*, an early novel, that 'memory is in one sense or another the clue to all things. It is the continuum, the ambience in which all our disjointed moments cohere into a whole'[10] and more recently has written that 'In my own life and in respect of other people's lives, I have become increasingly preoccupied by the past within a present which moves forward constantly into a previous future, so that

the past resides at every moment...' (*IP*, 215), one can understand
why he slyly notes in *The Fourfold Tradition* that Kierkegaard's 'way of
writing was as important to him as his ideas. A novelist might still learn
something from him about methods of narrative presentation'.[11]

What Heppenstall learned from Kierkgaard about narrative method
and the dialogue between an individual's past, present, and future states
of being can be seen in *The Connecting Door*; however, I believe it is even
more successfully assimilated into the companion novel, *The Woodshed*,
also published in 1962. *The Woodshed* presents Harold Atha's childhood
and adolescence, a still earlier stage of his life than those used in *The
Connecting Door*, and lovingly evokes the memories of his father, his home
town, and his gradual maturation. Mainly, it is the story of a young
man who has always hoped to break away into the new forced by his
father's sudden death to recognize and to come to terms with the old,
especially in terms of his gradual estrangement from a father he loves.
The Connecting Door devotes one paragraph to this crucial moment:

> A thing which the near future held in store for me was that my father
> died. This left me, technically, head of the Atha family, although my
> mother is still alive and although I shall never quite feel head even
> of my own brood while my father-in-law, Idwal John, J. P., lives.
> (*CD*, 133).

The Woodshed focuses tightly on four days in the life of Harold Atha in
1948, a Thursday as he hurries by train from his vacation on the west
coast of Wales to his Hinderholm home where his father lies dying, the
Friday on which he walks around the town while the funeral is arranged,
the Saturday of the cremation, and the Sunday with a second walk and
a visit to his aunt. There is a very short coda separated in time from
the rest of the book in which the new knowledge shaped by his father's
death is assimilated into the evolution of yet another stage of being.
The novel grows directly out of memories of childhood, photographs,
evocations of the past sparked by streets, houses, and the Yorkshire
landscape in general, and the books still standing in the glass cases in
his parents' house. More particularly, *The Woodshed* records Heppenstall's
own experiences. Heppenstall said the novel 'started off with my father's
death and thinking very much about him, while I was taking a long
journey across Wales and northwest England, and the few days that I
remember of his funeral, and that naturally led to a consideration of
everything that would have been connected with him and the remote
past...'.[12] Harold's journey home is a physical journey across Wales

o Yorkshire, a journey back in time to his roots, and a metaphysical coming to terms with his past. Indeed the journey from Gwaelod to Hinderholme in the West Riding of Yorkshire structures the novel metaphorically: Harold names the towns through which he passes just as he names the events in his earlier life as he approaches a fact in his past, and just as his father dies, a part of himself dies during the experience.

Metaphors stress the significance of this particular journey. Harold toys humorously with the idea of writing a stream-of-consciousness novel:

> In a train, your consciousness streams like a cold. Mr A. regrets. Mr A. is confined to his carriage with a streaming consciousness. If I had a secretary sitting opposite with shorthand notebook, or a dictaphone, I could just talk like this. They reckon about ten thousand words to the hour. In a journey of eight hours, you could finish a book. Change the names, and you'd have a stream-of-consciousness novel. A man travelling somewhere for a purpose. What had led up to it, hopes and fears, retrospect and apprehension mingling, things noted as the landscape slid by. At the end, some kind of pay-off (*W*, 17–18)

His thoughts provide a paradigm for the novel except that he does not confine the occasional structuring within the train ride itself. When the Birmingham men he has snubbed walk past his compartment, Harold believes that his open exercise book, pen, and spectacles might lead them to believe that 'I was doing my accounts. I am, in a way' (*W*, 23). Near the end of the novel, he briefly contemplates a roots metaphor but breaks it off with the comment, 'Men are not plants' (*W*, 187), and at the very end of the novel as his train steams by Hinderholme, he thinks, repeating the William James image:

> If consciousness streams, it is backward. Or, rather, it is like the slack tide in an estuary.... At present, it is almost as though I were out on the open sea, glassily calm, If I again let down the deep trawl of memory, I should bring up dabs and elvers by the ton. The catch would only be to throw back. (*W*, 189).

Roots, dredges, trawls, accounts, journeys – these central metaphors coalesce into the figurative structuring of an otherwise plainly written, even rhetorically flat, story of a young man who has put considerable intellectual, emotional, and even economic distance between himself and his earlier selves but who, nevertheless, still fears something from his past. His journey is his own peculiar Swann's way and his Guermantes way in childhood (see *W*, 66).

A father's death is, of course, one of the most stressful and anxiety-producing moments in a son's life, perhaps even more so when a separation has not been healed for one reason or another. Harold's retrospection becomes, then, not only an evocation of memories but a reassessment of his father's life, a recognition that he himself contributed to his father's failure, and an escape into a sense of freedom as he confronts in memory the woodshed whose role in the 1927 summer of the eclipse is as important in his life as were the belladonna to Leo Colston and the lightning-struck tree to Sylvia Carter.

The 1948 Harold Atha has become fairly successful in journalism and publishing. *The Connecting Door* explored his career as a journalist which brought assignments in post-war France and Germany and brought him into contact with Sartre, Camus, Jouhandeau, Gide, and other members of the literary and philosophical circles in Paris. Lectures at Oxford on the publisher's points of view, travel, a more pleasant house in London, and vacations in Wales mark the distance the West Riding son of a co-operative manager reduced in retirement to an income of two guineas a week has travelled on his outward journey away from his lower-middle-class family and the constricting environment of Hinderholm.

As he travels back to Hinderholm, we quickly learn that he and his family have largely broken off communication. We learn that he 'had kept up no connection...even by letter' (*W*, 24) with his parents during the late 1930s because he 'did not want their eye upon my life at all' (*W*, 24). All attempts at communication betwen himself and his father during 1936 were 'simply meaningless, as had been all our exchanges for many years' (*W*, 26). Even though he still felt affection for his father at this time, there was 'no real communication, no means of demonstrating affection. Neither of us could, in even the simplest way, help the other' (*W*, 27). It occurs to Harold 'astonishingly how little [he] had succeeded in loving [his] father after the age of ten' (*W* 31). One searches in vain for some dramatic break between father and son in this novel. The hatred of Lawrence's Paul Morel for his coal-mining father has no attraction for Heppenstall who has Harold recall of a brief encounter in the 1930s:

At that moment, I truly loved my father. But indeed I had never as I should later discover to be almost common form among the young men I knew in London, 'hated' him. When I first heard of a young man hating his father, I thought what a very odd thing that was to do, though clearly a certain *chic* attached to it. (*W*, 146)

Harold and his father simply grow apart as generations with differing ambitions do. A quarrel over a philosophical point 'radically damaged the relation,' leading Harold to treat his father 'with inward disdain' (*W*, 145); otherwise they simply differ as Harold grows up over Harold's love affair, his flirtation with Catholicism, his brush with socialism, later with communism, and his ambition to attend a university rather than to take a job as a junior clerk in the Town Hall – the usual fodder for quarrels between fathers and sons.

More serious perhaps is Harold's estrangement from his home town and the narrowly defined future it offered him. The novel could appropriately carry the subtitle 'To Be Young, Talented, and Ambitious in a Provincial Industrial Town' and does bear numerous similarities to the Angry Young Man fiction of the 1950s, especially the novels of John Brain and Alan Sillitoe. The sociological divisions and tensions within Hinderholm are carefully delineated, not only in terms of Harold's younger life but also in terms of his family's history. Heppenstall traces the subtle dividing lines between families which had to use the public muck-cart and those which did not, between those that attended chapel and those that attend church, and between young men who wore 'proleptic caps and mufflers' and those in 'collars and ties' (*W*, 65). Harold's 'first lessons in sociology' (*W*, 64) come painfully when childhood friends reject him, telling him "Nay . . . you're a High School lad now. . . . Go and laik with Leslie Balmforth' (*W*, 65). More tellingly, Heppenstall conveys even the smells differentiating classes. Poverty has 'the smell of verdigris' (*W*, 68) coming from brass taps and copper pipes. Ethnic divisions also figure in the picture. Harold puzzles over stereotypes of Irishmen when his mother calls Johnny Lenihan Irish because Johnny's 'face spoke eloquently of soap and a sharp razor. His hair and cothes were spotless. He was not drunk. He had not shouted, spilt anything on the tablecloth, spat in the fire, thrown his overcoat on the couch, kicked up the mats, trailed in mud or done anything Irish, so far as I could see' (*W*, 82). School at Carlin Beck introduces Harold to the even more subtle differences in accents, so important in his culture; 'the great division [which] runs across Yorkshire, at somewhere about the latitude of York' (*W*, 120). As his friends reject him, his schoolmates rag him, and his interests in music and philosophy direct his attentions elsewhere, Harold becomes alienated from

Hinderholm. He becomes 'very solitary, partly... from necessity, partl' from choice' (*W*, 127). His provincial environment rises in its mos threatening form, however, when Harold is sixteen. He knows his fathe will not let him go to the Royal College of Music, and he doubts whethe the university is a possibility. At this moment, Harold hopes to atten Oxford for a while 'then leave it like Matthew Arnold's scholar gips' and be a mysterious, wandering poet or musician or both' (*W*, 168) At the age of fifteen, though, reality threatens in the form of a situatio vacant advertisement. Knowing that 'work in the Town Hall representec the height of [his] father's ambition,' (*W*, 168), Harold feels trapped He knows that his life threatens to take 'a direction [he] had not chosen (*W*, 170) and quotes Tennyson for comfort:

> ...And I, I know not if to pray
> Still to be what I am, or yield, and be
> Like all the other men I see. (*W*, 170)

Like Tennyson's 'few [who] / Escape their prison, and depart', Harolc escapes the potentially constricting, stultifying job in the provincia bureaucracy by brilliantining his freshly washed and fluffed hair, putting on a very tight collar and fumbling the questions during the interview

These and many other memories flood in by association upon Harolc as he rides home, as he sits that Friday morning 'in the chair by th shoe-cupboard, with the cardboard box of small albums and photograph and my exercise book' (*W*, 42) – the archetype of retrospection and a act which figures significantly in a number of post-war novels – and a his walks around the town awaken Fellinesque recollections of the past During his walks it even occurs to him to knock at a door and sa' "'Please forgive me, I lived here as a child, when the house was new. suppose you wouldn't let me just peep inside....'' (*W*, 46–7). The wall awakens memories of trading anatomical views with Sylvia Jagger, o early crushes, of Sidney Webb and Peter Holmes, of the feel, sound smell, and taste of Hinderholm between the earliest memories of 191. to the moment of his departure in 1936. He recalls, for example:

> Down to Waterside Lane was the walk my father and I took o' alternate Sunday mornings. This was the way my mother and I wen' on Saturday afternoons, unless it was raining or she wanted to bu' boiled sweets at Dobson's in the covered market. Then we'd go u' to Holt End by tram, by two trams, or into town, one up Kirkgat and past the main entrance to Grange Park. Sometimes, my fathe

came up after tea and walked home with us. The Shop closed at four
on Saturdays. (*W*, 66)

The percipitious streets and byways of Hinderholm and vicinity are
recalled with accuracy and detail associated with *Moll Flanders, Oliver
Twist,* and *Ulysses.*

Harold Atha has distanced himself from his past because of fear–fear
of repetition, of failure, and of the ominous secret of the woodshed.
Harold's family history contains an alarming number of parallel incidents
which can be read as startling coincidences or disturbing patterns. Often
they involve deaths. He thinks it odd, for instance, that his 'Rhineland
pilgrimages' should always conclude by involving him with his father
but brushes this aside, saying 'that is looking for coincidence and a
pattern... this time there is no casual connection of a natural kind.
The only conceivable link would be metaphysical' (*W*, 23–24). We
learn, however, that his mother wears a leg brace because a lorry struck
her during the first night of the wartime blackout and fractured her leg
severely and that his A'ntie Beulah 'had been in irons since she fell off
a 'bus at the stop in Bradford Road' (*W*, 28). He discovers that A'ntie
Jean collapsed from a stroke two days before a stroke killed his father,
a fact Harold finds troubling:

> One is accustomed to imitative crimes and 'waves' of suicides. It is
> difficult to see mere coincidence in these two parallel calamities.
> There must, I feel, at least have been 'suggestion' of a kind. It is all
> a bit eerie. (*W*, 35)

A search of his and the family's past reveals a number of other 'eerie'
similarities. His A'ntie Ada had an illegitimate child, his cousin Roy,
who died agonizingly of meningitis; he learns later that his A'ntie Beulah
also had an illegitimate child which had died. Births, accidents,
marriages, catastrophies, and deaths seem to come in pairs in his world.
and Harold may well be wondering exactly with whom and with what
his fate is paired.

He fears perhaps that it is paired with his father's. After all, he
physically resembles his father, even down to the same scar on the upper
lip,and most particularly in 'breaking away'. His father was the first
member of the family to work in a collar and tie, and his son is the first
member of the family to attend a university. The son broke away from
the provincial middle class just as the father broke away from the
working class. The father's ambitions, however, led nowhere. To Harold,

his father has not had 'much of a life' (*W*, 23), being proscribed by his own limitations and economic conditions. Once he attempted a major break: he moved his family from Hinderholm to take a promising job in Carlin Beck, a North Riding town. Harold admits that his father 'had felt at home in Carlin Beck' (*W*, 99) and had enjoyed its wider sphere of opportunity. His job paid well; he was well received in the community; he almost became a public figure since he was encouraged to stand as a Liberal for the town council. Carlin Beck posed a threat to Harold and his mother, though, and they bear a large responsibility for getting Atha to return to Hinderholm after only two years. Harold's mother wept persistently and made few friends. Much later she confessed to her son, "'I held him back. I s' never forgive myself'" (*W*, 137). 'The only thing she ever found to say in favour of the small, flat town', Harold remembers, 'was that her curtains didn't need washing as often there' (*W*, 100). The date of moving, 18 October 1923, remains fixed in Harold's mind because it marked a betrayal in his mind. His life had been disrupted. As he walks through the Hinderholm house on that day, he thinks:

> I should never again come home at tea-time on Tuesday to the smell of hot loaves and tea-cakes spred out on that table. There would never be sarsparilla boiling again in the copper, or, if there was, it would not be I who drank it to cool my blood. Not that my blood needed cooling at the moment. (*W*, 105)

Carlin Beck brings 'the worst moment of my life to date' (*W*, 117), he thinks, as he recalls the school ragging during which his cap was taken and his face was blackened with shoe polish. He remembers that after the return to Hinderholm his father was 'yet a disappointed and wounded man. His face, sufficiently handsome but without boldness, had set in weak lines of disappointment' (*W*, 31) and then Harold admits, 'It is him I take after, not my mother' (*W*, 31).

Another form of patterned repetition and failure also haunts Harold, much like the boggart that he once imagined lived beneath 'the shelves of jams and pickles' (*W*, 19) in the house. Harold approaches his moment in his past cautiously, telling himself, 'I must go carefully now about the order in which things happened' (*W*, 165). At the end of June, 1927, when Yorkshire citizens witnessed a total eclipse of the sun, Harold experiences a much more serious personal eclipse. His parents take a short trip leaving him alone. One evening he visits the home of his newly married cousin, Gertie, only recently returned from her honeymoon, for dinner and, finding the door locked and apparently no one home, goes into the backyard to a woodshed to see if a spare key can be found. As he comes out of the woodshed, he sees his Uncle Gordon at the kitchen window and smiles. Gordon sticks out his tongue; Harold laughs. Harold decides

> I must have offended him by what I had said ten days ago about not being very interested in footballers any longer. He certainly didn't mean to let me in. He didn't shout at me, but clearly he was sending me away. In fact he seemed in a towering rage. He glared. His eyes almost popped with fury. His face was more darkly congested than ever. He shook his head angrily and then more slowly and decidedly from side to side. (*W*, 177)

Only later does Harold discover that he happened onto his uncle at the very moment he was committing suicide by hanging himself from a meat-hook in the kitchen. Still later, when the scandal concerning homosexuality involving the Hinderholm United team and Law Barraclough breaks does Harold fit all the pieces together and associate Gordon with the scandal. Even this suicide is paired, since Mr Allendale, Master of the Carlin Beck school Harold attended, shoots himself with a cavalry carbine the same summer. Confronting the memories of the suicide near the end of his four days at home, Harold is tempted to ask his mother questions but refrains:

> I might have been led on to tell her what I had seen at Gertie's back window. She might have raised again the question I asked myself then, whether it really would have been too late for me to do something if I had not so quickly been driven away by what I took for so improbable a bit of mere face-pulling. (*W*, 181)

The suicide and the later scandal deeply troubled Harold, perhaps because he had flirted unashamedly with Peter Holmes and once Law Barraclough had encouraged the relationship. The novel invests Gordon's suicide with an importance it might not otherwise have had since Harold erects signals around the episode, stresses the importance of recalling it carefully, and postpones it until last. Also, the title of the novel. functioning much as do the elaborate puns in the Raymond Roussel stories Heppenstall admires, broods significantly over the entire novel waiting completion, explanation, and recollection for both Harold and the reader.[13]

Sylvère Monod has concluded that Harold emerges from the recollection with 'a consciousness of patterned life', but only glancingly suggests what the pattern involves.[14] Harold encounters the impermanence of self, the bewildering array of coincidences which hold no key as to his own fate, similarities between his own and his father's lives, and a recognition that he has influenced lives in ways he never recognized before. He has also come to terms with 'the essential sweetness' (*W*, 31) of his father and his own indebtedness to his father. His literal patrimony may be insignificant – 'a light overcoat of red tweed, a suit which fits me perfectly, an umbrella with engraved silver ring and a box of tools, less a diamond glass-cutter promised to the deaf young man next door' (*W*, 139) – but his patrimony, he realizes, also includes a sense of values and a cluster of poignant memories of a man he loves.

Patrimony also includes freedom. Heppenstall has sometimes been criticized for the endings of his novels. He has admitted that 'a painful *accidie* normally supervenes just past the halfway mark [in the composition of a novel]. This has to be accepted and the book, however pointless it may have come to seem, pushed on with and completed by an effort of will, after which the novelist should go away for a holiday' (*FT*, 149). Sylvère Monod writes that in *The Woodshed* 'the most attractive and ingenious of narrative devices comes to be somewhat perfunctorily resorted to'.[15] The Coda to *The Woodshed* seems an essential statement, necessarily brief, of Harold's insight wrung from the experience of his father's death and his visit home. In it, Harold is once again on a train, journeying away from Hinderholm and hence completing the journey begun in the opening section of the novel. Like a quest hero, he has descended into the underworld and now is escaping with his new boon of knowledge. Like the accountant he imagined himself taken for, he draws the closure lines to the episode: 'And so I suppose I have finished with Hinderholm. It won't matter. That is not the centre of my life' (*W*, 188). He feels nothing about the town as the train passes it; he knows no 'anthromorphic cry' from the whistles; he senses that as he approaches London 'no doubt new urgencies will begin' (*W*, 189).

5 Brian Moore, *I Am Mary Dunne:* 'memento ergo sum'

A survey of the last six novels of Brian Moore underlines a particular interest in the past and its relationship with the present which has deepened and broadened from a tightly focused one-day novel concerning a woman's pending breakdown to the confrontation between a twentieth-century failure and his nineteenth-century ancestor and double. In *I Am Mary Dunne*, the protagonist who once suggested that Descartes' *cogito ergo sum* should have been *memento ergo sum* recalls in troubling detail her marriages to three very different men and the resulting collapse of her own sense of identity. The other five novels even more particularly concern this confrontation between the past and the present, whether in the fantastic recreation of a collection of Victoriana or a wife striving on a second honeymoon to find something missing from the first or a dying man reliving his past. In such novels as *Fergus* and *The Doctor's Wife*, Moore explores the relationship between the individual and his past, seeing therein a redemptive process, a self-redemption, whereby the character comes to terms with self and is freed by the dialogue with the past. In *The Great Victorian Collection*, he explores the responsibility of the present for the artifacts of the past, paradoxes raised by authors as diverse as Jorge Luis Borges and John Fowles, concerning the contemporary recreation and adaptation of past artistic forms. In *Catholics*, he probes the implications of a present culture demanding of itself a complete renunciation of its past heritage as Father Kinsella demands that the monks of Muck Island cease saying Latin Mass. Most recently, in *The Mangan Inheritance*, the protagonist returns to Ireland to discover if he is descended from James Clarence Mangan, Europe's first *poete maudit*, and unexpectedly to encounter, while on this search for roots, his historical double. Perhaps the confrontation with the past raises autobiographical questions for an author who has moved from one culture to another; more significantly, Moore's novels affirm the necessity of a culture, an individual, and an artist addressing the past, not as a nightmare, but rather as a vital memory which one cannot and should not escape. Through this impressive collection of novels runs the thought, voiced emphatically by Fergus: 'Until now, he had thought that, like everyone else, he had exorcised his past by living it. But he was not like everyone else. His past had risen up this morning, vivid, uncontrollable, shouldering into the present.'[1]

In at least four interviews, Moore has spoken at length about *I Am Mary Dunne*, explaining problems he encountered in writing it, voicing his intentions, and sounding once very much like Gustave Flaubert. For the *Literary Guild Magazine* — the novel was a Literary Guild selection in 1968 — he commented:

> I am Mary Dunne because I have taken my own life and transmogrified it into hers.... For two years I have wakened in the mornings, gone into a room, sat at a typewriter and, like an actor going on stage, like a medium trying to induce a trance, I have tried to think myself into the skin and into the mind of a young, troubled, pretty woman, And, like a medium speaking in a voice of another person, I have written the book in the first person singular, in her voice, the voice of Mary Dunne.[2]

Moore probably began writing the novel in 1966 at the latest — he said once he usually liked to work for two years on his books — and definitely not in the first person. He told Hallvard Dahlie in a June 1967 interview. 'I started my current book in the third person, and then I went back to the first person, and by that time I had done a lot of work. Then I decided that the interesting way to do it was to put it all in the historical present, and so I rewrote nearly two-thirds of the book in that way. And then I read it all over again decided that first-person, non-historical present was and most interesting way and gave me the most interesting feeling...'.[3] A month later, he told Richard B. Sale that he was unhappy with the last third of the book and intended to rewrite it as well.[4]

Setting the narrative point of view was perhaps the most important decision Moore made while working on the novel, because the novel poses particular difficulties. It is, first of all, a doubly retrospective narrative in which Mary Laverty née Dunne lies, at the end of a confusing and frightening day, in her bed. She forces herself to recall in minute detail everything which happened to her during the day and as she does she also recalls the major events of her life up to the day. The cogs of the short retrospective of twelve hours mesh firmly and smoothly with the long retrospective of thirty-two years, except perhaps for the final scene, as Mary recalls her encounters with three people from the past and, by association, all those other events in her past directly and indirectly related to these three individuals. Fitting past and present together in a retrospective narrative is a delicate task demanding technical expertise. Sometimes, authors emphasize the break as when, in Wilson's *Late Call* and Hartley's *The Go-Between*, the books' divisions segregate past and present as formally as the premises in a syllogism; other authors, among them Heppenstall and Moore, chose to present the past and the present fully intertwined on virtually every page of the work thereby creating a slightly different perspective on the past impinging constantly on the present. The technical problem lies in transitions, associations, and juxtapositions which must remain true to the mind generating them.

Putting his reader within the thought processes of Mary Dunne is the second technical problem. Retrospective narratives frequently have a knowing, experienced, aware narrator looking back at an earlier, less experienced, often ignorant self and evaluating the inadequate responses of this earlier self. The first-person point of view bristles with difficulties. One easily understands why authors such as Henry James rejected it.[5] It offers intimacy and verisimilitude, but it also raises the spectre of authority, reliability, and distance. The events may be filtered through the somewhat comfortable smugness of Jane Eyre, the paradoxically defensive and celebratory view of Moll Flanders, or the garrulous ramblings of Molly Bloom, whose famous soliloquy may stand as an immediate ancestor to Moore's novel. In his attempt to put himself 'into the skin and into the mind of a young, troubled, pretty woman', Moore has intensified the problems of first person narrative while at the same time communicating fully his character's tensions, frustrations, and fears. But to what extent is the reader to trust Mary Dunne's recollections? She herself ponders the problem of her own reliability, thinking at one point,

When people say they remember everything that happened in their lives, they're deceiving themselves. I mean if I were to try to tell anyone the story of my life so far, wouldn't it come out as fragmentary and faded as those old snapshot albums, scrapbooks, and bundles of letters everyone keeps in some bottom drawer or other? What would I remember about my life, wouldn't it be just some false, edited little movie, my version of what my parents were like, the places I lived in, the names of some of the people I've known, and would any of it give you any idea of what I feel about, say, sex, or children . . . ?
(*MD*, 10)[6]

Mary Dunne raises the central problem discussed over twenty years ago
by Wayne C. Booth in *The Rhetoric of Fiction*.[7] How does an author
establish a secret communion with the reader when the narrative itself
originates within the mind of a not totally perceptive and occasionally
outright devious character who wishes to gloss over, to ignore, or to
hide certain important facts or events? The question is not unimportant
if we are to emerge from our saturation in her stream of consciousness
with some clear understanding of her plight and her condition at the
end of the day, for Mary Dunne is more than troubled; she may be
verging on madness. Moore confessed his own ambivalence concerning
his character's condition, telling John Graham: 'Well, I dunno if this
woman is going to make it. I dunno if she really is clinically mad. I
mean she may be gonna get worse because he's [the third husband] too
solicitous, for instance'.[8] Indeed, more than one reviewer objected about
the point of view, sometimes stressing the limitations of the technique,
as did Nora L. Magid who simply commented that 'a human being is
more than the sum of his remembered parts', hence implying that there
is far more to Mary Dunne than the character herself perceives, and
sometimes objecting to the success of Moore in insinuating himself into
his character, as did Katherine Gauss Jackson who found herself
'unpleasantly overpowered by so much feminine psychology and
feminine physiology as well, and the fact that it was written by a man
gives the sense of participating in a kind of weird and unwelcome
transvestitism'.[9]

I Am Mary Dunne is filled with both psychology and physiology. Mary
is in the midst of a serious 'Down Tilt' brought on by premenstrual
tensions. Throughout the day, she suffers from dizziness, trembling,
blanking out, and moments of panic, problems which have increased
for the last two years since her second divorce. Onset of menstruation
fragments her personality; for years 'the Curse that comes once a month
making me murderous one minute, suicidal the next, weepy, sick, silly,
confused, and I sit here appalled, feeling some other self within me
begins to go berserk' (*MD*, 21). Premenstrual tension polarizes her into
a hostile self which sees violence, criminal acts, and chaos threatening
her and an appalled 'Sensible Self.' Unreasonable terror alternates with
embarrassed shame. Moore chose this moment, he told Graham, as a
symbol of the tensions surrounding the individual in the modern world:

> This woman is not mad, but all women go through varying degrees
> in a period of each month when they are more or less upset, some
> women very little. The pre-menstrual tension is in a way the symptom
> of the madness we all feel, the tension of normal life.[10]

Her physiological tensions magnify her psychological tensions. She sees the day as her 'crack-up' (*MD*, 12) — not a clinical breakdown but rather the crack-up suffered by cartoon characters. She fantasizes Sigmund Freud looking at her saying '*Paronoia, Liebchen, ja, ja!*' (*MD*, 83) and senses that she is on 'the cliff edge' (*MD*, 135) which may mark the descent into insanity. She fears that she may be committed to an asylum by Terence, her third husband.

Mary Dunne had lost her sense of identity and hence feels she has lost her sense of purpose and her hold on sanity. She is experiencing a severe identity crisis, a problem Erik Erikson has identified as the major crisis facing the individual in the twentieth-century world.[11] In Moore's opinion, identity may be a far more crucial issue for women than for men; he told the interviewer from *Publisher's Weekly*, 'Everyone is writing about alienation and problems of identity. The tendency since Camus had been to treat them abstractly. Women lose their identity much more than men', and, for some time, the novel carried a working title 'A Woman of No Identity'.[12] Moore planned to treat a woman who 'has reached a point in her life at which she begins to wonder who she really was, who she really is, and who she is going to be . . . I feel that gap between the different selves we are at different times of our lives very strongly . . .'.[13] When the receptionist at the beauty parlour asks Mary her name and Mary momentarily forgets, Mary's inability to recall and then her blunder of giving her first husband's name shatter her awareness of self. She remembers thinking, 'I am no longer Mary Dunne, or Mary Phelan, or Mary Bell, or even Mary Lavery. I am a changeling who has changed too often and there are moments when I cannot find my way back' (*MD*, 98). She asks Terence, '"Who am I any more! All these names, who am I?"' (*MD*, 133). Remembering becomes a desperate search for identity since memory defines being for Mary. Mary thinks, 'If I can remember that far back and so clearly then shut up, heart, calm down, there's nothing to be afraid of' (*MD*, 9) and begins 'that fleeting Indian wrestle' (*MD*, 25) with memory to affirm her identity by tracing her various discontinuous selves. Her 'mulish, unbiddable memory' yields up 'sudden, isolated moment[s]' (*MD*, 147–8) which enable her to get some grasp on who she is.

Memory quickly establishes three central qualities to her personality: fear, sexuality, and guilt, all intertwined complexly. More specifically, she fears her future and feels guilt for her past. These feelings are exacerbated by rather rude invasions of her privacy by the New York City environment. Throughout the day, she is buffeted by rude cab drivers, rude *maître-d's*, less than friendly waiters, and a surly maid.

Three men treat her as a nameless, personalityless sex object — a well dressed man on the street suddenly grabs her wrist and in a breathy advance says, ' "I'd like to fuck you, baby" ' (*MD*, 12) a delivery man in the Delight Dry Cleaners 'began making sucking motions with his lips, pretending to kiss through the windowpane' (*MD*, 75), and a pimply faced student 'accidentally on purpose, rested the back of his hand against my thigh' as they board on a bus (*MD*, 89). New York provides further tensions for the lonely individual in an urban world; it becomes 'an aggressive character in the novel'.[14]

Assaulted by the present, Mary Dunne also fears the future, because she sees how her society ruthlessly discards older women. Her own mother, widowed and alone in her small house in Butchersville, Nova Scotia, worries her. Even more, she cannot understand why a woman as interesting as Mrs Dowson has been pushed aside by her daughter and son-in-law. Now an 'unwanted old widow who sits staring into the sad, coloured glooms of a television set in the lounge at Briarwood [an expensive nursing home]' (*MD*, 50), Mrs Dowson once met Rasputin at tea in the Tsarina's apartments, once worked as governess for the Duc de Mirepont, and once knew Marcel Proust. Time, marriage, and society have stripped these women of their identities, so it is easy to see why Mary fears that the future will also strip her and leave her a nameless discard in some asylum. In one of the many rephrasings of Descartes which dominate the book, Mary fantasizes:

> I will get worse, I will lose not only my memory, but my mind and at the end I will be that vegetable squatting on the floor of the asylum's disturbed ward, unable to say its name, any of its names, for it has forgotten, therefore it is not, it has no name, it cannot even clean itself. (*MD*, 185–6)

Guilt rises from the past to join the present dangers and fears of the future. Mary Dunne is perhaps the most guilty feeling character in English fiction since Thomas Hardy's Tess, and with as little reason as Tess. She scourges herself with whips of hardly deserved guilt. She sits in her bedroom, unable to confront her maid, 'like a condemned person awaiting the execution party' (*MD*, 21). In one of the most telling allusions in the novel, she sees her face in the mirror as Macbeth's, 'the face of the murderer and no matter how I tried not to think of that night I could not exorcise it' (*MD*, 89); she imagines herself, at one point, speaking to a jury but instantly becomes her own judge, ruling 'it is still *mea culpa, mea culpa, mea maxima culpa*' (*MD*, 90). In her opinion, she is a 'rotten person' (*MD*, 106), and, under the gaze of Dostoyevsky, Proust, Tolstoy, and Yeats, portraits of whom hang in Terence's study, she tells herself, 'I was again guilty of something, I knew not what, but guilty, yes guilty. Self-condemned' (*MD*, 134). The guilt is self-inflicted and exaggerated because she has willingly accepted the guilt other people have forced on her.

Mary's anguished search through her past to find and clasp to her some sense of identity quickly reveals both her desperate drive for success and escape from something and the adolescent trauma which casts a sinister cloud over her own sexuality. At several points in the narrative, she thinks, 'If Red Davis had not told Dick and Dick had not repeated the story to me, I would never have known it. I would be a different woman today' (*MD*, 163), and again 'I wonder has he [Dick, her brother] any idea how that ugly little story has affected my life, how, all through my teens, any time a boy made a pass, I froze, afraid that I might become like my father' (*MD*, 19). The 'ugly little story' concerns her father's death. When Mary was ten, Daniel Malone Dunne, 'a charmer', died of a cerebral haemorrhage in New York's Park Plaza Hotel while coupling with a prostitute, who left him deserted, naked, and dead for the maid to find the next morning. Mary's brother tells her the story when she is fifteen, a most impressionable and sexual age, and the death becomes entangled in her one recurring dream. Mary understands that her dreams of being naked with naked men in hotel rooms 'are mixed up in my mind with that story Dick told me about my father and with my fear that, somehow, I am like my father' (*MD*, 19) but she has not made the essential connection that she blames her father for destroying her innocence and consequently heaps guilt on herself for seeing his death as an appropriate punishment, and, just perhaps, for feeling some desire for her father. In either case, her father's death sours life in Nova Scotia for her, 'when simple things were funny, when life was ordinary and often dull. When I was Mary Dunne' (*MD*, 15). Lost innocence brings a desire to flee just as she had once fled after breaking a neighbor's window. Her BA degree brings only 'an offer of a filing clerk's job at the government forestry lab at Fredericton' and her life seemed 'stretched ahead . . . like an empty horizon' (*MD*, 103). Acting seems a way out and a way to success.

To achieve success, later to be spelled 'suckcess' (*MD*, 137) in the novel, Mary has to use people and to allow people to use her, a dual motif in her memories. Mary first uses James Patrick Phelan, her first husband, to escape from Butchersville to Toronto. She does not love him, and he only lusts after her. A 'twenty-one-year-old boy with a big

Adam's apple, laughing with a nervous bark' (*MD*, 103), Jimmy involves
Mary in one of fiction's strangest elopements and desperate poverty.
They elope in a rented car, charged with driving Tom Dawkins, a
retarded man, from Halifax to Toronto. Tom, offended because Jimmy
tries to make him sit in the back seat and slighly drunk from the
wedding-breakfast whiskey, convinces the landlady of the motel where
they are spending the night, that he is the groom's father, takes the car
keys, and lands everyone in trouble at the border crossing station. Even
worse than the confusion and poverty, Jimmy ejaculates prematurely
and convinces Mary that she must be at fault. Mary tells herself on the
disastrous wedding night 'well you've done it now, this is the first real
mortal sin in your life . . . you *are* a rotten person, Mary Dunne, you've
married him, yet you don't even want to kiss him, let alone live with
him the rest of your life' (*MD*, 106). She accepts responsibility for the
sexual failures which come to separate them and believes Jimmy when
he accuses her of being frigid, of being 'a virgin . . . as cold as a bloody
plaster saint' (*MD*, 142).

Life with Jimmy also brings her into contact with Ruth 'Mackie'
McIver, a research librarian at *Canada's Own Magazine*, who attempts
to mold Mary to her own liking along even more drastic lines. Mackies'
power and wealth corrupt by enticing Mary and Jimmy to move from
Blodgett's to Mackie's spacious, well-appointed home, by offering
servants and cars, and by providing an entry into acting school. Mackie
secures Mary a better-paying job, turns her into 'Maria', and transforms
her into a creature of her own design. Mary realizes later that 'no man
ever tried to change me as much as Mackie did, no man tried so
ruthlessly to suppress the Mary Dunne I was in order to transform me
into a creation of his imaginings. . . . It was as though she had decided
to destroy my old identity by inventing a new one for me' (*MD*, 119).
When Mary begins to reject her gifts and stultifying care and when
Mary coldly repulses Mackie's tactfully and guardedly worded lesbian
overtures, Mackie avenges herself by telling Jimmy that Mary is having
an affair with Hatfield Kent Bell.

Hat, as Mary calls him, offers an escape from both Jimmy and
Mackie, but the escape becomes equally nightmarish. Mary moves up
the ladder of success with this affair and marriage, but with it she moves
into a world of alcoholism, further sexual failure, and increasing guilt.
From their first moments alone in the La Salle Hotel in Montreal, Mary
knows something is sexually wrong: when she emerges naked from the
bathroom, her long hair swirling around her hips, she finds Hat waiting
but he has no erection. Immediately, she blames herself: 'he admires

me in my clothes, he always says I look like a model, maybe my body is a disappointment to him?' (*MD*, 34) Sex with Hat becomes a succession of 'litanies I would come to know as the prayers of failure' (*MD*, 35) and she intensifies her guilt, telling herself, 'the jokes and giggles were mild hysteria. I know it, yet I did not want to know it and that was my fault, my fault, my most grievous fault' (*MD*, 35) though she struggles along in the marriage, following Hat to New York when he lands an important job with *Life*, staying with him when he is fired for his heavy drinking, and returning with him to Montreal when he is hired by *Canada's Own*. She goes even more reluctantly than with Jimmy, thinking 'I will spend the rest of my life locked up with him . . . I thought of those horror films where ordinary people turn into vampires and, for a moment, Hat seemed a vampire and I wanted to scream, and though a scream would release me, end the panic, let it all out (*MD*, 65).

Hat's insecurity causes him to blame Mary for all his failures and inadequacies, blame he transfers to her far more successfully and far more damagingly than Jimmy had ever done. Mary so willingly accepts his judgement, because she knows she should never have married him. His judgement constitutes her punishment. When Janice Sloan betrays Mary's affair with Terence Laverty to Hat, he turns on Mary bitterly, telling her

> You know what you are, you're a bitch, a bitch, you don't give a curse about affection or love or marriage or any normal, decent emotion, all you want is to be fucked, fucked, fucked, until the come is running out of you, that's why you left poor Phelan, because he couldn't satisfy you, and now you're running out on me for the same reason and after the poor Beatle bugger has fucked you blind, you'll ditch him too . . . (*MD*, 91)

Guilt increases, because Hat dies, a possible suicide, definitely a confirmed alcoholic, and people blame Mary. They say she killed him. Even Janice Sloan, supposedly a good friend but the one who betrayed her, in anger says '*Look what you did to him when he was down*' (MD, 57).

Mary even feels guilt with her third husband, perhaps partially in reaction to her success. She has now arrived. She is married to a successful English playwright, has a well appointed apartment on East 78th Street in New York, has no worries over money, and obviously enjoys a most comfortable life. Sexually, she and her husband are compatible and happy. She goes so far as to tell Hat '"Terence is my

saviour. I shall not want, he maketh me to lie down in green pastures,
he restoreth my soul"' (*MD*, 92), yet she feels guilty even with him
and feels she has failed in some way. Most obviously, her premenstrual
tensions remind her that she has no child, though she desires one with
Terence. Even Terence has taken away her shreds of identity, as when
he jokingly introduces her as Martha to some colleagues. Mary knows,
too, that Terence has compromised his talent, abandoning a serious
play for a 'little revue' because ' "they" had said audiences wouldn't
like it' (*MD*, 136), a compromise she feels she may have caused. Mary
finally admits 'I feel guilty with Terence' (*MD*, 140) because she has
asked him to do so many things for her — to rescue her, to save her, to
fulfil her.

Each of these three men has, in his own destructive way, remade
Mary and in so doing stripped her of her precious identity. She realizes
that she has become an actress playing a different role for each husband,
'with special shadings demanded by each suitor':

> For Jimmy I had to be a tomboy; for Hat, I must look like a model:
> he admired elegance. Terence wants to see me as Irish: sulky,
> laughing, wild. And me, how do I see me, who is that me I create
> in mirrors, the dressing-table me, the self I cannot put a name to in
> the Golden Door Beauty Salon? (*MD*, 32)

Peregrinations from Butchersville to Toronto to Montreal and finally
to New York and from Jimmy to Hat to Terence have destroyed Mary's
self-image. She literally does not know who she is any more.

The 'day of reckoning' though sees Mary encounter Karl Dieter
Peters, who reminds her of her acting days, then Janice Sloan, an image
of the neurotic, disappointed woman she could have become, who takes
her back to Jimmy and Hat, and finally Ernie Truelove, nicknamed L.
O. Macduff, who, while dining with Mary and Terence at the end of
the day, tells Mary that Hat may have committed suicide after writing
her a very long letter the day of his death. By accident, the letter never
reached Mary. The day closes with the residue of its beginning. Mary's
mother calls from Butchersville. Earlier in the day Mary had atempted
to call her, worrying over the news that her mother was to have surgery
for the removal of a tumorous growth.

In his interview with Sale, Moore spoke of the Joycean epiphanies
and indicated his own interests in writing:

> I feel that when ordinary people are forced to examine themselves
> and when they're lucky enough to have that moment of insight — of

seeing themselves — it's astonishing how they manage to get up and go on. It's their endurance I admire, the guts that ordinary people have, the guts that the least likely people have.[15]

The comment's ambivalence may explain the divergent opinions over the ending of the novel. In *Late Call, The Go-Between* and *The Woodshed*, the moments of recognition and of insight created by the past impinging on the present brough growth, freeing knowledge, and release from tormenting guilt. Moore's remark implies that an individual 'lucky enough' to gain insight into the true nature of his being and his condition is benefited, but his comment that 'it's astonishing how they manage to get up and go on' suggests that insight may be destructive.

Reviewers and later critics have been unable to agree whether the conclusion of *I Am Mary Dunne* involves a breakthrough in understanding that matures Mary or whether it records a defensive retreat and a defeat. Moore himself seems a bit unsure in his interviews. He told Sale he was 'unhappy' with the last third of the novel but that Mary 'isn't a loser in the Judith Hearne sense'. He also stressed that endings pose crucial moments of artistic judgment for him: 'at the point where I must decide the ending, I get hung up, very depressed. That's often the point at which I reject a novel, because I realize that though I have gone a great way with this character, something has gone wrong; I haven't succeeded in creating a character close enough to my ideal of the sort of person I wanted to write about to make my ending viable'.[16] Moore believes that novels should be directed towards a decision and that a novelist evades his responsibilities if he settles for certain anti-novel innovations. A happy ending may veer the book into unwarranted sentimentality and falseness, but no ending at all may simply be a failure of nerve. 'I feel', he told Sale, 'I would be cheating the reader at the end because I'm not going toward something at the end. I'm going toward the idea of what happened, and I have to take that chance ... my books are structured toward a decision which I make at one point or another and which I haven't made about my new book yet. '[17] A month earlier, he had affirmed his interest in endings, saying 'I feel that I am working towards answers for myself' and again pointing to his discontent with the 'end section' of the novel.[18]

Reviews written in haste for deadlines often err, but the reviewers were genuinely puzzled by the ending as have been the later, more considered, critics. James R. Lindroth read the ending negatively, seeing it as a life coming to a close, while Philip French writes that Mary had contemplated suicide and 'moved on'.[19] The anonymous reviewer for *Time* saw 'no resolution' while Richard Gilman concluded that 'nothing much has happened' and George Woodcock saw a cyclical decline into progressively more serious identity crises.[20] Hallvard Dahlie, Jeanne Flood, and John Wilson Foster, who have discussed Moore's work at length, voice equally divergent readings. In 1968, Dahlie called the ending an affirmation and an 'attainment of calm', but in 1974 Foster replied that Dahlie had missed the irony because the ending testified to Mary's 'utter insecurity, not to any degree of certainly whatever'.[21] Flood, too, infers Mary's failure to find answers.[22] The ending, however, partakes the same ambiguity as the informing metaphor of the novel — menstruation. Is menstruation a beginning or an ending?

Close reading, within the necessary qualifications, reveals both affirmation and negation, similar to that in Moore's own life as he completed the novel. When questioned about his happier outlook on life, Moore responded:

> My new book was written and is being finished in this new happiness which is my present life … People's lives change them. I don't know whether this great change in my life will make me a better; or worse writer. But I'll be a different writer.[23]

Mary's life poises similarly: she will certainly be different, but the tip of the scales is not entirely resolved. Qualifications are necessary in reading the ending because Moore chose to have a limited and somewhat unreliable narrator, a point initially suggested by the epigraph taken from William Butler Yeats' 'Among School Children':

> O body swayed to music, O brightening glance,
> How can we know the dancer from the dance.

When Mary casts her 'brightening glance' almost in terror over her past, she reaches certain conclusions before she finally affirms:

> I did manage to remember most of the thoughts, words, and deeds of today, and now I will not panic, these dooms may just be pre-menstrual, I will not over-dramatize my problems, I am not losing my memory, I know who I am, . . . I am the daughter of Daniel Malone Dunne and Eileen Martha Ring, I am Mary Patricia Dunne, I was christened that and there is nothing wrong with my heart or with my mind . . . (*MD*, 187)

Mary continues to delude herself in that she has changed and changed considerably. She is no longer Mary Dunne nor can she recapture her lost innocence, and, indeed, more than pre-menstrual tensions threaten her. On the other hand, she has confronted her fear of death and overcome it; she has considered suicide and rejected it; she has demonstrated to herself what she is *not*, a necessary clearing of the ground so she can begin to re-establish who and what she is. In this sense, her journey through her past has been both purgative and reconstitutive. She has been led, in part, to see that she is no more tied to her earlier, discontinuous selves than her present self will be to some future self. Finally, she accepts that existence need not have a particular purpose other than existing, the capacity 'to get up and go on' Moore admires. The excursion into the past has not redeemed, freed, and transformed Mary yet, but it has brought her to a central recognition that she is who she is and not who others say she is. She is what she remembers, and there is still a firm bedrock of her earlier provincial, Catholic, and innocent self on which to build an identity. She decides to fight her dooms and recall a past she does not like to remember. At one point she provides the answer to the debate over the novel's ending:

> This is a story of how I lost part of my innocence, lost part of that Mary Dunne who left Butchersville and never can go back. It is a story of what money did to me. If I am to learn anything from past mistakes, then there's no sense blaming it all on Jimmy. (*MD*, 121–2)

Nor, she might have added, on Hat or Janice or Ernie or herself. She is not as guilty as she assumes, nor is she guiltless. Paradoxically, Moore's novel asks its readers to affirm growth through negation.

Part III
Challenged Comparisons

In John Fowles' *The Ebony Tower*, his 1974 novella dealing, among other things, with the meeting between an analytical critic and a synthetic creator, David Williams stands before Henry Breasley's masterpiece *Moon-hunt* thinking:

> As with so much of Breasley's work there was an obvious previous iconography — in this case, Uccello's *Night Hunt* and its spawn down through the centuries; which was in turn a challenged comparison, a deliberate risk . . . so the memory of the Ashmolean Uccello somehow deepened and buttressed the painting before which David sat . . . behind the modernity of so many of the surface elements there stood both a homage and a kind of thumbed nose to a very old tradition.[1]

Before his meeting with Breasley concludes, David senses that the true strength of the artist's creativity lies in his 'umbilical cord to the past'.[2]

In this brief passage, Fowles strikes to the heart of a crucial literary problem for our age which insists that 'poetry can only be made out of other poems; novels out of other novels'.[3] What relationship or relationships can or does the contemporary author strike in terms of his predecessors? David Williams considers several alternatives and suggests an ideal solution. *Moon-hunt* and *Night-hunt* stand in direct relationship with one another, one as a descendant and in some ways an amalgamation of a tradition, the other as a progenitor of the tradition. If *Moon-hunt* were merely a 'homage' to the Uccello painting, David would dismiss it rather quickly; indeed, he would never have come to Coëtminais to interview an imitative painter in the first place. The annals of art are littered with the remains of talented imitators, sometimes of outright forgers, whose talents never escaped the shadows of their more talented predecessors and whose abilities were consumed by the earlier works.[4] Frank homage is a dead end, but the 'thumbed nose' of parody, David hints, is also a dead end. Susan Sontag pinpointed the difficulties

inherent in the 'decadent response' of parody when she commented tha
'it's not an answer. It's a response. The glut of cultural goods creates a
kind of fatigue — having too many models, too many stimuli. And
parody is one way of handling the problem and copping out at the same
time'.[5] *Moon-hunt* successfully navigates through the Scylla of imitation
and the Chardybdis of parody by simultaneously being both. In it, one
talent challenges another and uses the earlier work to provide an
intensified purpose and a deepened perspective for his own creation.

Moon-hunt stands as a paradigm for numerous contemporary novels
which stand as deliberate challenges to earlier novels, most usually
Victorian novels. The 'umbilical cord to the past' is deliberately evoked
in the reader's mind, and the phenomenon is not peculiar to English
fiction. In 1971, for example, Joyce Carol Oates told an interviewer
that she planned a group of short stories which would be 'reimaginings
of famous stories'; Tom Wolfe contemplated writing a novel 'that
performs something of the same function of Thackeray's *Vanity Fair*',
and John Hawkes recalled that his novel, *The Blood Oranges,* consciously
offered 'a somewhat different version of Ford Madox Ford's *The Good
Soldier*'.[6] One thinks, too, of John Barth's The *Sot Weed Factor* and Erica
Jong's *Fanny,* those very different recreations of eighteenth-century
fictional conventions. In other words, Oates, Wolfe, Hawkes, and Barth
offered 'counter-books' obliquely 'completing' the works of Joyce, Kafka,
Chekhov, Thackeray, Ford, and others, revealing, as Jorge Luis Borges
pointed out in 'Tlön, Ugbar, Orbis Tertius', that 'a book which does
not include its opposite or "counter-book", is considered incomplete'.[7]

'That a present-day book should derive from an ancient one', the
narrator of Borges' 'The Approach to Al-Mu' tasim' reminds us, 'is
clearly honorable: especially since no one . . . likes to be indebted to his
contemporaries.'[8] The relationship between the contemporary book and
the ancient one is defined by the same complex issues David Williams
sensed as he stood before Breasley's painting. There is always an
ambivalent love–hate connection as the contemporary struggles to create
a symbiotic rather than a parasitic relationship. Consider, for a
moment, two modern 'forgeries' which claim to be newly discovered
manuscripts — Nicholas Meyer's *The Seven-Per-Cent Solution* and George
MacDonald Fraser's *Flashman Papers.* In both works, the authors relegate
themselves to editorial sidelines, claiming only to have corrected obvious
factual errors, to have struck redundancies, and to have supplied
necessary annotations, Meyer's narrator may offer striking relevations
about Sherlock Holmes but he plays the game comfortably within the
boundaries already defined by A. Conan Doyle in that he does not

question the general ideas, perceptions, methods, and tenor of the Doyle stories. George MacDonald Fraser's *Royal Flash,* the second volume of the *Papers,* however, presents a more complex situation. When specifically asked if *Royal Flash* was intended to debunk *The Prisoner of Zenda,* Fraser responded: 'Turning the "Prisoner of Zenda" sunny side up was just an idea, because Flashman in Ruritania seemed too good to miss. But I wouldn't describe Hope's book as a "target"; I admire it far too much for that.'9 Fraser's comment, like David Williams' perception, underlines the complexly ambivalent ties. On the one hand, Fraser could not resist turning the tenuous ideas and actions of Hope's romance 'sunny side up'; on the other hand, he admires it 'far too much' to make it a target of withering parody.

Breasley and Uccello, Meyer and Doyle, Fraser and Hope epitomize what Harold Bloom has so persuasively written of as 'the anxiety of influence'. The original work may intimidate, threaten, and provoke, yet it may also evoke a new voice. Bloom has argued that

> Poetic influence — when it involves two strong, authentic poets — always proceeds by a misreading of the prior poet, an act of creative correction that is actually and necessarily a misinterpretation. The history of fruitful poetic influence . . . is a history of anxiety and self-saving caricature, of distortion, of perverse, wilful revisions without which modern poetry as such could not exist.10

Bloom's analysis may be a more abstract and sophisticated mediation than that of David Williams, but the issues are identical in their focus on homage, parody, confrontation, misreading, and escape. In Chapter One, David Lodge and Angus Wilson spoke eloquently on the anxiety of a contemporary author finding his or her own voice, and when asked if she still accepts her early preference of being at the end of a dying tradition she admires to being at the fountainhead of a new tradition she may deplore, Margaret Drabble said her perceptions of tradition were much more complex than she had earlier thought. 'And now I see', she said, 'that one can take, one can combine elements from all these people. That is not a question of committing yourself to rewriting or to being James Joyce. There is a sort of huge middle area where you are conscious of all these traditions and with any luck you can find your own voice . . .'.11

Paradoxically, then, certain authors wish both the umbilical cord to the past and their own independence, their consciousness of tradition and their own voice, their particular pattern and their own unique creation — they wish to create new *Moon-hunts*. Brian Aldiss, George MacDonald Fraser, and Jean Rhys are but three contemporary novelists who have chosen deliberately to emphasize their connections with particular works of the past and to create within the shadows of masters while defining their own voices. They have offered readers 'counter-books' to such works as *Frankenstein*, *The Prisoner of Zenda*, and *Jane Eyre*.

5 George MacDonald Fraser, *Royal Flash*, 'the course of history'

Imagine for a moment the excitement which would sweep the literary world if a catalogue of Sotheby-Parke-Bernet or Christie's announced for sale the long-lost memorandums of Moll Flanders, the journal of Razumov, or the business of papers of Leopold Bloom and suddenly a heretofore fictional character were translated from one realm of reality to another. The seven volumes of George MacDonald Fraser's *Flashman Papers* posit just such a discovery. According to the explanatory note prefacing each volume, Harry Paget Flashman, the notorious bully of Thomas Hughes' *Tom Brown's Schooldays*, was an actual Englishman who wrote his multi-volume memoirs in the early years of the twentieth century, probably between 1900 and 1905.[1] These were discovered by his relatives in 1915 after his death and lightly edited in parts by his sister-in-law, Grizel de Rothschild, who 'modified his blasphemies, but has not otherwise tampered with the old soldier's narrative'.[2] Totally unknown outside the immediate family, the papers were rediscovered 'during a sale of household furniture at Ashby, Leicestershire, in 1965', and were claimed by Flashman's nearest known living relative, Mr. Paget Morrison of Durban, South Africa, who subsequently asked George MacDonald Fraser to edit the papers for publication (*F*, vii).

Like many other such 'editors' ranging from Charlotte Brontë to Iris Murdoch, Fraser plays the role of the objective, detached historian convincingly but with perhaps a bit too much protest concerning the truthfulness of the papers he is editing. He tells the reader of *Flashman*, 'I have no reason to doubt that it [the journal] is a completely truthful account; where Flashman touches on historical fact he is almost invariably accurate' and he modestly assigns himself a minor role of correcting 'some minor spelling errors' and the addition of 'a few historical notes' because 'Flashman had a better sense of narrative than

I have' (*F*, viii). The editor claims no larger role in later volumes. In *Royal Flash* he once again confines himself to correcting 'occasional lapses in spelling', adding 'such notes and comments as seemed appropriate', and marvelling over Flashman's remarkable accuracy in relation to 'known history'.[3] By the fourth volume he has come even more to trust his author, claiming 'his general accuracy where he deals with well-known events and personages, and his transparent honesty, at least as a memorialist, are evidence that the present volume is as trustworthy as those which preceded it',[4] and in *Flashman in the Great Game*, the fifth volume, he complains 'his narrative tallies closely with accepted historical fact, as well as furnishing much new information, and there has been little for his editor to do except correct his spelling, deplore his conduct, and provide the usual notes and appendices'.[5]

Both Mr Paget Morrison and the editor quickly recognized the importance of the *Flashman Papers* for our knowledge of and understanding of nineteenth-century history and Victorian literature, for not only was Flashman involved in a number of significant historical events but also provided material for several important novels of the period. The *Who's Who* entry prefacing the first volume suggests the range of his adventures:

Flashman, Harry Paget. Brigadier-general, V.C., K.C.B., K.C.I.E.; Chevalier, Legion of Honour: U.S. Medal of Honour; San Serafino Order of Purity and Truth, 4th Class. b. 1822, s. H. Flashman, Esq., Ashby, and Hon. Alicia Paget; educ. Rugby School. m. Elspeth Rennie Morrison, d. Lord Paisley; one s., one d. Served Afghanistan, 1841–42 (medals, thanks of Parliament); Crimea (staff); Indian Mutiny (Lucknow, etc., V. C.); China, Taiping Rebellion. Served U.S. Army (major, Union forces, 1862; colonel [staff] Army of the Confederacy, 1863). Travelled extensively in military and civilian capacities; a.d.c., Emperor Maximilian of Mexico; milit. adviser, H. M. Queen Ranavalona of Madagascar; chief of staff to Rajah of Sarawak; dep. marshal. U.S. Chmn, Flashman and Bottomley, Ltd.; dir. British Opium Trading Co.; governor, Rugby School; hon. pres. Mission for Reclamation of Reduced Females. Publications: Dawns and Departures of a Soldier's Life; Twixt Cossack and Cannon; The Case Against Army Reform. Clubs: White's United Service, Blackjack (Batavia). Recreation: Oriental studies, angling. Add.: Gandamack Lodge, Ashby, Leics.

So far, much of this has been verified in detail in the *Papers*. The volumes cover the following:

Flashman, 1839–42 – First Afghan War
Royal Flash, 1842–3, 1847–8 – Schleswig-Holstein Affair
Flash for Freedom, 1848–9 – Anglo-American slave trade
Flashman at the Charge, 1854–5 – Crimean War
Flashman at the Great Game, 1857–8 – Indian Mutiny
Flashman's Lady, 1842–5 – Rajah James Brooke in Borneo; Queen Ranavalona I in Madagascar
Flashman and the Redskins, 1849–50, 1875–6 American gold rush; Battle of the Little Bighorn

Yet to appear are those portions of the memoirs dealing with Flashman's involvement in and adventures in the United States Civil War (1861–5), the Taiping Rebellion, the Zulu uprising, and the Boxer Rebellion (1900) to which Flashman refers in passing in the published volumes. Here, then, is an historical treasure – eye-witness accounts of many of the century's most crucial military engagements. The editor notes, 'when the Flashman papers, that vast personal memoir describing the adult career of the notorious bully of *Tom Brown's Schooldays*, came to light some years ago, it was at once evident that new and remarkable material was going to be added to Victorian history' (*FC,* 5).

The papers also add 'new and remarkable' material to literature. Here is Flashman's own reaction to Arnold and Rugby so idealized by Thomas Hughes. More importantly, here are the 'true' adventures behind works as diverse as *The Prisoner of Zenda* and *Uncle Tom's Cabin*. One of the editor's notes in *Flash for Freedom* tells the readers:

> There can be little doubt that Harriet Beecher Stowe, who was living in Cincinnati at the time, must have heard of Cassey and Flashman crossing the Ohio ice pursued by slave-catchers, and decided to incorporate the incident in her best-selling *Uncle Tom's Cabin*, which was published two years later. She, of course, attributed the feat to the slave girl Eliza; it can be no more than an interesting coincidence that the burden Eliza carried in her flight was a "real handsome boy" named Harry. But it seems quite likely that Mrs Stowe met the real Cassy, and used her, name and all, in that part of the book which describes life on Simon Legree's plantations. (*FF,* 287, n.39)

And in *Royal Flash*, Flashman complains in his narrative:

> Only once did I tell the tale, and that was privately some years ago, to young Hawkins, the lawyer – I must have been well foxed, or he

was damned persuasive — and he has used it for the stuff of one c
his romances, which sells very well, I'm told. (*RF,* 242)

To this, the editor appends the note:

Whether Flashman's real-life experiences in Germany provide
Anthony Hope with the basis of his famous romance, *The Prisoner O
Zenda,* is a matter which readers must decide for themselves. (*RF*
247)

If the reader has begun to entertain doubts, he is fully justified, fo
the *Flashman Papers* are an elaborate and all too convincing *trompe l'oeil*
Notice how skillfully Fraser manipulates his readers, though, int
believing they are reading the 'real thing'. By discrediting *Uncle Tom'
Cabin* and *The Prisoner of Zenda* as being mere fiction spun from Harry
Flashman's true life adventures, Fraser allows the *Flashman Papers* t
validate themselves as 'reality' rather than 'fiction'. Moreover, the edito
repeatedly insists that there is no discrepancy between the historica
record and Flashman's version as there is in so many novels. Flashman'
account of the Afghan retreat, for instance, 'tallies substantially wit
those of such contemporaries as Mackenzie, Lady Sale, and Lieutenan
Eyre. This is also true of his version of affairs in Afghanistan generally
(*F,* 249). Flashman's account of slave trade is, the editor confides
'accurate enough, but obviously he does not give more than a hint c
the compliant system of treaties and anti-slavery laws by which civilise
nations fought the traffic' (*FF,* 284), and Flashman's account of th
Charge of the Light Brigade 'disagrees with other eye-witnesses no mor
than they disagree among themselves, and these discrepancies are min
ones' (*FC,* 284). In discussing General Duhamel's 1854 plans for
Russian invasion of India through Persia and Afghanistan, the edito
notes that 'at various points in Flashman's account Ignatieff repea
passages from Duhamel and Khruleff almost verbatim' (*FC,* 286). Thi
note of authenticity snared more than one reviewer and perhaps explain
some of Fraser's cult appeal among historians. Andre Michaiopoulos
writing for the King Features Syndicate, announced that 'Flashman'
account . . bears the stamp of authenticity'; and J. V. Neilson suggeste
that the papers 'rank with Samuel Pepys Diary and the Boswell papers'.
Perhaps the ten reviewers who accepted the first volume as an authenti
memoir can be forgiven in view of the traps set in the texts for them
In fact, so seriously did reviewers listen to Flashman, that Fraser'
American publisher felt compelled to issue a statement avowing th

fictionality of the books, a statement Fraser then turned to doubly ironic uses when he declared in *Flash for Freedom* that 'if any doubters [of the historical veracity of these books] remain they are recommended to study the authoritative article which appeared in the *New York Times* of 29 July, 1969, and which surely settles the question once and for all' (*FF*, explanatory note). Here we find a never-ending reflection in the mirrors of history, fiction, and reality as works of fiction and newspaper disclaimers become the authenticating documents for further fiction.

Behind this debunking, however, stand more firm ideas concerning history and the use of historical facts. In *The Steel Bonnets*, Fraser's history of the Border counties and the Border reivers from the time of Hadrian's Wall to the accession of James VI to the throne of England, Fraser makes clear his quarrel with two schools, the romantic, who, following in the line of but not fully understanding Walter Scott, turned the Border into 'a land of brave men and daring deeds, of gothic mystery and fairytale beauty, of gallant Scot and sturdy Saxon, of high ideals and sweet dreams' and hence glamorized 'the blood and the terror and the cruelty and the crime'.[7] They lack perspective, as do the historical specialists, the other school, who in dealing exhaustively with international politics, administration, military history, genealogical research, and a host of much smaller topics . . . examined in minute detail' (*SB*, 7) have lost sight of the human interest. After sketching his quarrel with these two approaches, Fraser comments:

> The Scottish policy of Henry VIII is a fascinating thing, offering as rich a field to the psychiatrist as to the historian, but I am less concerned with the effect that it had on, say, Franco-Scottish relations than with the more immediate and dramatic impact which it had on the good wife of Kirkcudbright who, during a skirmish near her home, actually delivered her husband up to the enemy for safekeeping. Obviously one must take account of the machinations of Walsingham and James VI and I, but the prime consideration for me is how Nebless Clem Croser went about his business of cattle-rustling, and how the Grahams came to dispossess the Storeys, and how old Sir John Forster's wife got the door shut in the nick of time as a band of reivers came up the stair. (*SB*, 7)

The concern for the human and the disdain for the theoretical, the abstract, the statistical, are embodied in Flashman's outlook on history. In one of his most insouciant observations, Flashman argues that trifles, not plans nor policies, shape history.

Scholars, of course, won't have it so. Policies, they say, and the subtly
laid schemes of statesmen, are what influence the destinies of nations;
the opinions of intellectuals, the writings of philosophers, settle the
fate of mankind. Well, they may do their share, but in my experience
the course of history is as often settled by someone's having a
belly-ache, or not sleeping well, or a sailor getting drunk, or some
atistocratic harlot waggling her backside. (*RF,* 11)

Similarly, throughout the novels, Flashman insists on the human
dimensions of historical action. An incident in *Flashman in the Great Game,*
he tells us, 'led to an encounter that was to save my life, and set me on
one of the queerest and most terrifying adventures of my career, and
perhaps shaped the destiny of British India, too' (*FGG,* 69).

Another and equally important aspect of Fraser's concept of history
is his belief — much like Walter Scott's — that manners and fashions
change while the human being remains much the same. Concluding his
history of the Border reivers, Fraser writes:

There may be lessons to be learned from them, wicked and yet not
unattractive ruffians that they were. As long as there are frontiers
there will be people something like them — I dare say one could
relate some of the Warden's problems to what happens along the
Suez Canal and the Jordan today, where governments are unable to
control their irregular people. (*SB,* 377)

Although by education and inclination Flashman lacks the historical
perspective of his author, he occasionally enjoys similar moments of
insight, and the idea that man changes little infuses all six volumes.

Fraser apparently believes the people of the Victorian age were
governed by two main forces — the desire to get what one could for
oneself and the desire to survive at all costs — but had evolved a highly
protective rhetoric and an insulating social etiquette. Man is, at heart,
a sexual bully, a coward, a con man; at least Flashman who cheats,
steals, lies, flees, betrays, and yet rises to prominence is all these and
more. Flashman signals the shift in values to repression. suppression,
and hypocrisy when he says of Victoria: 'the young Queen was newly
on the throne then, and people still believed as they had under the
Prince Regent and King Billy; not like later on, when mistresses had to
stay out of sight' (*F,* 18–19). The indictment becomes even more severe
in the second volume of papers: 'It was the end of the great days of
buck and blade; we had a queen on the throne, and her cold white

hand and her poker-backed husband's were already setting their grip on the nation's life, smothering the old wild ways in their come-to-Jesus hypocrisy. We were entering into what is now called the Victorian age, when respectability was the thing . . . the age of the Corinthian, the plunger, and the dandy was giving way to that of the prig, the preacher, and the bore' (*RF*, 12–13). Among the prigs, preachers, and bores singled out for particular attack by Flashman are Thomas Arnold, Tom Brown, and Anthony Hope Hawkins who epitomize the failures of the Victoria age in reconciling philosophical ideals with human realities. In Flashman's world no one does anything for glory, for patriotism, for duty, for honour, for any grand abstraction unless he is a fool or is accidently trapped in a situation which suggests he has acted in accord with the abstractions. Abstractions are made as appearances, to be worn, used, manipulated, and discarded at will. Flashman maintains that he is the norm and much better equipped to survive in a world of hypocrisy, duplicity, betrayal, and unbelievable cruelty than such moral aberrations as Tom Brown. This explains why the first words Flashman supposedly wrote were 'Hughes got it wrong . . .' (*F*, 11). Unashamedly, Flashman admits that his papers are 'the portrait of a scoundrel, a liar, a cheat, a thief, a coward — and, oh yes, a toady' (*F*, 11).

From volume one to volume six, Thomas Hughes is repeatedly alluded to, attacked, cajoled, villified, and dismissed as having misread, misunderstood, and misrepresented the truth behind the masks, and myths called honour, duty, bravery and a dozen other noble-sounding abstractions. In his study of the English public schools, Johnathan Gathorne-Hardy discussed the phenomenal success of *Tom Brown's Schooldays* sale of 11 000 copies the year of its publication, its run through fifty-two editions by 1892 — and rightly saw its moral fervour as leading to the apotheosis of Thomas Arnold.[8] It is, in truth, a secular hagiography: a 'remarkable book', Brigid Brophy, Michael Levy, and Charles Osborne called it, though they then added 'remarkable for the viciousness of its moral attitudes, and the numbling dullness with which these attitudes, are expressed'.[9] Flashman's papers stand in relationship to Hughes' novel in much the same way that William Golding's *Lord of the Flies* does to Ballantyne's *The Coral Island*, as an assault on its moral and ethical assumptions about man and society. In *Flashman at the Charge* which tells of the Crimean War, Flashman, encounters Scud East, of Hughes' fame, and muses:

> I know my Easts and Tom Browns, you see. They're never happy
> unless their morality is being tried in the furnace, and they can feel

they're doing the right, Christian thing — and never mind the consequences to anyone else. Selfish brutes. Damned unreliable it makes 'em, too. On the other hand, you can always count on me. I'd have got the news through to Raglan out of pure cowardice and self-love, and to hell with East and Valla both; but your pious Scud had to have a grudge to pay off before he'd abandon me. Odd, ain't it? They'll do for us yet, with their sentiment and morality. (*FC,* 192)

When Flashman meets East again a few years later in India, he has a moment of revenge and shatters East's reputation, soiling his abstractions. While they were held captive together in southern Russia, they managed to acquire full information concerning a Russian grand plan to sweep through Persia, Afghanistan, and India, once and for all establishing Russian dominance in the sub-continent. East wants to escape and to attempt to get the important information back to British authorities — for duty, honour, and country. Unexpectedly, because of a rebellion of serfs, East and Flashman get the opportunity and flee in a sled with Valla, the Russian lord's daughter, ostensibly to save her. Eventually Russian cavalry pursue the sled, and Flashman pushes the naked, drunken Valla out of the sled in an attempt to slow and to distract the cavalry. Flashman convinces East that he was motivated solely by duty. Several years later, East believes he has pierced the true depths of Flashman's sacrifice. He admits his own failure to live up to his ideals and blushingly blurts out:

I've wondered if perhaps you too loved Valla . . . if you did, and placed duty first. . . . Did you . . . love her, Flashman?

Flashman's reply devastates him:

About four or five times a week . . . but you needn't be jealous; she wasn't nearly so good a ride as her Aunt Sara. You should have tried a steam-bath with that one. (*FGG,* 182)

Arnold and Brown haunt Flashman's later years. Several times, when trapped, Flashman assumes the identity of Thomas Arnold, and on occasion, even the tone. Applying for a job as an overseer on the Mandeville plantation in *Flash for Freedom,* Flashman introduces himself as Tom Arnold, from Texas; when he is captured by the Eider Danes, he tells them he is Captain Thomas Arnold, A British Army officer.

Hughes' book dominates his life. We are led to believe that Flashman wrote in reply to it. Indeed, at the very moment he achieves his highest award, the Victoria Cross and a knighthood, for his actions in the Indian Mutiny, Hughes' book arrives to taunt him and remind him how others perceive him. Lord Raglan, in a vengeful moment, sends a copy to Flashman who realizes 'How could I ever hold up my head again, after this poisonous attack — my God, just in my moment of supreme glory, too! What would my Cross and my Knighthood be worth now, with this venom spewed on me by "an Old Boy"' (*FGG*, 295). At this point in the memoirs, torn sheets and 'several explosive blots' attest to Flashman's anger.

Fraser never quarrels with Thomas Hughes' assessment of Flashman:

Flashman, be it said, was about seventeen years old, and big and strong of his age. He played well at all games where pluck wasn't much wanted, and managed generally to keep up appearances where it was; and having a bluff offhand manner, which passed for heartiness, and considerable powers of being pleasant when he liked, went down with the school in general for a good fellow enough. Even in the School-house, by dint of his command of money, the constant supply of good things which he kept up, and his adroit toadyism, he had managed to make himself not only tolerated but rather popular amongst his own contemporaries . . . Flashman left no slander unspoken, and no deed undone, which could in any way hurt his victims, or isolate them from the rest of the house.[10]

Beneath these qualities, however, Fraser perceives a soundrel whose ingenuity and flair for surviving, coping, and prospering in a hypocritical world command respect, some sympathy, and even admiration. Flashman knows he has only three talents — horses, language, and fornication (*FL*, 3) — but he is never dishonest with himself. The vein of admirable qualities is underlined in *Flashman's Lady* when Tom Brown suggests he is a self-destructive type: 'The German doctors are doing a lot of work on it — the perversity of human nature, excellence bent on destroying itself, the heroic soul fearing its own fall from grace, and trying to anticipate it. Interesting . . .' (*FL*, 7). These are not matters Flashman wishes to pursue; but they are matters his audience will wish to consider. Flashman is a troubled soul, unloved by his father, expelled by his school, cuckolded by his wife, betrayed by his superiors in their bungling, ineptness, and incompetence. He has been cast out for very minor 'sins' and bitterly and cynically decides to exploit the masks hypocrisy offers him. Paradoxically when most a failure, his society greatly rewards him.

The book to read in the spring of 1894, late in Flashman's life, was Anthony Hope Hawkin's *The Prisoner of Zenda* which 'swept the reading public off its feet' and 'took the hearts of the reviewers and the world by storm' sweeping all along in a 'breathless spirit of interest and admiration from the first pages to the last'.[11] Robert Louis Stevenson left a letter on his writing table the day he died praising the 'very spirited and gallant little book' and by 1934, 760 000 copies had been sold in England and America.[12] From that moment, 28 November 1893, when the word 'Ruritania' took shape in Hawkins' mind as he walked from Westminster County Court to his rooms in the Temple,[13] the connotations of romantic neverneverland, mistaken identity, royal impersonation, and love thwarted by duty has been before the public in one form or another as a book, a motion picture, or a television adaptation.

For all its popularity, *The Prisoner of Zenda* is a surprisingly thin and superficial novel offering its readers high adventure and rather shallow characters caught up in the abstractions of love and chivalry, for the tale is nothing if not an epitomization of dashing honour and devotion to duty narrated by a pining lover who, once a year, exchanges a single red rose and a message, 'Rudolf — Flavia — always' with his beloved.[14] In the novel, Rudolf Rassendyll, second son of a noble English family, finds himself unexpectedly caught up playing the game — soon a very serious game — of impersonating the King of Ruritania. The true king has been captured and is being held prisoner in the castle of Zenda by his morganatic half-brother, Michael, a truly Victorian melodramatic villain who wishes to gain the throne for himself either through direct assumption or more indirectly through marriage to Princess Flavia, the next rightful heir to the throne. Because of an intermingling of Elphberg (the Ruritania royal family) and Rassendyll blood in an eighteenth-century scandal, Rudolf is the living image of the King. He goes through the coronation ceremony, courts his cousin Flavia, finding to his despair that she loves him only slightly less than he loves her, and finally plots a successful assault on Zenda to rescue the King, restore him to the throne and to Flavia, and then retire quietly to England. Interspersed throughout are sword fights, attempted assassinations, and daring deeds all in the best swashbuckling tradition, muted by the ill-fated love affair. Constantly the actions and thoughts are defined in terms of honour and duty. Marshall Strakencz tells Rudolf, for instance:

I have known many of the Elphbergs . . . and I have seen you. And, happen what may, you have borne yourself as a wise king and a brave man; aye, and you have proved as courteous a gentleman and as gallant a lover as any that have been of the House. (*PZ*, 149)

The usually taciturn Rudolf admits that his code is keeping 'faith with man, and honor with women' (*PZ*, 173), and the true king tells him '"You have shown me how to play the king"' (*PZ*, 283). In perhaps the most affecting scene, titled, 'If Love Were All', Flavia and Rudolf part, affirming their constant love but sacrificing it to public duty. Flavia's words capture the essence of their code: '"Honor binds a woman too, Rudolf. My honor lies in being true to my country and my House. I don't know why God has let me love you; but I know that I must stay"' (*PZ*, 289). In the sequel, *Rupert of Hentzau,* published in 1898, Rudolf once again has a chance to take the throne and to marry the now unhappy Flavia, but he is assassinated.

Aside from adding the word 'Ruritania' to the literary vocabulary, *The Prisoner of Zenda* provoked Fraser into writing his magnificent send-up of its values, its actions, its characters, and its characters' motivations. Moreover, Fraser grounded his send-up firmly in known boundaries of space and time, taking not the mythical kingdom of Ruritania, but rather selecting the Schleswig-Holstein affair, Dano-German political tensions in the 1840s, Otto von Bismarck, Lola Montez, and the revolutions which swept Europe in 1848. One reviewer called it a 'considerate sort of parody that allows a double-tracking reader to enjoy his old chestnuts even while he roasts them'.[15]

Royal Flash early hints its relationship with a famous novel but never insists on this so heavily as to burden the joke. The editor's 'Explanatory Note' suggests an historical as well as a literary importance to the packet he is presenting because 'it also establishes a point of some literary interest, for there can be no doubt that a link exists between Flashman's German adventure and one of the best-selling novels in the Victorian period' (*RF,* 7) and returns to this in a brief appendix:

Whether Flashman's real-life experiences in Germany provided Anthony Hope with the basis of his famous romance, *The Prisoner of Zenda,* is a matter which readers must decide for themselves. Flashman is quite definite in the text in two places — especially where he refers to "Hawkins", which was Hope's real name. There is certainly some similarity in events, and names like Lauengram, Kraftstein, Detchard,

> de Gautet, Bersonin, and Tarlenheim are common to both stories.
> Flashman's "Major Sapten' is literary twin brother to Hope's
> "Colonel Sapt", and no amateur of romantic fiction will fail to
> identify Rudi von Starnberg with the Count of Hentzau. (*RF*, 247)

As the editor notes, references to Hope in the text are sparse and
unobtrusive except for one. Flashman once says that without the
'glorious chapter' a certain famous novel would never have been written
(*RF*, 53) but does not identify the novel until the closing pages of the
memoirs when he confides that he only once told the tale, excluding it
from his many other 'garrulous reminiscences' (*RF*, 242), and then to
'young Hawkins' who 'used it for the stuff of one of his romances, which
sells very well, I'm told' (*RF*, 242).

One must admire the imagination capable of ingesting the work of
another novelist and then retelling it with such a tone of authenticity
that it impeaches the earlier work as a mere whimsical fantasia. Fraser's
skill is perhaps nowhere so apparent as when he hews closely to his
target and with straightfaced affrontery seduces his reader. After all,
there are no Ruritania, no Duke Michael, no King Rudolf, Zenda, nor
Antoinette de Mauban, but there are a Schleswig-Holstein, a Prussia,
a Bavaria, an Otto von Bismarck, a prince Carl Gustaf of Denmark, a
Schonhausen, Karl Marx, Franz Liszt, Richard Wagner, and Lola
Montez. Indeed, there is scarcely a fact, a character, a locale, or a
thought in Hawkin's novel which does not experience a wonderous
validation as Fraser's wit transforms, and realigns them. Even the
horrible pipe through which King Rudolf's body is to be disposed
reappears in a slightly new, even more horrifying, guise.

Royal Flash enjoys a complexity, a particularity, and a believability
one might expect from the true version of such a highly romantic novel,
now revealed to be a *roman à clef*. In 1842, Flashman, the adulation of
his Afghan exploits paling in London society, finds himself fleeing from
a police raid on the Minor St. James Club where in true Flashman
fashion he had been drinking, gambling, and wenching with Speedicutt,
another refugee from *Tom Brown's Schooldays*. He hides in a cab taken
by Otto von Bismarck and Rosanna James. Bismarck takes umbrage at
his presence and Flashman soon finds himself in Rosanna's bed feeling
as though he 'had been coupling with a roll of barbed wire' (*RF*,
22). When this affair breaks off, Rosanna disappears, but Flashman
encounters Bismarck again at a country house. Their original dislike for
one another intensifies and Flashman tricks Bismarck into boxing with
a national champion. Returning to London Flashman finds Rosanna

has metamorphosed into Lola Montez, Spanish dancer, and in an hilarious recreation of the actual event, Flashman gets his revenge on her by getting Lord Ranelagh to expose her as plain Betsy James. Four years pass, and a letter from the Countess of Landsfield summons Flashman on 'a matter of the most extreme delicate' (*Rf*, 57) to Munich. Needless to say, disaster for Flashman follows. A trumped-up rape charge lands him in the hands of Rudi von Starnberg in a coach ride across the German states to Bismarck's castle. Bismarck sketches the Schleswig-Holstein political tangle and his plans to use Flashman to impersonate Prince Carl Gustaf at his marriage to Irma, ruler of the Duchy of Strackenz since Carl Gustaf has unceremoniously contacted 'Cupid's measles' (*RF*, 98). Rigorous training follows, during which time Bismarck avenges the boxing match by having two schlager wounds inflicted on Flashman. The wedding occurs and Flashman carries off the impersonation successfully except for one tense moment, and, of course, given Flashman's experiences and prowess, the honeymoon succeeds as well. During the honeymoon at Strelholm lodge, Bismarck's co-conspirators attempt to murder Flashman and use the resulting disorder to forge a unified German state, but, with his usual luck, Flashman escapes only to fall into the hands of the Sons of the Volsungs, a patriotic – some would say fanatical – group sympathetic with the Danes. Flashman admits his impersonation, telling them he is Captain Thomas Arnold, an English army man blackmailed into the dastardly action. His neck virtually in a noose, Flashman agrees to assist the group in rescuing the true Prince Carl Gustaf who is held captive in the dungeons of Jotunberg, a gothic castle brooding over the lake. After several chapters of greasing, swimming, knifings, sword-play, broken bottles, and sheer luck, Flashman succeeds and then recklessly returns to the palace, seizes the crown jewels, and flees to Munich just in time to witness Lola Montez's downfall as mistress of King Ludwig I of Bavaria. They flee together, briefly reassuming their affair; then Lola flees alone with the jewels leaving Flashman with a little money and a letter closing with her motto, 'Courage! And shuffle the cards' (*RF*, 241). Flashman returns to London from the adventure with none of the glories of the Afghan campaign, none of the loot from the Lucknow campaign, but at least with the Order of the Elephant which mystifies the Danish Embassy.

The summaries reveal just how close yet how distant the two novels are. Fraser's anti-heroic view thrusts home many times, exploding the heroics of *The Prisoner of Zenda*. Hope's Rudolf Rassendyll has moments when his Flashman side can be glimpsed. He experiences doubts, fears, and ambitions, but brushes these aside for honor and duty and the 'game'. He ponders forcing Michael's hand so the real King will be killed, leaving him on the throne ready to marry Princess Flavia, thoughts he later calls 'wild and black . . . that storm his brain when an uncontrolled passion has battered a breach for them' (*PZ*, 143). Flashman on the other hand knows he is a brutish, selfish, conniving coward, but he also knows that these qualities may also be his virtues. He calls himself a 'dishonest poltroon who takes a perverse pride in having attained to an honoured and admired old age, in spite of his many vices and active lack of virtue — or possibly because of them' (*RF*, 12). More than a mere seventy-six years separate Rudolf Rassendyll accepting the challenge partly out of the thrill of the adventure and partly out of an obedience to the rules of the game with a stalwart ' "Yes, I'll go" ' (*PZ*, 47) Tom Brown would have been proud of and Harry Flashman, seized, cherrypicker pants at his knees and literally coerced on fear of death into the impersonation; or Rassendyll actually plotting and leading the assault on Zenda to a shivering, grease-coated Flashman prodded at knife-point across the moat, his leg knotted in cramps, while he whispers ' "I'll freeze, I tell you — I'm dying — I know I am. God damn you, you scabby-headed Danish swine . . ." ' (*RF*, 188). Heroics are once again laid bare as cowardice trapped into desperate action, honor caught in the necessity of skilled duplicity, and duty as self-preservation at all costs, never mind what lies, what actions, or what compromises must be used. Years later Flashman says he can be philosophical about the adventure because ' — I'm still here' (*RF*, 243).

A detailed comparison of a few of the scenes demonstrates Fraser's ability to take even minute details from Hawkins and render them perfectly plausible and believable. In *The Prisoner of Zenda*, Rassendyll stops in Paris on his way to Ruritania. While there, he sees Antoinette de Mauban, a woman so in love with Black Michael, he later learns, that she warns and assists him several times in his rescue of the King. Antoinette is described as 'a widow, rich, handsome, and, according to repute, ambitious' (*PZ*, 15). Later, 'bound to [Michael] by the chains of shame and hope' (*PZ*, 266), she attempts to thwart Michael's plans, and still later she returns to Paris to live 'in great seclusion — a fact for which gossip found no difficulty in accounting' (*PZ*, 295). She and Rassendyll exchange letters, hers a 'very affecting' one concerning the king's generosity and her high regard for Rassendyll (*PZ*, 297). How much more colourful, exciting, believable and plausible is Fraser's Lola Montez, drawn carefully from real life; as one of the notes reminds us:

The account of Lola's disastrous appearance at Her Majesty's Theatre (June 3, 1843) is splendidly accurate, not only in its description of Lord Ranelagh's denunciation, but even in such details as the composition of the audience and the programme notes. . . . This is a good, verifiable example of Flashman's ability as a straight reporter, and encourages confidence in those other parts of his story where corroboration is lacking and checking of the facts is impossible. (*RF*, 252)

A check of the standard biographies 'substantiates' the editor's claim. The debut of Lola at Her Majesty's Theatre occurred as Flashman records, because Fraser has taken the opera, the dance, the audience, the programme advertisements for 'Jackson's patent enema machine' and 'Mrs. Rodd's anatomical ladies' stays,' even Lumley's card, and Lord Ranelagh's unmasking of Betsy James from Horace Wyndham's *The Magnificent Montez: From Courtesan to Convert.*[16] Even Franz Liszt's *bon mot*, 'As soon as you meet Lola, your mind leaps into bed' (*RF*, 75) apparently is Flashman's version of Aldous Huxley's comment, 'When you meet Lola Montez, her reputation made you automatically think of bedrooms', which Wyndham uses as an epigraph to his biography. The Munich crowd's chant of '*Pereat* Lola' and Flashman's description of Lola's daring walk through the mob, as well as her motto apparently originate in Ishbel Ross's *The Uncrowned Queen: Life of Lola Montez.*[17] Compare, for example, Flashman's description of Lola's debut with the description in Wyndham. Flashman mentions that the Queen Dowager, Wellington, Brougham, the Baroness de Rothschild, Count Esterhazy, and many others attended the performance of *The Barber of Seville*, less for the opera, than for Benjamin Lumley's promised attraction. A contemporary reviewer wrote that Lola was

a lovely picture . . . to contemplate. There she is before you the very perfection of spanish beauty — the tall handsome figure, the full lustrous eye, the joyous animated countenance, and the dark raven tresses. You gaze upon the Donna with delight and admiration.[18]

When Flashman looks, he sees much the same, but with the usual Flashman attractions to the fleshly and the sexual:

Her striking beauty brought the pit up with a gasp: she was in a black bodice, cut so low that her breasts seemed to be in continual danger of popping out, and her tiny pink skirt showed off her legs to tremendous advantage. The slim white neck and shoulders, the coal-black hair, the gleaming eyes, the scarlet lips curled almost in contempt — the whole affect was startling and exotic. (*RF*, 49)

Within the very real contexts of Lola Montez's adventures and Bismarck's machinations, especially the Danish nationalist movement of the 1840s which sought to annex the duchies,[19] Flashman's antiheroics propel him most unwillingly through a most important chapter of European history, simultaneously levelling a devastating satiric blast at *The Prisoner of Zenda* and probing the sleazy, suspect, essentially Hobbesian depths of the nineteenth century political events. Perhaps the most disturbing impression one carries away from a study of the novels and their sources is that no matter how brutal, cruel, bloody, and revolting the actions Flashman records, the historical reality is always much worse.

7 Jean Rhys, *Wide Sargasso Sea*, 'all belonged to the past'

In 1978, 313000 individuals visited the Brontë Parsonage in Haworth–five times as many as visited Shakespeare's birthplace in Stratford-upon-Avon–to see, to muse over, and perhaps to 'gloom about' the house of Charlotte, Emily, Anne, and Branwell Brontë, many of them drawn by their love of *Wuthering Heights* but perhaps even more because of their familiarity with *Jane Eyre*.[1] In the 137 years since its publication, homage has been paid *Jane Eyre* in numerous ways: motion picture and television adaptations, musical compositions, ballets, not to mention a continuous stream of comments by other novelists.[2] But *Jane Eyre* has inspired and even stranger set of progeny, mothered not by Jane Eyre Rochester herself but rather by Bertha Mason Rochester, the mad wife confined to the upper rooms of Thornfield Hall. Bertha has gripped the imagination of reader and novelist far beyond the power of a gothic mystery.

Although Bertha appears a number of times during the Thornfield Hall episode as a haunting and terrible laugh, as a shadowy presence, as a setter of fires, and as a potential vampire, she is not identified nor her story told until chapters 26 and 27. Here, when Richard Mason and his lawyer, Briggs, declare an impediment to the marriage of Jane and Rochester, it becomes necessary for Rochester to answer their charges with an explanation. Fifteen years earlier, Rochester tells his small audience, on 20 October, he married Bertha Antoinetta Mason in Spanish Town, Jamaica. Within four years she became nothing but 'a bad, mad, and embruted partner' to him.[3] Before satisfying his audience's curiosity about the marriage, he introduces them to Bertha, and, at first, Jane is uncertain whether or not she has met a human or an animal.

In the deep shade, at the further end of the room, a figure ran backwards and forwards. What it was, whether beast or human

99

being, one could not, at first sight, tell: it grovelled, seemingly, or
all fours; it snatched and growled like some strange wild animal: but
it was covered with clothing; and a quantity of dark, grizzled hair
wild as a mane, hid its head and face. (*JE*, 257–8)

Later that same day, Rochester tells the full history of the marriage to
Jane. His father, 'an avaricious grasping man' (*JE*, 268) and Rowland
his brother conspired to keep the Rochester estates undivided by
providing Rochester with a wealthy Jamaican bride having a dowry of
£30 000. Infatuated with her, Rochester hurries into the marriage, only
later realizing that he has been betrayed by all parties. He condemns
himself for 'being ignorant, raw, and inexperienced' (*JE*, 268), and for
being a 'gross, grovelling, mole-eyed blockhead' (*JE*, 269). Only after
the wedding does he discern that his brother-in-law is 'a complete dumb
idiot' (*JE*, 269), that his wife, 'a hideous demon' (*JE*, 277) is 'at once
intemperate and unchaste' (*JE*, 270), and that he has been bought and
sold by the fathers. His charges against Bertha mix intellectual, sexual
and racial repugnance with his own sense of betrayal. Quickly, he finds
'her nature wholly alien to mine; her tastes obnoxious to me, her cast
of mind common, low, narrow, and singularly incapable to being led
to anything higher, expanded to anything larger' (*JE*, 269). The
conversation of his 'Indian Messalina' (*JE*, 274) is 'coarse and trite,
perverse and imbecile' (*JE*, 269) and her 'giant propensities' (*JE*, 269)
repel him. To him, Bertha is 'most gross, impure [and] depraved' (*JE*,
270), and soon doctors pronounce her mad as well. In despair, his
self-image destroyed, Rochester contemplates suicide (*JE*, 271), but his
hopes aroused by 'a wind fresh from Europe' (*JE*, 271), he leaves
Jamaica, commits Bertha to the attic rooms, and, like a 'Will-o'-the-wisp'
(*JE*, 273), wanders for the next ten years across Europe seeking his
'ideal of a woman' (*JE*, 273) who will restore his sense of being and
worth.

Bertha, who apparently originated through an amalgamation of a
deranged English lady near Leeds, Ellen Nussey's mad brother, and
Branwell Brontë's setting his bed curtains on fire during a drunken
sleep, was defended by her creator in an 1848 letter to W. S. Williams

The character [of Bertha] is shocking, but I know that it is but too
natural. There is a phase of insanity which may be called moral
madness, in which all that is good or even human seems to disappear
from the mind, and a fiend-nature replaces it. The sole aim and
desire of the being thus possessed is to exasperate, to molest, to

destroy, and preternatural ingenuity and energy are often exercised to that dreadful end.[4]

ollowing this sympathetic reading of Bertha's madness, however, the tter reverses its terms and blames Bertha for creating her own madness; Mrs. Rochester, indeed, lived a sinful life before she was insane, but n is itself a species of insanity – the truly good behold and compassionate as such.' The demonically possessed Bertha, bearing her creator's isapprobation, appealed to Charles Dickens, D. H. Lawrence, and a nixture of minor popular writers such as Herbert De Lisser, who villingly adopted Brontë's judgement of Bertha, and saw her as mad, estial, non-human – a barrier to a true love.

Within four years of the publication of *Jane Eyre*, Charles Dickens ad used details of Rochester's mad wife in sketching Stephen Blackpool's vife in *Hard Times*. She is described in virtually the same terms as ertha:

Such a woman! A disabled, drunken creature, barely able to preserve her sitting posture by steadying herself with one begrimed hand on the floor, while the other was so purposeless in trying to push away her tangled hair from her face, that it only blinded her the more with the dirt upon it. A creature so foul to look at, in her tatters, stains and splashes, but so much fouler than that in her moral infamy, that it was a shameful thing even to see her.[5]

rapped, like Rochester, Stephen Blackpool recalls for Mr Bounderby ow the marriage degenerated through his wife's alcoholism until she isgraced herself everyways, bitter and bad' (*HT*, 66). In love with achel, who has the same regenerative effect Jane had on Rochester, tephen cannot legally escape from his wife. The Stephen Blackpool ubplot occupies relatively little space in Dickens' novel, but the shadow f Bertha Mason appears to dominate it.

D. H. Lawrence's public hostility towards Charlotte Brontë's novel as overshadowed his early preference for it and has thus obscured cognition of its influence on *Lady Chatterley's Lover*. In 'Pornography nd Obscenity', Lawrence favoured the 'fresh and wholesome'' Boccaccio Brontë because *Jane Eyre* verg[ed] towards pornography . . . much earer to pornography than in Boccaccio'.[6] Even Clifford Chatterley, 'hose interest in Racine and Proust aids in characterizing his physical eadness, finds hearing the once 'ridiculous' *Jane Eyre* 'more like a leasant ticking, that enervated rather than stimulated him'.[7] Barbara

Weekly Barr recalled the Lawrence 'thought *Jane Eyre* should hav
been called Everybody's Governess',[8] but in a more private momen
Lawrence wrote Blanche Jennings: 'I presume you are well acquainte
with *Shirley* and *Jane Eyre*, two of my favourite English books.'[9] Th
ambivalent attitude towards *Jane Eyre* is reflected in its probabl
influence on the several versions of *Lady Chatterley's Lover*, where Lawrenc
seems deliberately to invert much of Brontë's novel, but where he als
seems to have used Bertha Mason as a direct source of Bertha Coutt
the gamekeeper's wife.

In both *Jane Eyre* and *John Thomas and Lady Jane*, the second versio
of *Lady Chatterley's Lover*, a protagonist, yearning for sexual fulfillmen
and physical completeness, falls in love with an older man only to fin
the relationship complicated and frustrated by a wife who, though
wife only in the legal sense, has disillusioned the man and peculiarl
maimed him. In both novels, Bertha functions more as a symbol tha
as a character: as Mellors says, 'Be sure your sins will find you ou
especially if you're married and her name's Bertha.'[10]

Like Rochester, Lawrence's Parkin (Mellors in the third version) i
hurried into marriage with an older woman only to discover too la
that her coarseness and vulgarity repel him. Lawrence stresses Bertha'
lowness, and Parkin recounts how when he was 'a lad of about eleve
or twelve', Bertha 'unmanned' him; 'she lifted her clothes up an' showe
me – you know what. – They wore those split drawers then, girls did . .
she wanted me to come an' feel. But I never knowed afore then a
women had hair there. Black hair! An' I don't know why, it upset m
an' made me hate the thought of women from that day' (*JTLJ*, 225)
Sexually incompatible once they marry ten or so years later, Parki
and Bertha finally part. She returns to threaten Parkin and Connie
however, in a scene heavy with symbolic weight. She breaks into Parkin'
cottage in the woods and, sitting naked in his bed, demands to be owne
as his wife again. He locks her in the cottage, after taking all food fron
the house, but this only seems to drive Bertha mad. Ivy Bolton write
Connie: 'she's like a mad-woman, and keeps going to the wood for M
Parkin, raving at him . . . she is evil-mad. . . . It is a kind of hysteria
no doubt, but to my mind it is more evil than anything, and come
from having lived wrong' (*JTLJ*, 292, 293). Connie herself is mor
sympathetic, because she understands, perhaps even identifies with, th
mad woman: 'Poor woman! the extent of her reckless defamation, an
the fact that she talked about her indecent conjugal intimacies wit
him, showed the extent of her morbid love for him. It was a love gon
mad. But it was like a dog with hydrophobia, insane at the sight o

water for which she had been thirsty. . . . No wonder she was evil-mad' (*JTLJ*, 294). And, just as Bertha Mason's brother protects her 'rights', Bertha Coutts' brother intrudes to thwart Parkin by brutally beating him, leaving him 'sadly disfigured'. Interestingly, Bertha's role in *Lady Chatterley's Lover* is relatively small, and the direct references to *Jane Eyre* have been deleted.

Was Bertha Mason Rochester in Lawrence's mind when he created Bertha Coutts? Except when overwhelming evidence exists, such questions must be answered cautiously and speculatively. However, because the two characters share names, ages, sexual vulgarity, coarseness, drinking habits, and unfaithfulness, because they attack their husbands in closed rooms, because they both are mad to a greater or lesser degree, and because the protagonists sense an alter-ego in them, it seems highly possible that Brontë's character did fix herself in Lawrence's mind and make her way into the versions of *Lady Chatterley's Lover*.

Perhaps the strangest of Bertha's progeny are the novels of Herbert G. De Lisser whose *Jane: a Story of Jamaica* and *The White Witch of Rosehall* seem much influenced by Brontë's novel. The first, a rewrite of the Reed family-Gateshead Hall episode, presents Jane, a Jamaica girl coming to work for the Mason family (a mother, two daughters, and a son), gradually rising in society, and being rewarded by a handsome marriage–all because she heeded her father's advice to ' "Keep you'self up. . . . Keep straight." '[11] Little more complex in characterization, action, and theme than Nancy Drew mystery stories, the novel created a pattern which De Lisser expanded in *The White Witch of Rosehall*, the tale of Robert Rutherford, scion of an English family, who arrives in Jamaica to work, however unlikely, as a bookkeeper on a plantation prior to taking over the family plantation on Barbados. He works for Annie Palmer, whose first three husbands have died under mysterious circumstances and who obviously dabbles proficiently in the black arts, knowledge she acquired in Haiti. She snares Robert as her lover, kills Millicent, a young native girl who loves Robert, and then, in a climactic scene, is strangled by Takoo, the girl's father, during a native rebellion. Robert's assessment of the action bears more than a trace of Rochester's disillusionment:

Circumstances have stopped me. I did not know myself. I had all sorts of high hopes and resolutions. I was going to learn a lot while enjoying myself; I was going to have a fine time and yet become a competent planter. I was going to make my old man proud of me; show my strength and determination, and all that. But I haven't

[sic] been here a day before I was making love to a woman I knew
nothing about, and I hadn't been here a week before I was
philandering with one of the native girls, and drinking lots of Jamaic
rum, and neglecting my work, and beginning to ruin my constitution
And now one woman hates me like poison and threatens me, and
the other is dead, through me. A lovely record in less than a month!"

These three novels suggest the extent to which the story of Jane Eyre
especially the chapters involving Bertha Mason, has become a reservoi
for other authors to draw from in imitation or in homage. None of thes
works, however, embodies a creative reaction to Bertha; all three adop
Brontë's general attitude towards the character and present her as th
nonhuman villainness. Jean Rhys's *Wide Sargasso Sea*, a very short nove
which took Rhys nine long years from the moment of its inceptio
during a dinner with Selma Vaz Dias in 1957 until its publication i
1966 to complete responds to Brontë with the untold story of Bertha
her victimization, and her madness, with a sympathy foreign to th
original or to the various imitations.[13]

The early and slow progress of the novel is recorded in a series o
letters from Rhys to Vaz Dias. In the first, a letter of 5 October 1957
Rhys outlined the complex ancestry of her planned work and defended
her project:

> The idea of writing the story of the first Mrs. Rochester came to m
> when I was with you and yes, I think it is a fairly good one, but
> is not easy to write – especially for me – and I realised almost a
> once that it was beyond my powers to make it convincing as
> monologue for one actress: At present – I saw dimly that it *might* b
> done but it would be extremely difficult – technically.
>
> No it must be a novel & the story told by at least three people.
>
> I think that one sentence in your letter to me is significant. You
> write 'Of course it will be a fictitious Mrs. Rochester', But don't yo
> see, Charlotte Brontë's Mrs. Rochester is also fiction.
>
> The flash that came, linking up with much that I'd heard & know
> was that *this fiction was founded on fact or rather several facts*.
>
> At that date & earlier, very wealthy planters *did* exist, the
> daughters *had* very large doweries, there *was* no married woman
> property act. So a young man who was not too scrupulous could d
> very well for himself & very easily. He would marry the girl, gra
> her money, bring her to England – a faraway place – & in a yea
> she would be an invalid or mad. I could see *how* easily all this coul

happen. It *did* happen & more than once. So the legend of the mad West Indian was established. Who would help her? By the time her relatives got to her (if they ever did) she probably *was* mad or an invalid. Or dead. There have been one or two novels about this. One was called "The Little Girl from Dominica." It was silly Prettified out of existence. Still there was the same old legend.[14]

By 10 January 1959, she announced, 'I have finished the first draft of Mrs. Rochester *The first draft* you'll think. After nearly two years! Only please try to believe that unless it is quite right – as good as I can make it & as smooth & as *plausible* it will be useless – just another adaptation of "Jane Eyre". There have been umpteen thousand & [illegible word] already.'[15] Throughout 1959, Rhys continued to work on the novel and to 'read & reread' Brontë's novel, leading her at times to realize 'it was creeping into my writing. A bad imitation – quite dreadful. All had to be scrapped'.[16] By 25 May, she wrote Selma Vaz Dias 'She's [Mrs. Rochester] coming along & I live with her all day & sometimes dream of her at night. An obsession!'[17] The novel was more than a response; in many ways it was autobiographical with Rhys finding an objective correlative in Bertha Mason's sufferings. Diana Athill, Rhys's editor at André Deutsche, affirming that Rhys always wrote about herself and that she felt she shared Bertha's lonely isolation in England, recalled the strongest identification between author and character. Quite consciously, Jean Rhys took Bertha Mason as her historical double and perceived herself as a twentieth-century counterpart, an alien being in English society. In *Wide Sargasso Sea*, Antoinette's sense of inferiority, her experience of the riots, and her distaste for the English parallel Rhys's autobiographical memoirs.[18] Rhys's letters to Vaz Dias are particularly open in discussing this identification. She told Vaz Dias 'it is not easy to put yourself into the mind of a mad woman. It is even dangerous perhaps. And dark. I'm trying to get over that by making her dwell on her childhood. I think she would light in darkness' and followed this a few moments later with 'But don't lose your identities and remember that Antoinette Bertha Rochester is one of your identities. Will be and I hope soon'.[19]

Four sources of creative energy thus converged in *Wide Sargasso Sea*: a personal response to *Jane Eyre*, an autobiographical urge, an historical awareness that such things actually had happened in the West Indies, and echoes of Rhys's earlier novels, especially *Voyage in the Dark*. There can be little doubt, though, that reaction to *Jane Eyre*, was uppermost. Rhys reread *Jane Eyre* so much that she 'found it was creeping into

[her] writing. A bad imitation – quite dreadful. All had to be scrapped,
but she apparently did not desert her rereading, for on 9 April 1959
she confided: 'I've read & reread "Jane Eyre" of course, I am sure that
the character must be "built up". I wrote you about that.'[20] In the eyes
of the English reviewers, Rhys was justified in destroying the 'bad
imitation'. They welcomed *Wide Sargasso Sea* and at time excessively
declared its independence from *Jane Eyre*. Colin MacInnes wrote that
'the only connection with "Jane Eyre" is this . . . that Miss Rhys has
appropriated two of the chief characters, and evoked their youth: for
otherwise there is no resemblance at all to the rest of Charlotte Brontë'
Rivers Scott, writing for the *Sunday Telegraph*, and the anonymous *TLS*
reviewer concurred that 'the book is no mere "extension"' of *Jane Eyre*
but 'exists entirely in its own right'. Nevill Braybrooke saw it as 'at once
both an inspired piece of literary research and a superb creation in its
own right'. Only Kay Dick, perhaps unfamiliar with Rhys's other novels
and hence unaware of many parallels, demurred: 'perversely I wish she
had returned with an aspect of life she had observed and experienced
rather than by annotating Charlotte Brontë'.[21]

Wide Sargasso Sea is saturated with facts from Brontë's novel, facts
used consistently to mesh Rhys's story with Brontë's, and hence to give
the illusion that this is the 'other side', the other truth. Rhys has used
the insane, confined mother, the idiot brother, the parental duplicity
on the parts of Mason and Rochester's father, and the Spanish Town
marriage. More tellingly, she also hews closely to the themes of betrayal,
isolation, and alienation, and develops the motifs of sexuality, passion,
and fire. The facts are identical; the treatment and interpretation are
not, because they involve a telling of Bertha's childhood and squarely
place most of the blame for her madness on Rochester's shoulders.
Bertha is pictured as being a lonely girl victimized as much as is Jane
Eyre but lacking Jane's resilience and courage.

From the first, Rhys's attention was focused on Bertha – her Antoinette
– of whom Rhys once said, 'she seemed such a poor ghost, I thought I'd
like to write her life'.[22] Michael Thorpe has suggested that 'Rhys
expended her whole creative effort upon an act of moral restitution to
the stereotyped lunatic Creole heiress in Rochester's attic',[23] a judgement
borne out in Rhys's letters. She told Selma Vaz Dias:

> Jane Eyre's mad woman is very different. To start with Mr. Rochester
> wasn't a villain. He must have had good reason for thinking his wife
> mad (helped by prejudice no doubt, but good). I have got that I
> think. As I see it he must speak. Then she, the girl must have had

some tragedy in her life which she can't forget. As a child. I have got that. It helps on everything [illegible word] her behaviour confirms his suspicions – So do [illegible word] about her mother's death.[24]

Eighteen months later, she voiced more specific criticisms of Brontë's Bertha:

The Creole in Charlotte Brontë's novel is a lay figure – impulsive & not once alive which does not matter. She's necessary to the plot, but always she shrieks, howls, laughs horribly, attacks all & sundry – *off stage*. For me (& for you I hope) she must be right *on stage*. She must be at least plausible with a past, the *reason* why Mr Rochester treats her so abominably & feels so justified. The *reason* why he thinks she is mad & why of course she goes mad, even the *reason* why she tries to set everything on fire & eventually succeeds. (Personally I think *that* one is simple. She is cold – & fire is the only warmth she knows in England).[25]

Except for the ironic parenthesis, Rhys sets a difficult task before her. Maintaining a fidelity to Brontë's facts, Rhys desires to create a past, a psychology, a personality and a causality which will turn Brontë's melodramatic stock character into a complexly sympathetic character whose childhood and adolescence have been as horrifying as anything Jane encountered at Gateshead or Lowood.

Solitary and alienated, Antoinette fits nowhere. Neither black nor European, she is rejected cruelly as a 'white cockroach' by her society, a nuisance by her mother, and a fool by her sole playmate. Antoinette's father took a Martinique girl, Antoinette's mother, for his second wife and a few years afterwards died, leaving his wife, daughter, and son virtually penniless on the Coulibre Estate, decaying in the aftermath of the Emancipation Act. As Antoinette says: 'My father, visitors, horses, feeling safe in bed – all belonged to the past.'[26] Coulibri is imaged as an Edenic garden after the Fall, threateningly beautiful and sinisterly wild:

Our garden was large and beautiful as that garden in the Bible – the tree of life grew there. But it had gone wild. The paths were overgrown and a smell of dead flowers mixed with the fresh living smell. Underneath the tree ferns, tall as forest tree ferns, the light was green. Orchids flourished out of reach or for some reason not to be touched.

One was snaky looking, another like an octopus with long thin brown tentacles bare of leaves hanging from a twisted root. Twice a year the octopus orchid flowered – then not an inch of tentacles showed. It was a mass of white, mauve, deep purple, wonderful to see. The scent was very sweet and strong. I never went near it. (*WSS*, 19)[27]

With her fathers's death, Antoinette's world has fallen; safety has disappeared; and happiness seldom brightens her life. In their place are threatening poverty, the hostility of the natives, and a mother whose refrain ' "Now we are marooned" ' (*WSS*, 18) provide little security. More than anything, Antoinette desires security, since love and happiness seem denied; she sees her mother's hair as 'a soft black cloak to cover me, hide me, keep me safe' (*WSS*, 23) and once prays 'for a long time to be dead' (*WSS*, 58). Antoinette has good reasons for feeling deserted, abandoned, marooned, and unloved. No one visits Coulibri; the natives taunt her with cries of 'white cockroach' (*WSS*, 23); her playmate steals her dress; Christophine, one of the faithful servants, tells her mother, ' "She run wild, she grow up worthless" ' (*WSS*, 26), and she feels her own mother may be ashamed of her (*WSS*, 27).

Her world changes abruptly and apparently for the better when her mother marries again, to Mr Mason who brings money, power, and direction to Coulibri. Antoinette feels safe again but, unfortunately, Mason also brings an apparently limitless store of naiveté and ignorance with him. He fails to understand the extent of the native's hostility until Coulibri is attacked and fired. Safety once again escapes Antoinette as the mansion burns, her brother dies, and her mother goes insane. After a convalescence, the family breaks apart; Antoinette goes to a convent school, hoping to find refuge within its walls, but she is taunted with her mother's madness by children in the streets. When she is 'over seventeen' (*WSS*, 59), Mason returns from England, visits her often, and tells her, ' "I want you to be happy, Antoinette, secure, I've tried to arrange, but we'll have time to talk about that later" ' (*WSS*, 59). At this point in the story, the narrative perspective shifts abruptly to Rochester and the marriage, the arrangement Mason spoke of, not to return to Antoinette's perspective until the short closing section of the novel.

Antoinette is a fearful, insecure, repeatedly traumatized child having little relationship to the grotesquely gothic madwoman in *Jane Eyre*. Nowhere is this more succinctly captured than in her dream which recurs several times:

Again I have left the house at Coulibri. It is still night and I am walking towards the forest. I am wearing a long dress and thin slippers, so I walk with difficulty, following the man who is with me and holding up the skirt of my dress. It is white and beautiful and I don't wish to get it soiled. I follow him, sick with fear but I make no effort to save myself: if anyone were to try to save me, I would refuse. This must happen. Now we have reached the forest. We are under the tall dark trees and there is no wind. 'Here?' He turns and looks at me, his face black with hatred, and when I see this I begin to cry. He smiles slyly. 'Not here, not yet', he says, and I follow him, weeping. Now I do not try to hold up my dress, it trails in the dirt, my beautiful dress. We are no longer in the forest but in an enclosed garden surrounded by a stone wall and the trees are different trees. I do not know them. There are steps leading upwards. It is too dark to see the wall or the steps, but I know they are there and I think, 'It will be when I go up these steps. At the top.' I stumble over my dress and cannot get up. I touch a tree and my arms hold on to it. 'Here, here.' But I think I will not go any further. The tree sways and jerks as if it is trying to throw me off. Still I cling and the seconds pass and each one is a thousand years. 'Here, in here,' a strange voice said, and the tree stopped swaying and jerking. (*WSS*, 60–1)

In the British Library typescript, the dream is not connected with her stepfather's return or the wedding plans, but rather is a dream which recurs while she is secure in the convent school.[28] The symbolism of the dream mirrors Antoinette's deepest fears and deepest hopes. Enticed by three men from the safety of Coulibri, Antoinette is three times betrayed and deserted: her father's death, her stepfather's failure, and, finally Rochester's desertion. Antoinette wishes the safety of her childhood home, especially her room and the painting of 'The Miller's Daughter', and the sanctity of her self, symbolized by the long white dress she wishes to keep clean (literally, psychologically, and sexually). But the man in the dream leads her to a dark forest, smiling ambiguously at her tears and fears, as the dress gets dirty and the landscape becomes foreign. The man ('his face black with hatred') and even the landscape ("The tree sways and jerks as if it is trying to throw me off") reject her.

Recreating Rochester was even more of a challenge to Rhys, and she had serious problems in getting him right. We have already seen that she did not consider him a villain, but neither did she excuse him. She wrote Vaz Dias: 'I wonder why people are so Jane Eyre conscious? And why Wuthering Heights is neglected? I suspect it's because Rochester is whitewashed – the cruel devil. Heathcliff is not.'[29] In sketching his character, Rhys developed three characteristics which victimize Rochester but also turn him cruel – his fear of passion, his racial prejudice, and his crushing sense of betrayal by all concerned.

Rochester comes to feel betrayed by Mason, by his father and brother, and finally by Antoinette herself, and the shock of betrayal explodes in rage against them. He ponders writing his father"'I know now that you planned this because you wanted to be rid of me, you had no love at all for me. Nor had my brother. Your plan succeeded because I was young, conceited, foolish, trusting' (*WSS*, 162). He reads in the unblinking eyes, the dark hair, and the daily thickening lips of Antoinette an even more sinister betrayal, especially since he believes that the love potion she put in his wine was poison. 'They bought me, *me* with your paltry money.' he shouts at her, 'You helped them to do it. You deceived me, betrayed me, and you'll do worse if you get the chance. . .' (*WSS*, 171). He blames her for withholding the secret of the island from him (*WSS*, 87). Christophine, the obeah woman, sums up Rochester quite coldly with Antoinette, telling her he is 'Stiff. Hard as a board and stupid as a foot, . . . except where his own interests are concerned' (*WSS, 115*) and later tells him outright 'You are a damn hard man for a young man' (*WSS*, 157). His racial prejudice, passingly hinted by Brontë, surface even before the overwhelming sense of betrayal. He thinks of Antoinette's 'long, sad, dark alien eyes' (*WSS*, 67) and decides that she may be of pure English descent 'but they are not English nor European either' and chides himself for refusing to admit this earlier. Even more, he feels his sense of being assaulted by the landscape of the island. Something mocking, even threatening, intrudes itself, hinting that there is a side to life he has not reckoned on. The place is 'Not only wild but menacing' (*WSS*, 69), he thinks: 'Everything is too much, I felt as I rode wearily after her. Too much blue, too much purple, too much green. The flowers too red, the mountains too high, the hills too near' (*WSS*, 70). Even the fragrances are 'overpoweringly strong' (*WSS*, 150). The landscape with its aggressive sexual symbolism overwhelms his controlled sense of sexuality. As Clare Thomas has written, he is victimized by his own Englishness but 'never loses our sympathy to become simply, a heartless monster . . . instead we are given a terrifying record of a man progressively losing his hold on sanity and any capacity for the trust that might have saved them both'.[30]

Brontë's Rochester tells Jane he needs to restore his self-respect, and it is precisely this loss that Rhys fastens on in her portrayal. Rochester has come to the West Indies young, inexperienced, confident, and trusting – trusting not only in others but in his own abilities. The early months of the marriage destroy this trust and confidence and force Rochester to destroy Antoinette's sanity in order to salvage the remnants of his own. A bit uncertain about the marriage in his own mind, threatened by the tropical lushness, Rochester first loses his 'feeling of security' (*WSS*, 75), but continues to play 'the part [he] was expected to play' (*WSS*, 77). His 'short youth' (*WSS*, 84) wavers as he wonders if she has been forced to marry him, and crumbles when he received a letter from Daniel Cosway warning him of madness in the family and telling him '*You have been shamefully deceived by the Mason family*' (*WSS*, 95). This uncertainty, once planted, grows apace as he extends it outwards 'certain that everything [he] had imagined to be truth was false' (*WSS*, 168). Discovery of the ruins of Coulibri and reading about obeah and zombies force him to ask Antoinette questions and to visit Daniel. Daniel taunts him revealing the extent of madness in the family, other people's laughter at him, and Antoinette's incestuous sexual experiences with Sandi and perhaps others. Rochester rejects Antoinette, henceforth only calling her Bertha and now fearing for his life.

Simultaneously, Antoinette has undergone a transformation. The tensions in the marriage, aggravated by Rochester's increasing coldness and his infidelity with a servant girl, reduce her to the outlines of the Bertha encountered in *Jane Eyre*: 'When I saw her I was too shocked to speak. Her hair hung uncombed and dull into her eyes which were inflamed and staring, her face was very flushed and swollen. Her feet were bare' (*WSS*, 146). She accuses him of turning the place she loved into a place she hates and bites his arm, as she will later assault her brother in *Jane Eyre* (*WSS*, 149). A duel of minds begins between the two, each hoping for a show of love on the part of the other. Rochester thinks, 'I'll watch for one tear, one human tear. . . . If she too says it, [*adieu*] or weeps, I'll take her in my arms, my lunatic. She's mad but *mine, mine*' (*WSS*, 166), but decides to wait 'for the day when she is only a memory to be avoided, locked away, and like all memories a legend. Or a lie . . . ' (*WSS*, 173). At this point, Rhys's novel has moved almost full circle back to *Jane Eyre*.

With a precision and a sensibility which could only have come from having lived with and mediated over a text for some time, Rhys adapted the imagery of *Jane Eyre* to her own novel, taking Bertha's plunge from the burning walls of Thornfield Hall as her central image and investing it with a richly symbolic resonance which dominates her novel. In the first part of the novel, the natives fire the Coulibri mansion while

Antoinette, her brother, her mother, her aunt, and her stepfather are
in it. They escape only because Coco, the family's pet parrot is killed,
a sign of extreme bad luck. Antoinette recalls the scene: 'I opened my
eyes, everybody was looking up and pointing at Coco on the *glacis*
railings with his feathers alight. He made an effort to fly down but his
clipped wings failed him and he fell screeching. He was all on fire'
(*WSS*, 43). Later, while on their honeymoon, the couple have their
dinner interrupted by a large moth who 'blundered into one of the
candles' and fell 'more stunned than hurt' on the table (*WSS*, 81).
Finally, of course, the novel ends with the burning of Thornfield Hall.
Bertha watches the fire Grace Poole tends and considers it beautiful.
Soon, she fires the mansion, and Rhys brilliantly captures her last
moments in another dream which when she awakens, she sets out to
fulfil:

> Then I turned round and saw the sky. It ws red and all my life was
> in it. . . . I saw my doll's house and the books and the picture of the
> Miller's Daughter. I heard the parrot call as he did when he saw
> strangers, *Qui est la? Qui est la?* and the man who hated me was
> calling too, Bertha! Bertha! The wind caught my hair and it streamed
> out like wings. It might bear me up, I thought, if I jumped to those
> hard stones. But when I looked over the edge I saw the pool at
> Coulibri. (*WSS*, 189–90)

Antoinette's pyromania complexly amalgamates childhood trauma,
replaying the nightmare of the Coulibri fire, the consuming fires of
passion, and the hearth fires symbolizing love and affection. In her
dream, on the other side of the fire lie childhood innocence and that
lost security she has hoped so much to restore.

Must *Wide Sargasso Sea* be read in the shadows of *Jane Eyre* as no
more than an annotation or a footnote? Walter Allen has averred that
it must; however, *Wide Sargasso Sea* is no parasitic work sucking life to
sustain itself from the Brontë novel.[31] It is no more dependent on *Jane
Eyre* than Brontë's own *Villette* depends on her earlier *The Professor*, but
like these has numerous apparent and real connections which cannot
and must not be ignored. *Wide Sargasso Sea* takes a situation which, to
its author, epitomized the half-understood conflicts between diverse
cultures. She felt that Charlotte Brontë was 'beastly English' to Bertha
Mason and to the problems of culture shock in general. Indeed, from
the first, Rhys was intrigued by cultural conflict whether geographical
or economic. In *Voyage in the Dark*, Anna Morgan, a fictional study of

the Bertha Mason type, Rhys captured the conflict in her opening contrast between England and the Indies:

> It was as if a curtain had fallen, hiding everything I had ever known. It was almost like being born again. The colours were different, the smells different, the feeling things gave you right down inside yourself was different. Not just the difference between heat, cold; light, darkness; purple, grey. But a difference in the way I was frightened and the way I was happy. I didn't like England at first. I couldn't get used to the cold. Sometimes I would shut my eyes and pretend that the heat of the fire, or the bed-clothes drawn up round me, was sun-heat; or I would pretend I was standing outside the house at home, looking down Market Street to the Bay. When there was a breeze the sea was millions of spangles; and on still days it was purple as Tyre and Sidon. Market Street smelt of the wind, but the narrow street smelt of niggers and woodsmoke and salt fishcakes fried in lard.[32]

This was a truer perception of the conflicts than that retailed by Charlotte Brontë, and it was as true in 1966 as it had been in the 1930s and as it once had been in 1847. Rhys wished to restore the balance and tell the other side.

8 Brian Aldiss, *Frankenstein Unbound*, 'the past was safe!'

In the scant century and a half since its publication, Mary Wollstonecraft Shelley's *Frankenstein* has ubiquitously permeated the English-speaking world, whether the world has read the novel or not. It leers from the grocery shelves in America as a breakfast cereal, intrudes as allusions in journalism, surfaces in everyday speech, and forms one of the major images by which modern man thinks of and speaks of scientific research. In the same century and a half, it has been adapted for stage, screen, and television dozens of times.[1] Frankenstein has taken his place with Faust, Hamlet, Ulysses, and Oedipus in the popular mind, and Mary Shelley's novel, which has been called 'the most important minor novel in English . . . begins to look both inexhaustible and inexplicable'.[2] Frankenstein's fears that his daemon would thirst for children and 'a race of devils would be propagated upon the earth'[3] has more than been realized, but not all of the progeny have been monsters as deformed and as grotesque as *Abbott and Costello Meet Frankenstein, Jesse James Meets Frankenstein's Daughter,* and *Andy Warhol's Frankenstein.* At least one, Brian Aldiss's *Frankenstein Unbound* is a disarmingly frank act of homage which deftly balances eulogy, literary criticism, and a pointed topical analysis while closely imitating most of the major features of Shelley's novel.

Frankenstein would, of course, have a particular appeal to a writer of science fiction, but Aldiss has found it to speak with peculiar aptness to his generation, almost as if his generation were living during the fulfilment of the prophecies in the novel. In *Hell's Cartographers*, a collection of essays by science fiction authors, he recalls how the fact of the atomic bomb changed his perception of fiction and echoed the imagery of *Frankenstein* in his recollection. 'The Bomb', he wrote, 'dramatized starkly the overwhelming worship of science and technology, applied science, in our lives', and then continued on to muse:

So I perceived, and have been trying to perceive more fully ever since, that my fiction should be social, should have all the laughter and other elements we associate with prosaic life, yet at the same time be shot through with a sense that *our existences have been overpowered (not always for the worse) by certain gigantic forces born of the Renaissance and achieving ferocious adolescence with the Industrial Revolution.*[4]

The vision of a society overpowered by technology explains the continuing appeal and durability of *Frankenstein*, which, in Aldiss's words,

not only foreshadows many of our anxieties about the two-faced triumph of scientific progress, it is the first novel to be powered by evolution, in that God — however often called upon — is an absentee landlord, and his lodgers scheme to take over the premises.[5]

Mary Shelley and Frankenstein have an especial place in the works of Brian Aldiss. Aldiss vaguely recalls reading *Frankenstein*, along with Bram Stoker's *Dracula*, when he was about fourteen and living in Devon.[6] He expected a horror story and, though he responded warmly to *Dracula*, *Frankenstein* brought only a lukewarm response. Years later he went out of his way to visit Mary Shelley's grave in Bournemouth and even thought about picketing to get the grave cleaned and marked more prominently since it was unkempt. Between the early reading and the later pilgrimage, however, *Frankenstein* appeared a number of times in his work. In 'Journey to the Heartland', the narrator, coming into the untidy room of a teacher, notices Krawstadt's *Frankenstein Among the Arts* on a shelf of books, and in 'Enigma 2', technically one of the more important of Aldiss's short stories because it was written under the influence of the anti-novel, the protagonist groups Horace Walpole, Ann Radcliffe, Mary Shelley, and Robert Louis Stevenson together as writers of 'a certain type of fiction' who had drawn consciously on their dreams for sources.[7] In the early 1970s, when he undertook to write a history of science fiction, Aldiss engaged himself in a serious and lasting relationship with Mary Shelley. The chapter on Shelley is a celebration, crediting her with originating science fiction. 'The central contention of my book, supported by evidence', wrote Aldiss,

is that science fiction was born in the heart and crucible of the English Romantic movement in exile in Switzerland, when the wife of the poet Percy Bysshe Shelley wrote *Frankenstein; or, The Modern Prometheus.*

And I seek to show how the elements of that novel are still being explored in fiction, because they are still of seminal interest to our technological society. I seek to show that these elements were combined as they were, when they were, because Shelley's generation was the first to enjoy that enlarged vision of time — to this day still expanding — without which science fiction is perspectiveless, and less itself.[8]

Here defined in sharp relief against the general history of science fiction are two ideas Aldiss often repeats when talking of or writing about Shelley: her position as originator of a particular kind of fiction and her position as a prophet whose vision is peculiarly valid for the highly technical modern world. As a writer of science fiction, Aldiss naturally feels indebted to Mary Shelley for creating the fictive genre he practices. As a citizen in this technological society, he feels compelled to echo her doubts about the mixed blessings of scientific inquiry and to affirm, rather loudly at times, that her prophecies have come true. To Aldiss, Mary Shelley stands at the beginning of the 'once-for-once-only' stream of science fiction, that type which is 'a direct literary response to a new factor of a change in society, generally brought about by a technological development, as are most societal changes' which then descends through Jules Verne, Villers de l'Isle Adams, Samuel Butler, Edward Bellamy, H. G. Wells, Franz Kafka, Aldous Huxley, George Orwell, and B. F. Skinner to Aldiss himself.[9]

During the two and a half years of fairly constant work on *Billion Year Spree*, Aldiss discovered that *Frankenstein*, in addition to saying more to him than much later science fiction, constantly raised questions. Why had little critical attention been paid to it? Was it because its author was a woman? Was it because she was overshadowed by Byron and Shelley and later science fiction writers? It occurred to him that, in addition to the critical discussion in his history, one could write an 'exegetical novel' doing the groundwork, even the missionary work, she could not have done.[10] Unlike his earlier novels, the idea for *Frankenstein Unbound* arrived complete, with a sense of sudden discovery, though the idea had done much subterranean travelling through his mind before springing, like Athena, full grown before him. Aldiss admits that he spends much time at his desk and often revises a great deal. Sometimes he writes quickly, as when , provoked to argue about human stupidities over dolphins, he completed *The Dark Light Years* in a month. More often, time is essential. *Barefoot in the Head* took three years, and four revisions, perhaps too many, shaped *The Malacia Tapestry*. The fortuitous conjunction of *Frankenstein*, the historical perspective required by his critical investigation of science fiction, perhaps even the influence of J. C. Squires's *If, or History Rewritten*, a 1931 book 'full of alternative universes dreamed up by scholars and historians' which was reprinted in England in 1972, and most definitely Aldiss's earlier book on time travel, *Cryptozoaic*, prepared a richly fertile imaginative ground in which the idea for the new novel could nourish itself until it matured and demanded form.[11]

In Aldiss's words, *Frankenstein Unbound* is 'pastiche and something more'.[12] It is 'not realist but surrealist'.[13] In it, Joe Bodenland, a 'deposed presidential adviser' living in Houston in the year 2020 sees a world collapsing.[14] Nuclear war in space has disrupted the infrastructure of space and time, even of reality, and man knows not from day to day where he may be. After a few brief and totally unexpected encounters with the past, Joe experiences a major timeslip, disappearing on 25 August 2020, and finds himself in Secheron, near Geneva, in 1816, the day before the trial of Justine Moritz. He suddenly becomes aware that he is in the presence of the story of Frankenstein, even before he meets the monster. The idea of only one reality pales though, because he also exists simultaneously with Mary Shelley. After witnessing the trial of Justine, he attempts to recall the details of Shelley's novel and, needing 'desperately to get hold of a copy of the book' (*FU*, 62), seeks out the Villa Diodati. After almost shooting him, Byron welcomes him to the household, and he dines with Byron, Shelley, and Mary. The next day he and Mary talk at length, swim together, make love in a very tender scene, and then part. Bodenland returns to Geneva, bent on confronting Victor Frankenstein, but instead is arrested for murdering him. Another timeslip occurs, destroying the prison, and Bodenland finds himself free again. In a scene which perhaps owes more to *The Bride of Frankenstein* than to Shelley's novel, Joe Bodenland forces his company on Frankenstein and accompanies him to his laboratory in the woods in which a mate for the monster is being constructed. Understanding the 'sheer horror' (*FU*, 159) of Frankenstein's experiment, Bodenland plans to destroy all, but before he can, the female monster has been brought to life. Waiting in his Felder car, gun ready, Bodenland plans to shoot them both, but, transfixed by their grotesque mating dance, fails to do so. The next morning, however, he does shoot Frankenstein and, after firing the house, sets off in pursuit of the monsters, following them like Shelley's protagonist, across barren northern scenes for days until he finally manages to track them down. 'This ingenious fantasy', 'a highly original and thought-provoking work', and 'a convincing interpretation of *Frankenstein* for today' wrote American reviewers;[15] however, English reviewers were decidedly cool. Peter Ackroyd called the novel 'too self-conscious . . . too elaborate by half', and Piers Brendon lectured Aldiss on the dangers of straying beyond the borders of science fiction 'into an illogical realm of fantasy or surrealism' into an artificiality which spoils the book.[16] Few confronted the crucial question of the several relationships between Aldiss's novel and Shelley's work.

In assessing the opening lines of John Milton's *Paradise Lost*, Gilbert Murray once commented: 'in those first fifteen lines, there is not a phrase, there is hardly a word, which is not made deeper in meaning and richer in fragrance by the echoes it awakens of old memories, old dreams, old shapes of loveliness'.[17] With equal validity could this be claimed of Aldiss's novel on a somewhat narrower scope, because Aldiss has imitated the form, the characters, the actions, and the themes of Mary Shelley's novel as his reinterpretation and consciously intended popularizing took shape.

The demands of close imitation of forms require perhaps the most discipline and the most defense with agents and editors, a problem Aldiss seemed to anticipate in *Billion Year Spree* when he defended Mary Shelley's choices:

> To modern readers, Mary's methods of narration in *Frankenstein* may seem clumsy and confusing. Her early readers, to whom the epistolary style of novel as used by Richardson was still familiar, experienced no such difficulty; for them, the flow of documentation from several hands — the letters from Captain Walton to his sister in England, the manuscript by Victor Frankenstein, which contains six chapters of his creature's account of its own life, and finally Walton's narrative again — only added to the general vividness and verisimilitude.[18]

Aldiss's response to a number of queries by his Random House editor, however, shifts the ground of the argument slightly:

> My novel modestly echoes the methods of Mary's novel right down to concluding with the same phrase. The diversion of this letter is consistent with Mary's methods. In any case, it forms a complete chapter by itself, and is thus easily skipped by a hasty reader. As with the diaries and letters in *Frankenstein*, or the correspondence in Richardson's *Clarissa*, realism is hardly the effect aimed for.[19]

Imitation may be the sincerest form of flattery, but it may also be the most tricky because of the peculiar requirements for disciplined creativity. This becomes particularly evident when a novelist like Aldiss adopts the form of the novel in which form is so organically fused with theme. Much of *Frankenstein's* power originates in its tight, almost claustrophobic, structuring which wraps layer after layer of narrative after-the-fact around a central core. At the heart of the book, the monster witnesses the domestic tranquillity and happiness of the DeLacey family. Always an alien and an outsider, the monster takes this scene and his own story to Frankenstein who, adding his own story, tells Walton, who, adding yet another layer of limited perspective, writes all this to his sister. Letters and journals, each with its own claims to authority and authenticity, comprise the novel, and many other novels of this kind. *The Private Memoirs and Confessions of a Justified Sinner, Dracula, Lord Jim,* and *Under Western Eyes* confront their audiences with documents of competing and often complementary authority which assault reality in a number of ways. In *Dracula,* for example, Jonathan Harker and his friends are

> struck with the fact that, in all the mass of material of which the record is composed, there is hardly one authentic document! nothing but a mass of type-writing, except in the later notebooks of Mina and Seward and myself, and Van Helsing's memorandum. We could hardly ask anyone, even did we wish to, to accept these as proofs of so wild a story.[20]

And the somewhat imperceptive editor of James Hogg's *Confessions of a Justified Sinner,* ever ready to explain human action by political reasons, in virtual despair over his conflicting documents, exclaims, 'What can this work be? Sure, you will say, it must be a allegory; or (as the writer calls it) a religious PARABLE, showing the dreadful danger of self-righteousness? I cannot tell'[21] He then quotes a letter, actually written by James Hogg and published in *Blackwood's Magazine* in 1832 as part of his fictional narrative.

Aldiss has handled not only the formal patterns but also the documentary nature of Shelley's novel and the later tradition with skill and sensitivity. Knowing that letters, journals, and diaries may well have disappeared in the McLuhanesque oral culture of 2020, he substitutes the documents a technological world generates — a few letters, newspaper leaders, cables, transcripts of telephone conversations, and, as the major part of the novel, a traped journal. Taking the exchange of letters between Robert Walton and his sister which open and close *Frankenstein* in his pattern, Aldiss presents his readers with several letters Joe Bodenland writes his wife, Mina (perhaps here echoing *Dracula*), in

Indonesia. A letter to 'dearest Mina' opens the novel, outlining an idyllic childhood scene with the grandchildren and defining the central thematic conflict: 'intellect will break in — crude robber intellect — and myth will wither and die like the bright flowers on their mysterious grave' (*FU*, 7). A leader from *the Times* then pinpoints 'the gravest crisis of [mankind's] existence' (*FU*, 8), the problems of instability in the infrastructure of space, followed by a letter detailing the first insignificant time slip and a Comp Cable to Mina announcing the disappearance of Bodenland. The taped journal itself follows, opening with the comment, 'A record must be kept, for the sanity of all concerned. Luckily, old habits die hard, and I had my tape-memory stowed in the car, together with a stack of other junk' (*FU*, 25), a less hopeful note than Walton's claim that 'this manuscript will doubtless afford you the greatest pleasure; but to me, who know him, and who hear it from his own lips, with what interest and sympathy shall I read it in some future day'.[22] After the deaths of Frankenstein, both novels return to more personal forms, *Frankenstein* to Walton's letters, *Frankenstein Unbound*, to more tapes, but Aldiss's novel abounds in other documents: a 23 May 1816 newspaper, poems by Byron and Shelley, a paraphrase of Shelley's 1831 Preface to her novel, a lengthy letter from Bodenland to Mary, everything but direct quotations from Shelley's novel itself, as in the case of George MacDonald Fraser's *Flashman Papers*. Bodenland however, does keep one of Frankenstein's notebooks and 'preserved it in case [he] ever managed to return to [his] own time' (*FU*, 188) Imitation of form extends far beyond the division of the novel into letters, journals, and other documents, and the closing on the same phrase to include use of epigraphs and an allusive title. Aldiss's title complexly amalgamates allusions to Frankenstein, Prometheus, and *Prometheus Unbound* in ways, of course, that Shelley could not, and his choice of epigraphs from Byron's *Manfred* and Leonardo da Vinci's *Treatise on Painting* echoes even more sinister threats than Shelley's choice of Adam's rebellious words from *Paradise Lost* to which Aldiss alludes in the novel.[23] To Aldiss, the formal structure of Shelley's novel was neither immature nor clumsy nor dated, but rather was an essential aspect of her novel to be copied and echoed; it was a way of giving 'a cheer for Mary Shelley' and her accomplishment.

Since 1895 when H. G. Wells's anonymous time traveller confidently 'flung himself into futurity' expecting to find in 802 701 'strange developments' and 'wonderful advances', science fiction has been largely futuristic, looking backwards only occasionally and then only to the present moment of the writer and very rarely looking backwards from the present moment to the past.[24] Aldiss had already written about time travel to the past in *Cryptozoaic*, and, in *Frankenstein Unbound*, deliberately selected the past in preference to the future, partly in reaction to H. G. Wells, and more pointedly because he likes the sense of remoteness and geography much science fiction makes impossible. Time travel is imaginative in action, and time travel to the past provides an escape into a world before it became entrapped and entangled in the regulated world made possible by the verge and foliot escapement clock invented in the thirteenth century, an invention which, to Aldiss, embodies a wrong philosophy of time. This concern is mirrored in the action of the novel in that the early letters and newspapers are dated precisely, but this precision lapses slowly into a telling of time by the rhythmical return of the sun and moon and the seasons. Bodenland experiences a time shock, and his 'new disposable watch, powered by a uranimum isotope and worth at least $70 000 at the current going price in USA, 2020' (*FU*, 41) becomes an object of no use except to be pawned for money. 'Its undeviating accuracy in recording the passage of time to within one twenty-millionth of a second' has little use in a world 'that still went largely by the leisurely passage of the sun' (*FU*, 42), and, in an act that seems symbolic to him, Bodenland pawns the creation of the technology of North Korea for a 'derisory sum' (*FU*, 42).

Wells's time traveller set off thinking the future was safe; his belief in progress encouraged this assumption. Similarly, Joe Bodenland, excited about being the first man displaced backwards in time, feels 'How much nicer to go back. The past was safe' (*FU*, 28). Similar disillusions soon follow. Bodenland presumes 'that the orthodox view of time, as gradually established in the Western world, was a mistaken one' (*FU*, 74), closely related to the technological disruption threatening his world of 2020.

The remote past also provided the haunting landscape of Aldiss's novel. Of course, Shelley's novel fully exploits landscape in its striving for the sublime — the glacier at Chaminoix, the isolated island in the Orkneys, the arctic ice — but these settings inspire awe at the force within nature and the natural; they do not hint the desolation Joe Bodenland finds in the truly boding northern lands:

> The country over which I travelled reminded me of the tundra I had seen in parts of Alaska and the Canadian Northwest. It was all but featureless, apart from an occasional lonely pine or birch tree. The surface consisted of uneven tussocks of rough grass and little else. (*FU*, 193)

The frigid northern land with this sparse vegetation, gloomy sky, and peculiar lighting owes nothing to Shelley, but everything to the landscapes of Caspar David Friedrich (1774–1840), a German painter contemporary with Shelley. In 1972, from 6 September to 15 October a major exhibition of his paintings was mounted at the Tate Gallery and Aldiss visited the exhibition, finding in the landscapes the visual effects he wished to achieve in descriptions of the barren lands of his novel.[25] 'Griefswale in Moonlight 1816–17' seems to have been in Aldiss's mind when he described cities through which Bodenland travel in his pursuit of the monsters. One landscape he describes thus: 'A mournful beauty infiltrated this period, in which the only persistent qualities were the most amorphous. Banks of mist, towers of cloud, layers of silvery fog, nondescript pools which reflected the curtained sky – these were the durable features of that place' (*FU*, 195). In this 'phantasmal landscape', he mistakes the 'spires of old churches, old cathedrals, old towns, ancient cities' (*FU*, 196) at first for tall conifers and then for 'masts of ancient sailing ships' (*FU*, 196), precisely as one can do with Friedrich's paintings, and Bodenland specifically underlines the visual allusion, saying,

> Always, their spires floated on the beds of mist which blanketed the land. I recalled the paintings of a German Romantic artist, Caspar David Friedrich, with his embodiments of all that was gloomy and meager about Nature in the north. I could imagine myself in the still world of his art. (*FU*, 196)

Although reacting against H. G. Wells, Aldiss writes from the same disillusionment. The suicide of the intellect, the time traveller finds, is a direct result of the 'perfected science and . . . logical conclusion to the industrial system' of his own time.[26] Aldiss stresses the causality even more emphatically. The world of 2020, actually a very near future, is the logical consequence of certain forces unleashed during the Romantic movement. He writes firmly in an apocalyptic tradition, seeing around him collapse and decay. In *Hell's Cartographers*, he attacks the naive philosophy of science fiction in which

> the writer takes for granted that technology is unqualifiedly good, that the Western way of life is unqualifiedly good, that both can sustain themselves for ever, out into galaxy beyond galaxy. This is mere power-fantasy. As I have often argued, we are at the end of the Renaissance period. New and darker ages are coming. We have used up most of our resources and most of our time. Now nemesis must overtake hubris, for this is the last act of our particular play.[27]

This darker age will be caused by 'our own innate violence' which we have already seen in World War II.[28] The coming darkness Mary Shelley hinted is, in Aldiss's view, already upon us, and it is the fulfilment of the fears of her novel which gives his novel its peculiar validity as a reading of contemporary attitudes towards science. Some have dismissed Aldiss as seeing Frankenstein as only a mad scientist. In *Billion Year Spree*, Aldiss discusses other dimensions of the character, but, clearly, turns fascinated again and again to the scientist unleashing, with the best of intentions, horrors on his world.[29] At the level of theme, *Frankenstein* and *Frankenstein Unbound* become synchronous, and it is at times difficult to tell from which novel thematic comments concerning the scientist have been taken.

Three themes dominate *Frankenstein*: the primacy of the heart over the head, the capacity of the intellect to isolate and to destroy, and the necessity for human society. Once Victor Frankenstein turns intellect against death and sexuality, two aspects of human existence which have destroyed his happy childhood, a number of other themes, some of which Mary Shelley seemed unaware of, are generated, but these do not displace the three major themes. In a crucial passage early in his attempt to warn and hence to rescue Walton, Frankenstein melds all three concerns into an extraordinarily powerful thematic statement:

> I do not think that the pursuit of knowledge is an exception to this rule. If the study to which you apply yourself has a tendency to weaken your affections, and to destroy your taste for those simple pleasures in which no alloy can possibly mix, then that study is certainly unlawful, that is to say, not befitting the human mind. If this rule were always observed; if no man allowed any pursuit whatsoever to interfere with this tranquillity of his domestic affections, Greece had not been enslaved; Caesar would have spared his country; America would have been discovered more gradually; and the empires of Mexico and Peru had not been destroyed.[30]

Frankenstein lives with a fear that mankind will curse him for allowing the monster to reproduce; Bodenland lives with the knowledge that he has produced wildly and irresponsibly. *The Times* leader picks up Bodenland's 'crude robber intellect' theme, proclaiming 'Intellect has made our planet unsafe for intellect. We are suffering from the curse that was Baron Frankenstein's in Mary Shelley's novel: by seeking to conrol too much, we have lost control of ourselves' (*FU*, 9) and Bodenland himself views Frankenstein as 'the archetype of the scientist whose research, pursued in the sacred name of increasing knowledge, takes on a life of its own and causes untold misery before being brought under control' (*FU*, 61). In reply to Percy Shelley's passionate and hopeful optimism, Bodenland attacks belief in progress and later tells Mary that her 'prediction of awful catastrophe' (*FU*, 101) is a complex allegory 'in which Frankenstein, standing for science in general, wishes to remold the world for the better, and instead leaves it a worse place than he finds it' (*FU*, 102). Bodenland knows that the 'Frankenstein mentality had trumphed by [his] day. Two centuries was all it needed. The head had triumphed over the heart' (*FU*, 161). But Bodenland is not a bleak pessimist or fatalist. He also knows that the intellect has, in many ways, bettered the conditions of the individual while simultaneously wreaking havoc in his world by destroying a certain primal harmony between man and his environment. Although Bodenland at first feels free in 1816, he quickly realizes that, in many ways, 2020 was better. He writes Mary:

> Between your age and mine . . . the great mass of people have become less coarse. Beautiful though your age is, many though the intellects that adorn it, and ugly though my age is, cruel many of its leaders, I believe that the period from which I come is to be preferred to yours in this respect. People have been educated to care more, upon the whole. Their consciences have been cultivated. (*FU*, 115)

He goes further to credit these advances to a checking of the intellect by the social conscience chiefly directed by poets and novelists, especially the socially aware novelists following Shelley in the nineteenth century 'who truly mirror the tremendous futurities and shape the hearts of the people' (*FU*, 119). Top most on a pile of notecards in Aldiss's study is a quotation from Percy Shelley's *A Defence of Poetry* which, in essence, is both Frankenstein's threat and Mary Shelley's fear about the intellect:

> We have more moral, political and historical wisdom, than we know how to reduce into practice; we have more scientific and economical knowledge than can be accommodated to the just distribution of the produce which it multiplies. The poetry in these systems of thought, is concealed by the accumulation of facts and calculating processes. There is no want of knowledge respecting what is wisest and best in morals, government, and political economy, or at least, what is wiser and better than what men now practice and endure. But we let '*I dare not* wait upon *I would*, like the poor cat in the adage.' We want

the creative faculty to imagine; we want the poetry of life; our
calculations have outrun conception; we have eaten more than we
can digest.[31]

In addition to imitating the forms and themes of *Frankenstein*,
Frankenstein Unbound adopts virtually all its important characters and to
these adds the Villa Diodati group in much the same way that the
prologue to *The Bride of Frankenstein* introduces Mary, Percy Shelley,
and Lord Byron. The responses to Shelley's characters involve several
crucial reinterpretations; the portraits of the novelist, the two poets, and
the others are, in Kingsley Amis's opinion, 'damned good portraits'.[32]
Mary Shelley has appeared in a number of stories and novels ranging
from Thomas Love Peacock's Stella of *Nightmare Abbey* (1818) and John
H. Hunt's Mrs Godwin Percy in 'Luigi Rivarola, a Tale of Modern
Italy' (1838) to more recent works such as H. C. Hartman's *Frankenstein
in Sussex* (1969) and a host of novelistic 'biographies' by Elinor Wylie
(1926), Catherine Dodd (1933), Frank Wilson Kenyon (1959), Rupert
Hughes (1935), and Gay Bolton (1961), but in none of these is she
presented more sympathetically than in Aldiss's novel. Peacock praised
her 'highly cultivated and energetic mind, full of impassioned schemes
of liberty, and impatience of masculine usurpation';[33] Aldiss chooses to
picture her delicacy, domesticity, and attractiveness. When she finally
appears, Bodenland calls her 'petite . . . fair and rather birdlike, with
brilliant eyes and a small wistful mouth . . . amazingly young' (*FU*,
77). Timid in comparison to the voluable and volatile personalities of
Byron and Shelley, Mary remains fairly silent until she and Bodenland
are alone the following day. He approaches her while she is
unselfconsciously nursing her infant son, William, and, while telling her
what her future holds, especially in terms of the fame of her work, he
finds himself falling in love with her, rhapsodizing 'Ah, Mary, Mary
Shelley, how dear you were and are, beyond all women — and yet what
was possible then was only possible because we were mere phantoms in
the world' (*FU*, 97). Byron and Shelley, who figure prominently for
only one chapter, are more quickly though no more less deftly sketched.
Byron enters, pistols drawn, threatening 'tourist-shooting season' (*FU*,
66), and Shelley, 'a slender young man shaking raindrops from his head'
(*FU*, 70), reminds Bodenland of Victor Frankensten, an argument
advanced in many discussions of Frankenstein and silently accepted by
the novel.[34] To Bodenland, 'Shelley was all electricity where Byron was
all beef . . .' (*FU*, 71).

Aldiss's handling of Shelley's characters may surprise some readers, for, like Bodenland, he feels Shelley was 'entirely too kind to Victor's betrothed, Elizabeth, and more than entirely too kind to his friend, Henry Clerval' (*FU*, 113). In Shelley, these two characters offer the positive moral norm counterpointing the isolation of the monster and Frankenstein. Always domestically inclined, benevolent almost to a fault, and dutiful to an extreme, neither Elizabeth nor Henry hesitates to sacrifice his own self-interest for the benefit of others. Clerval sacrifices one year of his life simply restoring Frankenstein to good health, and Elizabeth testifies on behalf of Justine Moritz. In *Frankenstein Unbound*, however, they are harsh, hard, and even dangerous. Elizabeth Lavenza, strikingly beautiful in both novels, has a coldness of features and haughtiness of behaviour lacking in Shelley's portrait, and Henry Clerval, indolent, uncivil, and unpleasant, appears more interested in Elizabeth than in Frankenstein. Frankenstein and the monster, who figure only slightly in the novel until the closing chapters, undergo no such transformation, though Frankenstein becomes more cowardly. Frankenstein still has that slightly hysterical edge to his personality frequently evident when he is recording his story or attempting to persuade Walton's sailors not to turn back. Perhaps more illusioned than his Shelleyean counterpart, he knows his life is doomed but rejects Bodenland's warning, passionately defending the right of disinterested pursuit of truth: 'My responsibility must be to that truth, not to society, which is corrupt. Moral considerations are the responsibility of others to pontificate on; I am more concerned with the advancement of knowledge' (*FU*, 148). Rather than willing destruction on himself and those he loves, he agrees to bring the female monster to life, and, in the very moment of his triumph when he tells Bodenland to 'fall silent on [his] knees' (*FU*, 184) before his power, Bodenland shoots him.

For all its close imitation of structure, theme, and characters, *Frankenstein Unbound* achieves an independence of its own, largely because its protagonist, Joseph Bodenland, belongs solely to Aldiss's novel. It is his personal story. Aldiss had been progressing steadily in his writing towards a 'wise man' figure missing in much of his earlier work. He had approached such a character in Joseph Bryner in several short stories, but wished to create a character, faintly like George Orwell, who, in Aldiss's view had the wrong opinions at times but who usually kept both head and heart in the right place. Then, too he saw necessary symbolic reasons for making his character an American. Power has shifted from Britain, and as the focus of the NASA space programme, Houston seemed the right background for Bodenland. Aldiss confided that Bodenland, a liberated individual with magic at his command is himself in his better moments — an alter-ego of the best kind.[35]

Ultimately, the entire novel revolves more around him than his meeting with Mary Shelley and Frankenstein.

In Shelley's novel, Frankenstein admonishes Walton, 'Learn from me, if not by my precepts, at least by my examples, how dangerous is the acquirement of knowledge, and how much happier that man is who believes his native town to be the world, than he who aspires to become greater than his nature will allow.'[36] No one admonishes Joe Bodenland, but his experiences with the past mature him in unexpected ways, completing, dissilluioning, and enlightening him as he encounters the Frankenstein family and the Villa Diodati menage. He moves from being the rational man outside mythic and religious feelings to a new perception of the complete being in whom neither head nor heart rules alone. Early in the novel while watching his grandchildren bury a scooter, decorate its grave, and then chant over it, he feels a pang of alienation from their 'innocent pagan outlook' and writes his wife: 'at first it caused me some regret that I have for so long stifled my own religious feelings in deference to the rationalism of our times . . .' (*FU*, 6). Later at one of the most frightening moments in the novel, when he confronts the female monster in the laboratory, an instinctive revulsion for what Frankenstein is doing and an instinctive religious feeling, long buried, overcome him, and he condemns Frankenstein's actions as blasphemy:

> And to say as much — to think as much — was to admit religion . . . to admit that there was a spirit that transcended the poor imperfect flesh. Flesh without spirit was obscene. Why else should the notion of Frankenstein's monster have affronted the imagination of generations, if it was not their intuition of God that was affronted? (*FU*, 160)

During this transformation, Bodenland moves through three discrete stages: quixotic throughout, but concerned first with rescuing Justine Moritz, then with destroying the monster, and finally with killing both Frankenstein and the two monsters.

Bodenland welcomes the timeslip because it offers him the opportunity of escaping from the world of 2020, which he partially helped make, to the nineteenth century, feeling that 'the past was safe' (*FU* 28), safe in it naiveté, its innocence, its lack of twenty-first century technological sophistication. Immediately before the timeslip, Dean Reede, Secretary of State under President Glendale, has condemned Bodenland, saying 'that many of the Western powers' present troubles could be blamed on [Bodenland], because [he] pursued such a namby-pamby role while acting as presidential adviser' (*FU*, 13). As soon as Bodenland steps over the time boundary, however, all weakness disappears as he experiences 'total euphoria! I was a different man, full of strength and excitement' (*FU*, 27). Part of his excitement comes from the superiority he feels to the world in which he finds himself, knowing, though never voicing this knowledge, that he is as foreign to this world as is the monster. His feelings of superiority come largely from his technology: in his nuclear-powered Felder are an array of advanced products ranging from tape-players to swivel guns. He feels himself 'a new man, fitted for decision and adventure' (*FU*, 28), once the initial shock of finding himself cut off from his own age has dispelled. In an initial moment of recognition, he recalls:

> My superior self had taken over — call it the result of time shock, if you will, but I felt myself in the presence of myth and, by association, *accepted myself as mythical*! It is a sensation of some power, let me tell you! The mind becomes simple and the will strong. (*FU*, 34)

Quickly disillusions follow, first with the innocence of the age, next with certain beliefs he has held. His sense of his own personality is assaulted, and he feels his identity 'becoming more and more tenuous' (*FU*, 51), because his conception of reality is undergoing assault not only in terms of the sudden timeslip but also because of the disappearance of boundaries between 'reality' and 'fiction'. From the moment Byron introduces Bodenland to Shelley, Joe knows that his 'severance with the old modes of reality was complete' (*FU*, 71). His first moments with Mary also bring 'a flash of revelation . . . I perceived that the orthodox view of time, as gradually established in the Western world, was a mistaken one' (*FU*, 75).[37] Much of the decisiveness of the first stage of development wanes, and Bodenland finds himself thrown into prison, accused of the murder of Frankenstein, much as Frankenstein found himself imprisoned for the murder of Henry Clerval. Confinement replaces the earlier sense of freedom, but Bodenland still trusts the intellect's power to solve problems. He plans to ally himself with Frankenstein, and, if possible, to persuade Frankenstein to destroy the monster and not to build the female monster. At this point, he still frimly believes that civilization has benefited from its exercise of the intellect. Bodenland's letter to Mary from the jail cell is a long impassioned apologia for the intellect.

In the last third of the novel, however, as Bodenland's original personality dissolves and as he feels his 'consciousness . . . slipping towards the extreme brink of disintegration' (*FU*, 190), Joe's perception of the intellect undergoes a major transformation. Two details loom large at the beginning of this stage, details minor in terms of action but crucial to the symbolic embedding of the themes. Someone — he never knows who — frees Bodenland from the jail cell, thus saving him from drowning in the water and mud pouring into the prison. 'Someone at least in that dreadful place . . . had a thought for others besides himself' (*FU*, 124), Bodenland tells himself. Later that day, his life is saved again, this time by the monster whom he is seeking to destroy. As Bodenland sleeps in a shallow cave on a hillside outside Geneva, two men attack him for his fire and leave him badly beaten. In the dim recesses of his memory, Bodenland recalls someone saying 'Here, fellow outcast from society, if thou canst survive this night, draw strength from one who did not' (*FU*, 130).

Bodenland's warnings to Frankenstein are rudely rejected throughout. Frankenstein at this time in the novel little resembles the tragic figure in Shelley's novel, confronting his own failures to respond to his creation. Aldiss's Frankenstein is cowardly, self-interested, and arrogantly Promethean; he becomes truly terrifying to Bodenland who sees 'starkly, for the first time, the villainy and the sheer horror of Frankenstein's researches . . . this moral madness placed him beyond human considera-tion' (*FU*, 159). Recognition about self rapidly accompanies this recognition about Frankenstein. Bodenland perceives that all his 'previous beliefs in progress were built on shifting sand' (*FU*, 161). More important, he experiences a devastating insight into his own age, recording on tape, 'What I experienced as I fell on my knees was a metaphor — I saw the technological society into which I had been born as a Frankenstein body from which the spirit was missing' (*FU*, 162). He internalizes this recognition, too, after murdering Frankenstein and beginning his pursuit of the monster:

> Nothing could refresh my soul; I was a Jonas Chuzzlewit, a Raskolnikov. I had lied, cheated, committed adultery, looted, thieved, and ultimately murdered; henceforth my only fit company was the two brutes who journeyed somewhere ahead of me, my only fit surroundings the frigid hinterlands of hell which I now entered. I had taken over Victor's role. (*FU*, 193)

Indeed, he has, and the novel recapitulates the pursuit scenes of *Frankenstein*, as Bodenland becomes the intellect attempting to destroy its own creation. In killing Frankenstein, he believes he has wrecked 'the *fatalism* of coming events' (*FU*, 189), but he knows with equal conviction that he has 'altered no future, no past' (*FU*, 190). He does manage to shoot and kill both monsters, but not before the monster eloquently tells him, 'though you seek to bury me, yet will you continuously resurrect me! Once I am unbound, I am unbounded!' (*FU*, 211). The novel ends ominiously with Bodenland 'biding [his] time in darkness and distance' (*FU*, 212), awaiting the expected attack from the Dis-like city on the horizon.

In *Broca's Brain*, the astronomer-philosopher, Carl Sagan sceptically considered if time travel into the past is possible and concluded that 'science-fiction encounters with alternative cultural futures may play an important role in actualizing social change' but that time travel into the past is impossible.[38] Aldiss is far less concerned with actualizing social change than he is with diagnosing a fundamental illness in Western culture. His Frankenstein still lives in the form of individuals such as the Chairman of the Board of General Electric who, when confronted with the many dangers created by modern technology, exclaimed, 'If science has brought us problems, as it has, then the answer is more knowledge, not less. If technology has brought us problems, as it has, then the answer is better-managed technology, not a slow slide back to the poverty and squalor that most people had to endure in the falsely idealized past.'[39] Aldiss, no modern-day Luddite, would agree in part. Through *Frankenstein Unbound* runs the idea that technology and knowledge become dangerous only when the Frankenstein head becomes divorced from the human heart, precisely Mary Shelley's intuition in 1818. Aldiss's memoir closes on a similar note:

> I regret having no faith — for belief in catastrophe is not faith — more especially since I have lost hope in the idea of Reason as a guiding light. Even a loving family does not entirely compensate for a sense of isolation; nor do beautiful women and good friends erase the knowledge that life and success are mere temporary accidents. The days come and go; the enemy is never forgotten.[40]

•

Part IV
Rich Evocations of the Past

Two recent books on British society and politics have proposed that Great Britain is currently experiencing an identity crisis, beginning in the 1960s, as it attempts to find its appropriate role in the post-war world. In a polemical discussion of British democracy, Stephen Haseler noted that 'today Britain is at another watershed in its long history. The Social Democratic Age which emerged from the First World War may now be in the early death throes of its own strange death . . . a new age is being born out of turmoil and change', and in *Britain and American*, Daniel Snowman portrays Britain as 'a society torn by self-doubt' whose 'self-image was fractured . . . her cohesiveness as a society was, if not seriously shaken, at least tested'.[1] Paradoxically, considering their diverse viewpoints, approaches, and intentions, Haseler and Snowman arrive at the same conclusion: that part of Britain's strength lies in tradition and a mature awareness of the uses of the past. Though he considers British democracy fragile, Haseler sees British 'social, economic and political history' as one of its 'powerful defenses' against a totalitarian future.[2] Though he does not necessarily approve, Snowman notes a reassertion of tradition and traditional values in the 1960s, enabling British culture to absorb new values during a crucial period of 'self-questioning'.[3] At times, Heseler and Snowman personify Britain as an individual experiencing a long-delayed mid-life crisis, or 'a turning point, a crucial period of increased vulnerability and heightened potential'.[4]

The novel has always been concerned with recreating the past, but in the works of authors such as Angus Wilson, Margaret Drabble, and John Fowles, particular metaphors have been created which yoke together the individual and the cultural pasts, finding in the relics of the past an objective correlative for the problems the individual faces and can only solve by meticulous recall of his or her past life. Margaret Drabble indirectly hinted this new metaphor, responsible in its way for the numerous historians, geologists, anthropologists archaeologists, and paleontologists who people contemporary novels, when she spoke of a glimpsing of St. Paul's Cathedral:

> One of the joys of living in London is that you can walk through layers and layers of history in one street. . . . I went to Fleet Street and looked out and saw a view of [St. Paul's] I have never consciously seen . . . and that must have been one of the things that was intended when this was built. . . . And that is wonderful, because I actually had a very keen sense of how generations of journalists, centuries of them, must have looked at this view and thought there it is. It is splendid, what a wonderful building.[5]

Concern with the past is evident in the biographies, guides, and landscape books these novelists have written. Angus Wilson has given us studies of Emile Zola and Rudyard Kipling. Drabble has added a biography of Arnold Bennett and studies of William Wordsworth and Thomas Hardy. In addition, Wilson wrote the text for *England*, a mediation on English landscape and historical buildings. Drabble's *A Writer's Britain* and Fowles' *Islands* and *The Enigma of Stonehenge* have extended and elevated the landscape guide along meditative lines. Fowles, drawn to the 'presentness of its past' in weighing the continued fascination Stonehenge holds, adds

> There remains something about the place that stays, even for the most convinced rationalist, religious or shrinelike, laden with echoes and undertones for which modern life may claim it has very little time, but which lingers on in all of us.[6]

And in *A Writer's Britain*, Drabble concludes:

> The past lives on, in art and memory, but it is not static; it shifts and changes as the present throws its shadows backwards. The landscape also changes, but far more slowly; it is a living link between what we were and what we have become. This is one of the reasons why we feel such profound and apparently disproportionate anguish when a loved landscape is altered out of recognition; we lost not only a place, but a part of ourselves, a continuity between the shifting phases of our life. Virginia Woolf knew that she would rediscover her lost parents in Cornwall, and she was right: for her readers, she is there too.[7]

Drabble's comment strikes to the heart of the thematic assumptions of *Anglo-Saxon Attitudes*, *The Realms of Gold*, and *Daniel Martin*, for in them the objective past of the timescape becomes symbolic of the individual pasts, not in a static way, as Drabble points out, for the present also 'throws its shadows backwards'. The artifacts and topography of the timescape become the analogy for the links between the various states of the individual's past, present, and future, and meditating on a ruin or site becomes the key to recapturing the past for present uses. In *Anglo-Saxon Attitudes*, Angus Wilson juxtaposes an historian's personal failures with an archaeological fraud; in *The Realms of Gold*, Margaret Drabble compares the discovery and excavation of an ancient city with the discovery and gradual disinterment of an individual's past long suppressed; and in *Daniel Martin*, John Fowles daringly exploits visits to ruins on four continents with a man's attempt to reconsider his entire life. The ruins metaphor figures centrally in each of these novels. Frances Wingate's comment in *The Realms of Gold* that 'Britain was so old, so crowded, so confined, so sated, so dug-up and reburied, so cross-threaded, all its interests were interdependent, so obscure' becomes the image of her own life, and the harmony she achieves by the end of the novel is imaged as 'not quite as spectacular a rediscovery and reclamation as Tizouk, but it offered many private satisfactions' – a successful archaeological and psychological 'dig'.[8] In *Anglo-Saxon Attitudes*, Gerald Middleton is forced to face the truth than an archaeological fraud foisted on the historical profession echoes his own fraud within his family. Indeed, one character sees 'Melpham [the site of the Anglo-Saxon find] simply as a symbol of a conflict inside him that needed to be resolved'[9] *Daniel Martin*, the most recent and perhaps the most ambitious of the three novels, explores the 'heightened sense of personal present and past' by opening a door on its protagonist's past, a man whose life is 'in ruins somewhere', and compelling him to recall with great accuracy his entire life.[10] As he does so, he projects the conflicting attitudes within himself outwards onto the ruins of Europe, Asia, Africa, and North America, culminating his search for 'whole sight' in a chapter entitled 'Future Past'.

Interest in the cultural pasts has not gone without its critics. More than one author has viewed it as an escapist tendency. Rayner Heppenstall, for instance, has said that 'life is becoming utterly intolerable and the life of any other kind seems preferable', a comment echoed by Richard Adams and George MacDonald Fraser, authors who in diverse ways have contributed major statements about the past to the

English novel, Fraser in *The Flashman Papers*, Adams in *Watership Down*.[11]
To Fraser, 'the present has so many disagreeable aspects that the past
looks like a blessed escapist relief, especially since one can pick and
choose the best bits'; to Adams, 'a lot of people are making frantic grabs
to try and retain their hold on the past' in the face of alarming rates of
change.[12] *Anglo-Saxon Attitudes*, *The Realms of Gold*, and *Daniel Martin*,
however, are not escapist works; rather they treat people who have been
escapists but who are now forced to re-evaluate and newly understand
their presents by measuring them against the pasts. In the novels of
Chapter 2, diaries, letters, and photographs aroused and freed memories
of the past. With the novels of Chapter 4, the reminders are cultural
artifacts and sites such as surround the Englishman and Englishwoman
in everyday life. When asked to name his favourite book of 1979, for
example, John Fowles turned not to a novel, a biograpy, a social treatise,
a philosophical work, but rather commented, 'the book I have enjoyed
reading this past year most of all . . . is John Aubrey's *Monumenta
Britannica*, his fascinating collection of notes on British prehistoric
monuments . . . . '[13] But perhaps the comment of Sir Alexander Glen,
Chairman of the British Tourist Authority, most perceptively identifies
the causes of the renewed interests in both personal and cultural pasts.
He notes that after World War II, 'the sense of the past was more
physically intact in Britain perhaps than anywhere else in Europe.
Surely that sense of the past was becoming important, almost a natural
resource, in a frantically developing future'.[14]

9 Angus Wilson, *Anglo-Saxon Attitudes*, 'echoes of memory'

Separated only by the mile between Bloomsbury and South Kensington but by immeasurable distances in terms of their importance are two of the most famous finds in British archaeology, finds which frame Angus Wilson's years at the British Museum and which cast long shadows over the inception, creation, and finished form of his second novel, *Anglo-Saxon Attitudes*. The first of these the Sutton Hoo treasure, Sir Thomas Kendrick called 'the most remarkable archaeological discovery ever made in England', and Rupert Bruce-Mitford exclaimed that it was 'a new rung established in the ladder of history'.[1] The second, the skull of 'Piltdown man', one of the most infamous forgeries in anthropology, unveiled 18 December 1912 'to a densely-packed and excited audience . . . [as] the ideal "missing link"', was unveiled in truth in November 1953 as 'an amalgam of a modernish skull with the jaw of a modern orang-utan'.[2] From such diverse materials emerged one of the most sustained and deeply inquisitive considerations of man's relationship with the past in recent fiction.

Angus Wilson began his career with the British Museum in 1937, two years before the Sutton Hoo discovery and retired in 1955 shortly after the Piltdown scandal broke. He has revealed that these two events were the inspiration of his novel, and alludes to both several times in the course of the novel, more frequently to Piltdown than to Sutton Hoo.[3] Clarissa Crane, a historical novelist, reminds Rose Lorimer of the fascination with and romance of such finds: 'think of Sutton Hoo! – the homage of the barbarians to civilization, that great Byzantine dish!' (*ASA*, 19). Professor Pforzheim, a visiting German scholar, tells Middleton: 'Alas, we historians have so little scandal. We are not paleontologists to display our Piltdowns' (*ASA*, 31) and less kindly reminds his audience of the joke against English scholarship: 'But in England . . . they specialize in Piltdowns' (*ASA*, 321). Even the paratexts of the novel underline the Piltdown references by fabricating *Times*

articles of November 1912 and January 1955 paralleling actual contemporary reports of the 'finds'. Wilson's pen has captured the tone of both
with incisive humour. *The Times* informed its readers in 1912 that:

> Excavations in Sussex by an anthropological student have brought
> to light the fragments of a human skull. The skull, said by experts
> to be that of a Palaeolithic man, is the earliest undoubted evidence
> of a man in this country. A detailed description of this and other
> discoveries will be presented at a meeting of the Geological Society
> to be held on 18 December. The skull would appear to carry
> anthropological knowledge back to a much more remote date than
> the human skeleton discovered by Mr J. Reid Moore in the Ipswich
> district last year.[4]

And in the summer of 1939, readers discovered that:

> It was learned yesterday that the burial place of an early Anglo-Saxon
> Chief, dating in all probability from the sixth century, had been
> unearthed in Suffolk. The body of the dead chief had been laid in a
> large rowing boat, which had been drawn up from the water and
> placed bodily in a deep grave. The grave dug for the reception of
> the boat had a length of 82 feet and a beam of 16 feet. Nothing
> remains of it but a pattern of iron clench nails in the ground, but
> finds of considerable antiquarian interest accompanied the body.
> These have been removed by excavation on behalf of the Ancient
> Monuments Department of the Office of Works.[5]

Wilson's pastiche captures the laconic tone exactly:

> It is now possible to make a tentative statement about the extensive
> archaeological excavations undertaken this summer in the former
> kingdom of the East Folk. The work was originally carried out by
> the East Coast Antiquarian Association under the direction of the
> well-known antiquary the Rev. Reginald Portway.... It is understood
> that negotiations are in progress for the sale of the objects between
> the owner and the Trustees of the British Museum. (*ASA*, 9)

Wilson's flair for pastiche is such that his pastiche of the forgery
revelation is virtually indistinguishable from the original:

> It now seems clear beyond doubt that the heathen idol found in the
> coffin of Bishop Eorpwald in 1912 was placed there as a practical

joke by Gilbert Stokesay, who assissted his father in the excavation. The full story of this lamentable affair will probably never be known. (*ASA*, 346)[6]

But why, one may validly ask, should Wilson have been interested by two important but recondite archaeological discoveries? Why should they have brought the urge to create over him? And why should he have combined them in the way he did so that Sutton Hoo and Piltdown underwent a sea-change to emerge as the Eorpwald burial at Melpham?

Wilson's interest in historians, archaeologists, paleontologists, and the past in general is readily explained. Wilson is by training an historian. His honours degree from Balliol College, Oxford is in history, coming during those years when the teaching of history was much influenced by Marx and Freud. Wilson was taught to look for the 'real power' and the 'real motivation', and he turned his satiric talents towards his academic discipline early in his writings.[7] In 'Totentanz', one of his most bitingly satiric looks at the academic world, he portrays Professor Cadaver:

> That long gaunt old man with his corseted figure, his military moustache and his almost too beautiful clothes; foremost of archaeologists, author of "Digging up the Dead", "The Tomb my Treasure-House" and "Where Grave thy Victory?" It was not only the tombs of the ancient world on which he was a final authority, for in the intervals between his expeditions to the Near East and North Africa, he had familiarized himself with all the principal cemeteries of the British Isles and had formed a remarkable collection of photographs of unusual graves.[8]

And one of the most prominent features of *Anglo-Saxon Attitudes* is its range of familiarity with types of academic historians and schools of historiography: Middleton, Lorimer, Clun, Roberts, Stringwell-Anderson, and Pforzheim sample the spectrum from history written toa bizarre thesis to documentary and statistical dullness to general cultural history. There are Sir Edgar Iffley for whom history is 'a discipline of the spirit, an act of faith in civilization' (*ASA*, 34) – a position shared by Gerald Middleton, Roberts, and Stringwell-Anderson – Clarissa Crane for whom 'the past speaks for us so much at this moment' (*ASA*, 18), and Clun, the technician whose 'hard research' involves figures and charts but no 'sweetness and light' (*ASA*, 32). The history papers being marked by Gerald suggest the range Wilson was exposed to during his career, because the questions include both the Marxist and the Freudian: '"Power follows trade routes." Discuss this statement in relation to the collapse of the Empire of Canute. "Feudalism is a pattern imposed upon mediaeval society by historians unversed in the difficulties of practical government." Discuss this view of feudalism in relation to English society in 1100' (*ASA*, 131). In addition to admiring the Dickensian scope and variety offered by the novel, especially in terms of its historians, the early reviewers also admired its satiric stance in sketching them. Kingsley Amis saw a potential twentieth-century Thackeray in Wilson's talents, and reviewers for *Time* and *Atlantic Monthly* agreed.[9] *Time* called the novel Wilson's 'longest, cleverest and most annihilating display of literary marksmanship to date', and Charles Rolo praised the cleverness of the 'satiric portraiture and the brilliant rendering of social milieu which are the heart of the matter'.

But there are more particular reasons why the specific historians surrounding Sutton Hoo and the Piltdown man appealed to Wilson. Both discoveries involved amateurs, a group instinctively distrusted by professional historians, and both contributed certain lines of thought to the novel. Sutton Hoo raised questions of interpretation. Indeed, debates over the relationship between the pagan and the Christian aspects of the burial still rage. The sheer force of the reputation of Thomas Kendrick in handling, validating, and interpreting the Sutton Hoo treasure fascinated Wilson. World War II broke out only nine days after the last day of excavation at the site, so there was little time for careful study and cataloguing of the treasures. Indeed, it was hurried, along with the Elgin Marbles and numerous other classical artifacts into 'a disused appendix of the London Tube system, the deep tunnel joining Holborn Kingsway and Aldwych station' where it remained until the end of the war.[10] Piltdown man raised questions of validity and nationalism, because more than a hint of national pride infused the early search for prehistoric man.[11] With the discovery of Neanderthal man in Germany in 1856 and the cave paintings in France in 1878–9, England lagged far behind in offering signs of prehistoric inhabitation. The Piltdown hoax reverberated not only through the halls of science but also through the halls of Parliament. On 25 November 1953, a motion was introduced in the House of Commons to the effect 'that this House has no confidence in the Trustees of the British Museum (other than the Speaker of the House of Commons) because of the tardiness of their discovery that the skull of the Piltdown man is a fake'.[12]

Wilson wears his considerable knowledge of these two findings lightly, but in his review of Peter Hunter Blair's *An Introduction to Anglo-Saxon*

England, he mentions the studies of Chadwick, Plummer, Hodgkins, Myers, Stenton, Kendrick and Whitlock with familiarity and sketches briefly why Anglo-Saxon culture may have appealed to him as a major symbol for his novel:

> But all these aspects of Anglo-Saxon history are additional to the central wonder – Anglo-Saxon civilisation itself. In the British Museum alone we can see the Lindisfarne Gospels with the Byzantine and Celtic traditions of art between the same covers the incredible riches of a sixth-century East Anglian king in the Sutton Hoo treasure, the Franks casket with scenes from three separate worlds, the rhythmic glories of the drawings of the Winchester school.[13]

His four references – especially the Lindisfarne Gospels and the Franks Casket – show the society unselfconsciously fusing diverse cultures, and it is this sense of fusion and wholeness which drew Wilson to the use of an Anglo-Saxon burial for his central symbol. Less complex than the modern world in many ways, the Anglo-Saxon world unified for one moment in time the beginnings of a new world with the remnants of a collapsing empire.

Sutton Hoo in Suffolk had attracted antiquarians' curiosity for centuries. Henry VIII's men had dug for treasure in one of ten mounds and John Dee, Queen Elizabeth I's Court Astrologer, apparently came to Sutton Hoo after having been commissioned to search for treasure on the east coast. No one, though, had significant luck until an amateur archaeologist, Basil Brown, began excavating in 1938 on the estate then owned by Edith May Pretty whose own interest in the mounds on her property had perhaps been piqued by the excavations she had seen in Egypt. After some interesting finds in 1938, Brown returned in the summer of 1939 for further excavations. He noted in his diary,

> Monday 8 May 1939 Arrived at Sutton Hoo and after leaving my luggage at Mr. Lyon's house where I lodged in 1938 interviewed Mrs. Pretty who accompanied me to the mounds. I asked which one she would like opened and she pointed to I, the largest barrow of the group, and said "What about this?" and I replied that it would be quite all right for me.[14]

Within three months, a ship burial, gold, silver, jewellry, and other grave furniture of a cenotaph, believed to be that of Raedwald (599–624) had been excavated. C. W. Philips, a scholar who arrived to help with the excavation, recalled that the find 'had the effect of an explosion, but world events were to muffle its full effect for some years . . .'.[15]

Here, then, are the essential ingredients of Wilson's novel: the amateur historian, the reputation of a respected scholar, the East Anglian estate, and its owner transformed into Gilbert Stokesay, Professor Stokesay, Melpham, and Lilian Portway. But Wilson's love for pastiche carried him even further into the creation of documents loosely spun around an actual Anglo-Saxon. The Melpham burial supposedly contained the coffin of Eorpwald, a 'seventh-century Christian missionary at the court of King Aldbert of the East Folk' (*ASA*, 8). The appendix of the novel contains 'extracts' from Bede's *History of the English Church and People*, a thirteenth-century *Anonymi Episcopi Vita Eorpwaldi*, and later historical documents.[16] Though they are fictive, they easily could have come from originals. There was an Eorpwald, an East Anglican Wuffinga king who ruled from 624 to 627 or 628 mentioned once in Bede in terms similar to those of the novel:

> So great was Edwin's zeal for the true Faith that he persuaded King Eorpwald, son of Redwald, King of the East Angles, to abandon his superstitious idolatry, and accept the Faith and Sacraments of Christ with his whole province. His father Redwald had in fact long before this received Christian Baptism in Kent, but to no good purpose; for on his return home, his wife and certain perverse advisers persuaded him to apostatize from the true Faith. So his last state was worse than the first, for, like the ancient Samaritan, he tried to serve both Christ and the ancient gods, and had in the same temple an altar for the holy Sacrifice of Christ side by side with an altar on which victims were offered to devils.[17]

While the Sutton Hoo treasure supplied the Anglo-Saxon background for the novel, the Piltdown man hoax supplied two crucial elements for the plot – the fraud and the mystery, a mystery which is solved in the novel, but which will apparently never be fully solved in life. The Piltdown excavations were begun by Charles Dawson, a Sussex solicitor, later revealed as a supremely audacious plagiarist, in February and March 1912. Five men participated in the excavation – Dawson, Pierre Teilhard de Chardin, Arthur Smith Woodward, F. J. M. Postlehtwaite, and Grafton Elliot Smith, whom informed scholars believe is responsible for the hoax. Even a hurried reading of the two primary discussions of Piltdown, J. S. Weiner's *The Piltdown Forgery* and Ronald Millar's *The*

Piltdown Man, reveals the complex mystery of the fraud and increases the suspicion that an amateur or a professional jealous of the reputation of other professionals attempted to embarrass or destroy them but was frustrated by circumstances.[18] It is only a short step to the Stokesay father-and-son relationship and Gerald's difficulties in reconstructing the events of 1912.

Gerald Middleton, the sixty-year-old (60, 62, and 64 at various points in the text) protagonist of Wilson's novel is at a moment of crisis in both his private and his public lives. The public crisis both mirrors and is intrinsically connected with the private crisis since similar things have gone wrong with his family and his profession. Separated from his wife and alienated from his three children, Gerald, though he established himself as a major scholar in his youth, has never realized his potential. He considers himself a 'failure, in fact, and of that most boring kind, a failure with a conscience...a family man who had had neither the courage to walk out of the marriage he hated . . . an ex-professor of medieval history who had not even fulfilled the scholarly promise of studies whose general value he now doubted' (*ASA*, 13). Gerald has failed because he has not had the courage to ask two questions, accepting self-delusion instead. As his son John tells his sister, '[There is] something we all guard desperately . . . the level at which we all prefer acceptance, because to fill it would mean facing something we prefer not to' (*ASA*, 130). Gerald does not wish to ask if his wife, Ingeborg, deliberately maimed their daughter by holding her hand in the fire, nor does he wish to ask if the Melpham burial excavated by Professor Stokesay involved a hoax. He has reasons for believing both of these fears to be true, but certain knowledge must be fended off. Hayden White has seen Gerald as a typical example of the 'modern writer's hostility towards history [in using] the historian to represent the extreme example of repressed sensibility',[19] but Gerald does not belong with such individuals as André Gide's Michel who finds a static deathliness in historical research and thought:

> When, in Syracuse and later on, I tried to resume my studies, to immerse myself once more in the detailed inspection of the past, I found that something had if not suppressed at least altered my enjoyment of it: the sense of the present. The history of the past now assumed, in my eyes, that immobility, that terrifying fixity, of the nocturnal shadow in the little courtyard at Biskra, the immobility of the death.[20]

Gerald's involvement with the past is a restorative and healing one as were the involvements of Leo Colston and Harold Atha. In *The Wild Garden*, his general survey of his writing habits, interests, and involvements, Wilson sketched just such a programme for his characters: 'I was enabled carefully to plan a technique of flashbacks and word echoes which would show how self-realization and the purging of guilt (or the acceptance of it) are inevitably a long process of re-living traumatic experiences in memory.'[21]

Arthur Edelstein has perceptively generalized Wilson's concern to cover several of the other novels, noting that 'at a strategically situated point in their lives, that last chance to locate the right direction despite a tangle of wrong turns behind them, his people are put to the test of awareness. They must rediscover the lost past in order to confront the unfound future'.[22] Both Frank O'Connor and Kingsley Amis, however, have raised serious questions as to whether Gerald is at 'a strategically situated point' in his life. O'Connor sees only artificial construction and little necessity in Gerald's retrospection: 'Here, in *Anglo-Saxon Attitudes*, you get a novel which would have been a good novel if it had begun twenty years earlier. A certain crime, a fraud, had been committed on archaeology, and if you traced the people from the fraud on, you'd have had a good novel. What happens? You get the crisis – the old gentleman who suspects a fraud has been committed – what are his moral problems in the last weeks before he decides he's gong to reveal the fraud?'[23] Amis castigated the novel for explaining art yet not explaining adequately: 'A grinding penury of invention saps the narrative, which in spite of its many discussions and explanations and long speeches . . . still fails to explain why Gerald stopped working and why, apart from having taken a rest-period for congitation and mulling over the past, he feels he can start again.'[24] O'Connor's quarrel with the novel can be readily dismissed. His desire for a process time-line novel is highly prescriptive; no valid reason demands that a novelist should follow such a time line if he, like Wilson, wishes to 'take a point in time' and develop the implications both backwards and forwards simultaneously. O'Connor would, by fiat, condemn most retrospective and epiphany fiction which depends on a significant starting point. Amis's charge is more serious because nothing is apparently unusual about 22 December 1954, the day on which the novel begins and continues for the first two chapters. The novel, however, supplies very good answers as to why Gerald should suddenly begin asking questions at this point in his life. Professionally, circumstances conspire to thrust more responsibilities than usual upon him. He has been asked to assume the editorship of a collective history of medieval England; privately, his Christmas visit with his wife and family makes him see that the tangled relationship between Robin, Marie-Hélène, Elvira Portway, and John closely resembles the destructive relationship established between himself, his wife, Dollie Stokesay, and Gilbert Stokesay three to four decades earlier, and that he should do something to rescue Robin from it. In addition, a letter requesting assistance with research on Gilbert Stokesay, Professor Pforzheim's discoveries at Heligoland, a casual mention of Dollie, Rose Lorimer's outburst at the annual Stokesay lecture, the annual visit with Mrs. Salad, and the unexpected meeting with Elvira Portway cause Gerald finally to think that 'the past seemed insatiable in its encroachments upon his life today' (*ASA*, 60).

Thus begins a scholarly detective story, similar to the unmasking of the forgeries of T. J. Wise, but played for Oedipal stakes since the detective will uncover the key to his own identity; as he attempts to solve one mystery, he will actually solve two. Elvira Portway, perhaps more perceptively than anyone else in the novel, understands that the one is a metaphor for the other, 'for she saw Melpham simply as a symbol of a conflict inside him that needed to be resolved' (*ASA*, 229). Indeed, this is one of Wilson's most commonly used approaches to symbolism. In *The Middle Age of Mrs. Eliot*, Meg Eliot, speaking of her husband's death, tells her brother:

> Oh, I don't think so, David. I've felt that this sudden blow from outside was only a symbol of my ignorance of the world. That I'd been punished for living in a fool's paradise. But to say that a thing is a symbol surely means in a way that it's something one should dismiss once one's seen what it's a symbol of, doesn't it? . . . And as to the possibility that such accidents have some meaning on another level, I know little enough about the surface reality without looking further.[25]

Edelstein has pushed the metaphor further, unfortunately in my view, arguing that 'aside from its function as an element of the plot, the Eorpwald excavation is a perfect effigy of Middleton's circumstances. Like his formerly inert consciousness, the tomb has enclosed the past in its darkness and has hidden those broken and decayed artifacts which can be disinterred only by digging beneath the level surface of the present'.[26] Though far too easy in its assumptions about the tranquil nature of Gerald's present and awkwardly ignoring the whole problem of the hoax, Edelstein's comments do underline the necessary connection between the two that the novel insistently reinforces. Early in the novel, before the reader senses the full extent of Gerald's failure, the connection is made by Gerald himself. He reminds himself that 'Never, after all, had he himself been prepared to face the truth in life, either in his family or in his profession' (*ASA*, 12) and, a few pages later, returns to this line of thought again: 'All this seeking for the truth of the past should be in abeyance until we had reached some conclusions about the truth of the present. In any case, who was he to dabble in truthtelling when he had evaded the truth, past and present, for most of his life?' (*ASA*, 15–16). Even more tellingly, at the end of Book One, Gerald pulls the two together in such a way as to force a decision and a judgment on himself:

> So that, he thought, was the whole of it. Suspicions engendered by the words of a drunkard and the actions of a hysterical woman. He had never dared to confront Gilbert with his words again nor face Inge with his suspicions about Kay's hand. And from these slender foundations it seemed he had woven a great web of depression and despair to convince himself that his chosen study of history was a lie and the family life he had made a deception. (*ASA*, 160)

Is it too late for Gerald to face the truths, to sweep away the falsehoods, deception, and masks, and to salvage some part of his life? Wilson specifically believes that it is not. He believes that 'Gerald leaves the book a happier man, relatively free even if his freedom is bought at the price of accepting irrevocable guilt, accepting his family's hostility, accepting loneliness . . .'.[27] And both books of the novel conclude with optimistic rhetoric and symbols. Book one, for instance, concludes: 'It seemed to him suddenly as though he had come out of a dark narrow tunnel, where movement was cramped to a feeble crawl, into the broad daylight where he could once more walk or run if he chose' (*ASA*, 161) Book Two concludes on a similar note of acceptance and action on Gerald's part. Paralleling his earlier decision to accept the editorship of the *History*, Gerald decides to accept the chairmanship of the historical association and to go abroad for lectures. His flight to his lectures in Mexico is not to be seen as an escape from problems but rather as 'an adequate symbol for adaptation to the modern rapidly changing world'.[28]

The conclusion to Book One has been misread and misrepresented, thus lending some credence to the charges raised by O'Connor and Amis. C. B. Cox has objected to the triteness of the imagery and the lack of dramatic force in the paragraph, maintaining that 'it is not clear why at this moment Gerald should have made this decision'.[29] Gerald seems, however, to make only a partial decision. He does not decide at this point to untangle the family mysteries nor does he decide to investigate Melpham, rather he decides to accept the editorship and to immerse himself in professional activities. Interestingly, the paragraph concludes with the clause 'he could once more walk *or run if he chose*'. Rather than seeing Gerald suddenly deciding to confront the entire range of his failures, I believe we should see Gerald as attempting yet one more escape from whole vision. By immersing himself in professional and scholarly activities, he can stave off the 'unspoken questions' yet a while longer. He selects a partial bondage in preference to a lonely and frightening freedom. The editorship brings an unusual 'clarity of mind that he had not known for years' (*ASA*, 201) and a new animation, but Melpham keeps demanding attention, even though Gerald thinks he has 'allowed the incident with Gilbert far too much influence in his life as it was; he could do far more for his chosen profession in getting on with the job in hand' (*ASA*, 223).

A more detailed look at Gerald's two failures of nerve reveals the connecting tissues between the various plots of this densely populated and complexly plotted novel. Dollie Stokesay summarizes the tangled web for the reader quite succinctly:

> As far as I can see, what you're getting at is this – Gilbert faked the burial as one of his ghastly jokes, mainly to spite the Pater. The Pater knew about it years afterwards but never let on for fear of seeming a fool. And the same goes for old Portway. That Baker man helped Gilbert, and he and his daughter blackmailed old Portway over it. (*ASA*, 313)

Gerald admits that 'roughly' this is indeed the story.

Closely paralleling the actual Piltdown find, the Melpham excavation of Bishop Eorpwald's tomb begins in 1912 on property owned by Reginald and Lilian Portway, a famous actress, under direction of Canon Portway in the early stages and later under direction of Lionel Stokesay, who builds his career on this find. The excavation uncovers a stone coffin bearing 'inscriptions and ornaments of great interest to historians of the seventh century' (*ASA*, 9) and containing 'a wooden fertility figure' (*ASA*, 11). Canon Portway knew that a find would be made on his property and told the excavators to 'dig' and when they found nothing to 'dig again' (*ASA*, 69). Gerald, a young graduate with

'a remarkable First in Tripos' (*ASA*, 151), arrives at Melpham late in
the summer following an invitation from Professor Stokesay, only to
slip and fall as he gets out of the car. He is confined to the house under
Dollie's care for the rest of his stay, but he does hear detailed reports
about the find and gradually falls in love with Dollie.

The wooden idol, Rose Lorimer tells Clarissa Crane, is a crudely
carved fertility god,

> Much cruder than the few finds they've made on the Baltic Coast.
> Due to native workmanship, no doubt with the Continental tradition
> almost lost. That accounts for the large size of the member. . . . But
> it's an Anglo-Saxon deity all right. A true *wig*. One of the *idola* Bede
> was so shocked about. (*ASA*, 21)

The implications of the find are as significant for medieval history as
the Piltdown skull was for anthropology. Here is proof of an uneasy
compromise between the pagan and Christian worlds of precisely the
kind that still informs discussions of *Beowulf* and the Sutton Hoo burial.[30]
On the basis of this one piece of evidence, an erroneous interpretation
of the past has been erected. As Gerald tells Lilian Portway: 'I'm afraid
it isn't a question of what happens to Melphan House. It's a far larger
question of historical truth. This lie, if lie it is, has become the cornerstone
on which a whole false edifice may be erected' (*ASA*, 244). Gerald has
every reason to believe that all is a lie, not because the excavation did
not meet the high standards of later professionalism, not because the
principals were unskilled, not because the idol was faked (it was not),
but because the drunken Gilbert Stokesay one night told him he had
deliberately concocted the hoax so that he could destroy his father at
his father's greatest moment of triumph – the awarding of a knighthood:
'I put it there. . . . I found the thing on the other site, among the pagan
graves, where you'd expect to find it. And, with a little help, I put it
in Thingummy's tomb' (*ASA*, 148). Gerald, however, decides that this
is simply 'another of Gilbert's aggressive drunken jokes' (*ASA*, 149) and
brushes it aside, though he does use it as an excuse for his seducing
Dollie, Gilbert's wife. The planned joke dies, however, quite literally
when Gilbert is killed in the war. Both Lionel Stokesay and Canon
Portway become aware of the hoax, but say nothing in order to guard
their reputations. Baker, who helped Gilbert, blackmails Portway. Thus
stands the affair in the early 1920s.

Gerald deeply suspects that Gilbert was telling the truth, but he
wishes to avoid the truth. Even though the past repeatedly breaks in

pon him during the Christmas of 1954, he 'felt a desperate desire to
ut it off' (*ASA*, 140) and 'determined resolutely not to open the
uestion of Melpham to his conscience' (*ASA*, 168) – further indications
hat acceptance of the editorship is a flight. The doubts persist, though,
'desperate brooding . . . that was to take hold of him . . . breaking
own his newfound ease' (*ASA*, 225), like an aberration which would
ot leave him' (*ASA*, 267). Gerald knows, too, that the doubts have
oisoned his affair with Dollie and hampered his scholarship, leading
im, in more than one sense, to betray his profession and its commitment
o truth about present and past actions.

Because the interpretations growing out of the Melpham burial
hreaten to broaden with the recent discoveries at Heligoland, Gerald
cts to save historical truth. Earlier he could think 'an odd freak of
Anglo-Saxon history was faked. What did that matter to the general
tudy of the subject?' (*ASA*, 161); now, though, he sees through Kay's
yes that 'It's a question of intellectual honesty... Oh, a small one
naybe. But you say yourself you don't know where it may lead, what
ccretions of untruth – if it *is* untruth – may gather round it. This is a
natter of historical truth, of course you must speak up' (*ASA*, 227). To
onstruct a pattern from the pieces involves detective work, specifically
isits to Lilian Portway, Mrs Salad, Mr Barker and his daughter, Frank
Rammage, and, ultimately, to Dollie. Gradually, the pieces assume
oherence, falling completely into place when he reads through the
Stokesay-Portway correspondence Dollie has lent him(*ASA*, 318). Even
roaching the subject with Dollie becomes restorative; it 'seemed a final
elease, the culmination of the long mental struggle' (*ASA*, 312). Freed
rom doubts and his self-inflicted guilt, Gerald suddenly finds himself
reed creatively – the *History*, his long delayed book on Edward the
Confessor, the chairmanship of the association – these await fulfillment.
Dollie tells him he '*had* to act' but now he must 'move on' (*ASA*, 330).

The professional inquiry proceeds alongside his private inquiry. The
extent to which his family life has suffered because he hesitated to
confront his wife with his doubts about Kay's injury becomes an
overriding question in his mind. He has no particular interest in the
ives of his two sons, his daughter, his estranged wife, or his son- and
daughter-in-law. He sees, dominated by Inge,

a world of indulgent sweetness and syrupy intimacy. He had done
nothing to reform it all these years; he could do nothing now.
Nevertheless, the failure of his family life added to his preoccupation
with his professional death and closed round him in a dense fog of

self-disgust. It seemed to him that his whole life had grown pale an
futile because it was rooted in evasion. (*ASA*, 98)

Gerald has some reasons for evading this cluster of 'darling dodos
Wilson's irony is as trenchant with Gerald's private side as with h
public side. John, his youngest son, writes reformist, socially-consciou
journalism, attacking government blunders and defending the wea
individual, believing that 'by God, we need another Dickens to blo'
them off the face of the country' (*ASA*, 108). He has dabbled in politi
and now hosts a television show. Robin, a Shavian industrialist, 'th
head of our greatest steel-construction business' (*ASA*, 107), Gerald ha
some feelings for, but is even more cut off from than with John. Ka
and Donald, her husband, are socialistically minded individuals; Donalc
unable to find a position in the academic world, finally unravels all
Robin's good deeds through an incendiary speech to the men at th
plant. Marie-Hélène, Robin's wife, is a society lion-hunter of considerab.
abilities. Ruling over all of these is Inge, whose charity, benevolenc
and compassion barely disguise the hardness and selfishness which mar
her as among the most destructive individuals to stalk through Wilson
canon. She is to the private plot much the same as Gilbert Stokesay
to the public plot. Advanced in thought and action, she invited he
husband's mistress to become part of the family, telling her childrer
'*you* will grow up and marry and leave me. Great big Robin and litt
Kay, and, yes, even, perhaps, little Johnnie. Your papa's love for Aur
Dollie is as natural as that will be. And if it is natural it must h
beautiful' (*ASA*, 121). Gerald knows that 'Freudians would probab]
have imparted some exceedingly unpleasant supressed motives to Inge
behaviour' (*ASA*, 121), and John finally tells her, 'You've neve
considered anyone else but yourself for a minute of your life.... You'v
tried to strangle me with your selfish love' (*ASA*, 265).

Finally galvanized into action because he wishes to save Robi
Gerald sees that he has allowed Inge to ruin his family life and decide
it is 'his duty . . . to give Robin a warning tip' (*ASA*, 216). In th
traditions of New Comedy, Gerald's awakened concern for his famil
would lead to revelations about Inge's maiming their daughter, he
attempts to manipulate John's life, and her suffocating love for Robi
Unmasked, Inge would be defeated; the children would be rescued fro
their vampirish mother, perhaps transfer some love to their father, bu
in any case, would be freed by the heroic actions of Gerald. Such is no
Wilson's way. Gerald finally confronts Inge with his suspicions only 1
learn that the children have long known the truth about the acciden

Inge appears to have won totally. John, crippled in a car accident, is in her care; Donald and Kay have moved in with Inge, 'and they are so happy and so pleasant with Old Thingy who has brought them this happiness that they are together again' (*ASA*, 331). Robin has, though, been saved. All Gerald has actually discovered, as with Melpham, is that he should never have hesitated as long as he did to seek answers. He has lived a life of evasion, refusing to see or to accept his own responsibilities in the two frauds. He has rescued himself and perhaps salvation of the individual is all that can be hoped for in a Wilson novel.

10 Margaret Drabble's *The Realms of Gold*, 'its lines were the lines of memory'

From her first to her sixth novel, Margaret Drabble's characters have sporadically worried about their pasts, even though the plots of the novels required no confrontation with it. In *A Summer Bird-Cage*, Louise tells Sarah, her sister and the protagonist of the novel, 'Whatever happens...you can't buy the past. You can't buy an ancestry and a history. You have your own past, and the free will to deal with it, and that's all', and Rose Vassiliou in *The Needle's Eye* is distressed by 'the callousness with which one discarded one's past self, the alacrity with which one embraced the wisdom of the present. Looking back upon one's past, one could disown it, with knowledge, experience, and judgement all augmented: but what if one had once been right and ceased to be so?'[1] However, it was not until *The Realms of Gold*, her seventh and perhaps most successful novel, that Margaret Drabble set herself and her protagonist, Frances Ollerenshaw Wingate, the task of coming to terms with the past, both personally and culturally.

With an archaeologist, a historian, and a geologist as main characters, the novel's concern with the past is never in doubt. The vocations were not chosen intentionally. Only after Drabble was well into the novel did she realize how useful it was to have the characters looking at different time spans.[2] The reviewers of the novel, however, pounced a bit overeagerly on the self-evident theme without actually exploring its depths and implications. Two American novelists, one sympathetic and one hostile, came dangerously close to over-simplifying the novel's complex engagement with the past. Joyce Carol Oates, writing with the warm admiration one would expect of the author of *Wonderland* which shares an interest in heredity and environmental questions with Drabble's novel, commented: 'its general theme is a simple and profound one: one may search for "gold" (sometimes quite literally) in distant lands and

152

in varying adventures, but he is most likely to find it close at hand, in his own ancestral past'.[3] John Updike, to whose *Rabbit, Run* Drabble alludes in her novel, saw that 'psychology, zoology, geology, history — all frame our heroine's energetic unearthing of the dead . . . the central reunion is not with her lover but with the ghost of her dead-aunt' but concluded that the wealth of archaeological metaphors brought only 'incidental illuminations to the book'.[4] Lore Dickstein saw Drabble's characters digging at the past 'sometimes literally, for its secrets and treasures', but finding 'that "the realms of gold" of antiquity evidence human frailties and failings as much as does modern life' — no escape to a golden age here.[5] Ruth Mathewson, pursuing over-rigorously a Darwinian reading of the novel found not even this negative consolation but rather a confusing mystery since Frances 'must settle for mysteries; the recent past is sometimes harder to reconstruct than a lost city. and just as the uncertainties of prehistory and history are the background of the present, so our present may be seen by future archaeologists as an elusive past'.[6] Eric Korn, in a review entitled 'Archaeology Begins at Home', concluded that the archaeological metaphor was apt 'for we all dig backwards through our own successive occupational levels'.[7] None of the reviewers, though, sensed the vital connections between the archaeological facts, the archaeological metaphor, and the title of the novel.

We do not learn of archaeologists' failures; we learn only of their successes. René Millon, Austen Henry Layard, Heinrich Schliemann, Arthur Evans, and Howard Carter are more or less known to the general public only because of the discoveries they made — Teotihuacan, Nineveh, Troy, Knossos, and the tomb of Tutankhamun. Margaret Drabble's novel, too, concerns successful discovery, a concern indicated immediately by the novel's title, taken from John Keats' sonnet, 'On First Looking into Chapman's Homer':

> Much have I travell'd in the realms of gold,
>   And many godly states and kingdoms seen;
>   Round many western islands have I been
> Which bards in fealty to Apollo hold.[8]

The sonnet, written in October 1816 after Charles Cowden Clarke had shared a 1616 folio of George Chapman's translation of Homer with Keats, celebrates not Chapman, not Homer, not the translation, but rather 'something much larger, more universal, the rapture of discovery itself', fusing into one complex metaphor the Spanish conquistador

searching for golden cities, Herschel astounded by the discovery of
Uranus, and the reader's discovery of a truer tone, style, and voice of
a favorite author available only through translation.[9] Keats is a daily
presence in Drabble's life, because the Keats house in Hampstead stands
immediately behind her own home. From her windows, she can look
into the garden and considers it 'wonderful . . . to have a view like the
back which is a historic view'. The title itself, though, was not actually
selected until she had virtually completed the novel.[10]

Frances Ollerenshaw Wingate, like Herschel and Balboa, has had her
moment of discovery, not so much when she actually unearthed the city
of Tizouk, but when the existence of such a city in the Sahara dawned
on her while she waited in the Rome airport:

> The triumph had been natural. All alone she had worked it out,
> putting bits together from here and there — the tablets at Carthage,
> the strangely Meroitic lion in Kano, the curiously Nok-like face on
> the tablet in Kush. A phrase or two from Athenaeus, who said that
> the Carthaginians had crossed Sahara eating barley. A sentence from
> Herodotus, a remark by Heinrich Barth, a visit with the children to
> the Ethnological Museum, a conversation about *négritude* with Joe
> Ayida, a vague memory of a heap of ruins. . . . And then, one night
> . . . suddenly she knew exactly where to look. She knew with such
> conviction that it was like a revelation . . . (*RG*, 28)[11]

During the course of the novel, Frances experiences several such
revelations, only this time they concern herself. Archaeology is, thus,
the dominating metaphor for the novel, just as the priestly metaphor
and the biological metaphor dominate James Joyce's *A Portrait of the
Artist as a Young Man* and Aldous Huxley's *Point Counter Point*. More
importantly, France's failure in her public vocation parallels her failure
in her private world, just as it did with Wilson's Gerald Middleton.

Frances does not wish to confront certain knowledge. She does not
like to be reminded of child sacrifice and slavery in the Carthaginian
empire. Following her lecture in Naples,

> she was asked if she agreed with the conventional historical and
> archaeological estimate of the Phoenicians: was it true that they were
> "a reactionary, mercenary, cruel, inartistic, and unsympathetic
> people, whose disappearance from history was a boon to mankind",
> as at least one eminent historian had stated? Frances always found
> this question alarming, because of the confusion of her own response.

It was a fact that she had first been drawn to the Phoenicians because of their bad reputation: no race could be as bad as *that*, she had decided while still at Oxford, and had set off from Carthage in her early twenties to prove it. But alas, she had found it difficult to do so. They had been, notoriously, destroyed: . . . It was with relief that she had moved further south, to peaceful trading outposts. . . . One couldn't really pretend her men had traded only in salt and pots and ironware. But she tried to, just the same. (*RG*, 32 – 3)

Like Virginia Woolf's Clarissa Dalloway, who has become more and more important in the novels of Drabble, she brushes aside certain facts about her children, her family, and her self as 'Nonsense, nonsense' (*RG*, 98):[12]

Morbid, morbid, said Frances to herself, as she curled up more comfortably, her hand tucked between her legs, ceasing to finger the irritating stitches. She felt better already. The prospect of action always cheered her up. (*Rg*, 99)

From its earliest inception, *The Realms of Gold* was planned around themes of the past and heredity. Sparked perhaps by her work on Arnold Bennett and her teaching of Jane Austen's *Mansfield Park* at Morley College, Drabble had begun to plan the book by October 1972. She told Nancy S. Hardin: 'I've got this new theory which I'm going to put in my new book that there's something wrong with the people living in the North of England. They're all depressive. They're all sour and it's something either in the water or in the chemicals or in the environment that is hostile to human happiness. . . . I'm going to start this new book in which I think I'll try and tackle hereditary depressions that run through three generations of a family.'[13]Some months apparently passed before Drabble actually began writing the novel. She vividly recalls sitting down to write, with a cluster of ideas in mind:

I remember very very clearly because I started it in this room [her living room/study area]; I hardly ever write here, and I wrote at that desk . . . it was Easter . . . and I sat and wrote for two or three days, and it was very exciting. I don't think then I had the whole plot in my mind. I decided she was going to be a successful woman.[14]

Other related sources also bespeak a concern with the past and family relationships. The woman in 'Crossing the Alps', a short story published in 1971, is reading a book 'about old people and kinship patterns in a perishing London working-class community'.[15] An earlier story 'Faithful Lovers', sketches character relationships developed more fully in the novel.[16] In it, two lovers, separated by the woman's choice for three years, decide on the same day, quite by coincidence, to visit the restaurant where they used to meet. The past differences are settled and the affair resumes with a new depth of understanding and commitment. Even closer to the actual writing of the novel is Drabble's visit to Sheffield which so clearly parallels Frances' visit to Tockley:

> I wrote the book [*Jerusalem the Golden*] which I had based on my childhood memories of Sheffield. I wrote the book from memory, and then decided I'd better go back and check up that I'd remembered right, so I went up for a night, arriving after dark and staying at the Station Hotel. In the morning I was expecting to look out of the window and see those soul-destroying grim industrial perspectives, but in fact I looked out, the sun was shining, the hillsides were glittering, green fields fringed the horizon, it was all bright and sparkling and beautiful.[17]

What the past says to the present, though, is ambiguous and complex.

The Realms of Gold is a story of discovery, reclamation, and reconstruction. At the beginning of the novel, we meet Frances Wingate, a successful, famous archaeologist in her mid-thirties, a respected academician, independent, free from her marriage, and energetic enough to manage the demands of her career and her four children. Privately, though, doubts, anxiety, and despair beset Frances who strives to stave off the 'darkness' through work and movement. The 'darkness' has been with her all her adult life, and 'she had by now a well-established program for the horrible thing that was about to get her' (*RG*, 6). This time, however, the 'darkness' assaults her mercilessly: she loses a tooth, has breast surgery, and then, 'after a month, she despaired, and fell ill' (*RG*, 55). Her future is imaged by her as 'the desert, hot and dry' (*RG*, 77). Frances images her despair and darkness as 'the stone in her chest' (*RG*, 221). This image may perhaps stem from Ezekiel xi:19: 'And I will give them one heart, and I will put a new spirit within you, and I will take the stony heart out of their flesh, and will give them an heart of flesh.'[18]

Frances is a wanderer, almost a Bunyanesque wanderer, facing emptiness, loneliness, meaninglessness, which she avoids confronting through activity. She travels with too many things, because 'it gave one something to do, packing, unpacking' (*RG*, 3). She clings 'to activity and movement as an escape, and on the whole her remedy had worked' (*RG* 97) — until now. She tells Hunter Wisbeck, a friend of a friend, that she works so energetically 'because I've got to keep moving. . . . I get so depressed if I don't. . . . But then I find it quite easy to cure depression by work. One just has to keep moving, that's all' (*RG*, 45). 'All one has to do', she tells herself, 'is to *keep moving, keep talking*, and don't spend too much time alone. And you'll survive. What for? Don't ask, don't be naive' (*RG*, 225–6).

Drabble presents Frances in terms of a myth — the expulsion from Eden and the wandering in the wilderness. Indeed, a religious terminology permeates the novel. She thinks of Karel Schmidt, the historian with whom she has broken off an affair: 'She had been rather afraid of him. He had been something of a salvationist, he had wished to save her, with evangelical passion, and she was afraid of disappointing him, and simultaneously rather afraid of being saved. So she had told him firmly that she was mad and beyond redemption and that he'd better leave her alone or he'd be in for some nasty disappointments. Out she had gone into the wilderness . . .' (*RG*, 11). More to the point, she imagines the cottage of her grandparents, where she spent many summers, as being like 'paradise, like the original garden' (*RG*, 102) from which growth, particularly sexual maturing, has excluded her: 'In the end, things had changed: inevitably, she supposed. It wasn't exactly an angel with a flaming sword that had expelled her: nor was it, as she had at one Freudian stage assumed, simply the sins of sex' (*RG*, 104). Driven from the cottage which 'had been the one fixed point in her childhood' (*RG*, 100), a place where 'one reached safety' (*RG*, 101), Frances has entered a wilderness, wandering rootlessly. Throughout the novel, we see Frances in hotel rooms, always in transit, never comfortably at home, and always accepting fragmentation.

France's life and self have been fragmented, and her physical ills symbolize the much deeper spiritual malaise which troubles her. Frances fears failure, she fears her 'darkness', and, most revealing, she fears wholeness. She has compromised in her marriage by marrying a man she knew she did not love, in her career by not extending her talents, and in her life in general by settling for fragments rather than attempting the wholeness to which Karel might possibly restore her. Like all Drabble heroines, she is torn between motherhood and career, managing both with energy and verve to hide an inner emptiness. She knows that she is hardening and watches her deterioriation with a calm detachment, almost clinical in its objective analysis. Her successes have seemed 'narrow' (*RG*, 29), and she thinks:

She'd rarely put it to the test, in case it failed her. She'd taken no chances; her guesses had been certainties. She applied for jobs she could not fail to get, she avoided too keen competition, she gave herself a wide margin, she covered her bets. She left Karel before he had a chance of leaving her. (*RG*, 56)

'Nothing ventured, nothing gained' is not her motto: there is a safety, a protection, in her life. She accepts fragmentation as inevitable: looking at a family bicycling by her, she concludes 'that she could no longer admit the concept of a two-parent family. Such symmetry, such ideal union utterly excluded her...she wanted them split, broken, fragmented' (*RG*, 234).

Oddly, for an archaeologist, Frances fears the past. She asks herself, 'what is it for, the past, one's own or the world's. To what end question it so closely' (*RG*, 121), reminding herself that the 'pursuit of archaeology ... is ... a fruitless attempt to prove the possibility of the future through the past. We seek a utopia in the past, a possible if not an ideal society. We seek golden worlds from which we were banished, they recede infinitely, for there never was a golden world, there was never anything but toil and subsistence, cruelty and dullness' (*RG*, 120–1).[19] Even in this denial, Frances glosses over her inability and her unwillingness to come to terms with individual and cultural pasts and hints of her own fear of individual mortality.

By the end of the novel, however, despair has been replaced by a peace if not a tranquillity; fragmentation by a balanced satisfaction; and celibate loneliness by a sexually fulfilling marriage with Karel. Restored to health and wholeness, Frances has no need to hide from reality in work and movement. Yet what brought about her cure necessitated an even deeper plunge into the darkness.

Halfway through the novel, Frances is invited to participate in a UNESCO Conference in Adra, an emerging Saharan nation. There is, of course, no country named Adra, just as in *The Ice Age*, there is no country named Wallacia. Drabble shows a tendency to use older political and geographical names in her novels, and she is 'passionately committed to making names up'.[20] Wallacia is a district in southern and south-eastern Rumania, and Adra does appear on the African maps as Adrar, a low central massif in the western Sahara, now part of Mauritania. Adra, however, is Niger. The novel's repeated references to its common border with Chad (*RG*, 231) and its national colors of orange, white, and green (*RG*, 229, 237, 241, and 255) leave little doubt of this. Niger's flag is a tricolour of orange, white, and green horizontal stripes with an orange circle in the center of the white stripe. Northern Niger is inhabited by nomadic peoples as is Adra, and Niger's tin mines at Agades produced seventy-eight tons in 1965. Tizouk, too, seems to be a coinage. Tizi appears as a prefix for a number of mountain passes and several towns in Algeria and Morocco, but no actual Tizouk associated with Carthage and the early history of Saharan Africa exists. The hotel in Adra, however, must be patterned after the Hotel du Lac in Tunis, 'a ziggurat turned upside down' in its shape and probably seen by Drabble when she visited Tunisia.[21] Drabble shares the tendency of Arnold Bennett and Thomas Hardy to rename the actual locales in her fictional works.

While at the Conference in Adra, Frances glimpses theoretical wholeness in the nation's rediscovery of its past and in its projected hopes for the future. Listening to Joe Ayida, Adra's Minister of Culture, Frances 'had glimpsed what it must be like to have lost one's past, and to stand on the verge of reclaiming it. . . . His nation was a small one, his country large. It needed culture, it needed water, and minerals, and oil, it needed past, present, and future' (*RG*, 222–3). At this point, Frances can admit the theoretical necessity for the country, without applying this insight to her own personal needs. Surrounded by talk of Adra's past and future, Frances, too, finds herself immersed in talk of kinship patterns. With others, she sits on the side of the hotel's swimming pool and in restaurants 'discussing endogamy and exogamy, and the nuclear family, and genes and heredity, and incest' (*RG*, 261). When Frances returns to her hotel room that night, she bursts into tears, scarcely anything new to the reader since Frances has done this several times during the course of the novel, but something is crucially different this time:

> The stone in her chest was dissolving, after all: fate was on her side, after all. The tears poured down. In the morning, or the morning after, when she got back from the tin mine, she would write to Karel, she would write him a long letter, explaining how much she needed him, asking him to take her back. There was no point, no point at all, in being alone. (*RG*, 263)

But fate has an even more demanding epiphany in store for Frances, one which forces the public lessons of the relationship of past, present, and future into her private life. In one of her finest scenes, Drabble summons Frances home to England to face a family scandal. Constance Ollerenshaw, Frances' great aunt, has died of starvation, and the Sunday

Examiner has taken the wealthy, privileged Ollerenshaw family to task for its callousness, insensitivity, and inhumane treatment within its family relationships — 'the collapse of family responsiblity' (*RG*, 275) it is labelled on a local news program.

Faced with the necessity of arranging the funeral and of settling the estate, since neither her father, mother, nor brother can handle the demands, Frances 'goes home' to Tockley. After talking with Harold Barnard, the lawyer, she visits Mays Cottage where Constance lived and died, and like Leo Colston rummaging through his attic, she finds fragments of the past:

> [the desk she had unlocked] was full of things, every little drawer and pigeonhole was full. Bits of paper, letters, photographs, medals, buttons, sewing eggs, bobbins, brooches, rings, old tickets, coins, pins, and bits and pieces of a lifetime — of more than a lifetime, she realized, as she started to go through them, for here were records going back into the dim reaches of the dusty Ollerenshaw past. . . . Nearly as indecipherable as hieroglyphics, nearly as sparse in their information as Phoenician shopping lists, they contained a past, a history. (*RG*, 299)

As skillfully as she pulled together Punic inscriptions, Frances resurrects Constance's past — a doomed love affair, an illegitimate child, an inexperienced and interfering clergyman, a possible suicide, and the years of embittered silence. But in all this Frances feels 'curiously at home, and private, feeding twigs into her own hearth' (*RG*, 303). Harold Bernard, who stops by Mays Cottage to check on Frances on his way home, exclaims: 'You gave me a fright. . . . You could have been Constance herself, fifty years younger. In this light' (*RG*, 304). What has saved Frances? A recognition that an individual, like a country, has a past, a present, and a future, all vitally and organically related. Her restoration of Mays Cottage, symbolic of her own restoration, is, we are told, 'not quite as spectacular a rediscovery and reclamation as Tizouk, but it offered many private satisfactions' (*RG*, 352).

Discussion of Frances has a completeness about it without mention of David, Janet, and Stephen which might lead one, as it led the reviewers, to reject their presence in the novel as irrelevant subplots having no particular connections with the main plot of the novel as a whole. *The Realms of Gold* tells not one but rather four stories, seemingly quite independent in their relationships. Faced with this structuring, more than one reviewer exclaimed 'incoherence'. The more cautious reviewers simply wrote that the characters' lives 'impinge on one another', that the narrative 'freely jumps from character to character', or that though the characters share a common past, 'such a connection seems arbitrary'.[22] Some agreed with Pamela Hansford Johnson who saw 'only the minimum of structure . . . really a string of incidents clustered around Dr. Frances Wingate. There are so many people and so many switches of place that five novels at least could have been made out of it', or Anatole Broyard who condemned the 'two or three unhelpful subplots. Subplot: the very word conjures up a nineteenth-century minor novelist conspiring to delay the reader's gratification until it has ripened to his or her satisfaction'.[23]

These complaints miss the mark. Janet Bird, David Ollerenshaw, Stephen Ollerenshaw, and, finally Constance Ollerenshaw are Frances' doubles. They present in pure forms the conflicting forces of her own existence. Originally, Drabble planned three discrete sections of her novel, of approximately equal space, which would be brought together through 'some kind of catastrophe' at the end of the book. (Recently Angus Wilson's *As If By Magic* and William Golding's *Darkness Visible* have used similar structures.) In words that echo Virginia Woolf's excitement as the merging of the Septimus Smith-Clarissa Dalloway plots approached, Drabble recalls that

> I got quite excited towards the end when I did manage to get them all in the same room because it had been very difficult, but I think one of my subjects was how a family can be so fragmented.[24]

A fragmented family they are, but Janet, David, Steven, and Constance function on one level as fragments of Frances' complex personality which must be brought together to free her from her darkness.

From her first novel, Drabble has shown an interest in complex replicating structures. In *A Summer Bird-Cage*, Sarah insistently contrasts Gill and Louise as she struggles to make the choices essential to her own being:

> It was so like her, so deliberately chosen: or perhaps people choose their own symbols naturally, for Gill always has in her room vast masses of green leaves, any leaves, chopped off trees or hedges, whilst Stephen and Louise have dried grasses in long Swedish vases. Simone, the flowers without the foliage, and Gill, the foliage without the flowers. I should like to bear leaves and flowers and fruit, I should like the whole world . . . (*SBC*, 70)

And in *The Waterfall*, Jane contemplates:

> that the ways of regarding an event, so different, don't add up to a
> whole; they are mutually exclusive: the social view, the sexual view,
> the circumstantial view, the moral view, these visions contradict each
> other; they do not supplement one another, they cancel one another,
> they destroy one another. (*W*, 47)[25]

These two passages bespeak the Victorian and the modernist strains in
Drabble's structures: the first, from a novel written under the influence
of George Elliot's *Middlemarch*, suggests the Victorian contrast and
juxtaposition methodology, what Charles Dickens so tellingly called the
'streaky bacon' theory of construction.[26] The second, reminiscent of the
several notebooks of Anna Wulf in Doris Lessing's *The Golden Notebook*,
hints the fragmentation of the modern self until, in Lessing's words, 'in
the inner Golden Notebook, things have come together, the divisions have
broken down, there is formlessness with the end of fragmentation — the
triumph of the second theme, which is that of unity'.[27]

Virginia Woolf's *Mrs. Dalloway* partially defines Drabble's method.
Janet, David, Stephen, and Constance stand in relationship to Frances
as Septimus Smith stands in relationship to Clarissa Dalloway.[28] For
fully two-thirds of the novel, these characters cross and recross one
another's paths. David Ollerenshaw attends Frances' lecture but does
not meet her. The narrator pointedly reminds us: 'Remember him, for
it will be some months before he and Frances Wingate meet again' (*RG*,
51). Janet Ollerenshaw Bird is pushing her baby in its pram along
Tockley High Street when Frances arrives in Tockley, but they do not
meet until later. Stephen, on the other hand, visits Frances rather
frequently at the home in London, while she is in the hospital, at his
father's home, and elsewhere. Not until the Adra Conference and the
death of Constance are Frances, Janet, and David drawn together in
community at dinner, at the funeral, and in the visit to Mays Cottage.
From these, Stephen is absent. These three characters represent the
demands of pure maternal domesticity, pure professional commitment,
and the wish not to be. The doubling relationship is most apparent with
Stephen.

Stephen, 'so delicate . . . so insubstantial' (*RG*, 85), though one
reviewer has called him a 'rhetorical character,' memorably embodies
a modern wish not to be, a latter-day descendant of Thomas Hardy's
Tess and Jude.[29] Fascinated by and faintly envious of Frances' energy,
he still believes 'that living is a crime' (*RG*, 88) and that 'the conditions

of survival were so dreadful that it was undignified to survive' (*RG*, 88).
Not 'addicted to living' (*RG*, 89) like his parents' generation, Stephen
still has managed to complicate his life greatly while still young. Married
to Beata, an oil millionaire's daughter who suffers from anorexia nervosa,
he has fathered a daughter whom he zealously cares for. Stephen has
read Freud's *Beyond the Pleasure Principle* and has taken to heart the death
wish. In a troubling scene in his father's country cottage, he discusses
Freud, Empedocles, and death with his father and Frances telling them
'Freud says . . . that the reason why things struggle so hard to stay alive
against all the odds is that they want to die *in their own fashion*' (*RG*,
188).

Significantly, Stephen disappears almost at the moment Frances
experiences her recognition and healing scene in Adra. When she returns
to England, Stephen has committed suicide, also killing his daughter,
leaving Frances a letter explaining 'that living was disagreeable, and
worse than disagreeable, humiliating and destructive' (*RG*, 345). He
has, we are told, had a 'revelation . . . like a light from heaven. It was
better to be dead than alive' (*RG*, 344). Frances, unable to understand
why he did not spare his daughter, just as she has been unable to
understand why the Phoenicians practised child sacrifice is devastated
by his death. It plunges her from the comforts she experienced in
burying Constance. She thinks: 'How can one make a friend of death,
how can one accept graciously the wicked deal? . . . Death and love.
How dreadfully they contradict all culture, all process, all human effort.
Stephen had been right' (*RG*, 346–7).

Perhaps the most significant passage relating Stephen to Frances is
Frances' gradual coming 'to see his death as a healing of some kind, the
end of a long illness, a sacrifice. Taken from them for their better health
. . . *Stephen had taken it all away with him*' (*RG*, 348; italics added). The
antecedent of *it* is revealing, because Stephen *has* 'taken it away with
him'. He gathers the Ollerenshaw 'darkness' into his own being and by
his death purges and frees the family from its destructive nature. Also,
he has been a propitiating sacrifice to the dark forces in life, offered up
with much the same intentions the Phoenicians had when they sacrificed
their children to Tanit and other gods. Stephen has enacted the facts
of Phoenician culture Frances refused to confront and, in doing so, has
freed her just as Septimus Smith's suicide freed Clarissa Dalloway.
Stephen is that side of her personality Frances considered 'morbid'.

Originally, Drabble tells us halfway through the novel, 'David was
intended to play a much larger role in this narrative, but the more I
looked at him, the more incomprehensible he became, and I simply

have not the nerve to present what I saw in him in the detail I had intended' (*RG*, 176). In the first draft of the novel, David was surrounded by 'lots of stuff about how he had been married and his wife' before Drabble decided to omit all the background material.[30] Like Stephen, David has little need of people; he loves the inorganic and considers man 'merely another agent of change, like wind or water, or earthquakes' (*RG*, 48). Unlike Stephen, though, David Ollerenshaw has a vocation. A geologist, he takes the longest view of the past and man's relationship to it of anyone in the novel. If Stephen is Frances' own wish not to be, David is her desire for pure commitment to her vocation and academic discipline without sexual, maternal, or family ties. David has apparently cut himself off from the Ollerenshaw family and tests himself constantly against the elements, He isolates himself on the Falkland Islands; he drives alone across the Sahara to the Adra Conference. He believes that to 'be completely free of all human contact was in itself a pleasure. People were all right: intermittently he enjoyed company. But solitude had its own quality' (*RG*, 136). He desires to be at the edge of nothingness, but unlike Stephen, has no particular desire to plunge into the nothingness, Like all the Ollerenshaws, he is after something – 'He wasn't quite sure what . . . but he pursued it with some perseverance' (*RG*, 177). He has the geological perspective which enables him to see the smallness of man. Driven by these forces, he likes to suffer, but 'he liked to overcome suffering' (*RG*, 252). During Constance's funeral, he fingers 'his stream of topaz,' because 'the inorganic was pure' (*RG*, 335). He, too, has escaped the human, with all its foibles, failures, frustrations, and denials, but he has channelled his energy into theoretical commit-commitment and pursuit of the earth's riches of gold, tin. copper, oil, and so on, existing pure and solitary. He sends Frances and Karel 'a lump of pale-yellow silica glass that he had picked up himself in the desert: scooped, pitted, smoothly irregular, carved and weathered by the desert wind, apparently translucent but finally opaque' (*RG*, 353) for a wedding present which, for Frances, becomes symbolic of the truly impenetrable nature of being human.

Frances, however, is a mother and a homemaker as much as she is a respected academic and a troubled depressive. Stephen, David, and Janet are fragments of this triune self. Janet Ollerenshaw Bird is more than just 'Frances' antithesis', or the typical Drabble heroine. As Johnson pointed out, she and her 'awful husband' could have been subjects for a novel which 'would have shown . . . Drabble at her very domestic best'.[31] Janet is what Frances, denied her vocation and her larger role as an individual, would have been, her purely domestic and maternal side, resenting the constrictions and confinements. Trapped in a housng development near Tockley with a teething, year-old son, orange drapes, a red piano, a formica dining table, and horrible recipes from *Femina*, Janet seethes frustration and disappointment. Like Frances, she married without love and now finds herself 'on her own, in a solitude that was so bleak that it was a thing on its own, almost a possession, almost company' (*RG*, 125). She shares 'the same envelope of darkness' (*RG*, 125) that engulfs her small baby and Frances; however, she does make some attempt to confront this darkness by visiting Constance at Mays Cottage and giving a propitiary offering of a box of chocolates. Otherwise, Janet is dismally pathetic. Insecure sexually, socially, and financially, Janet yearns only for some great disaster: 'she would quite have liked to see the warriors descending from the mountains, rattling their sabers, aiming for her heart' (*RG*, 127); 'she wished for a volcano or an earthquake . . . what if the great river Don were to overflow and wash them all away out to the cold North Sea? (*RG*, 171). She reads constantly about disasters, concentrating at present on 'the literature of the concentration camps, war memoirs, even Solzhenitsyn' (*RG*, 130). Like Frances, she has been driven by social and cultural change from a secure and edenic world, the world, of her parents' shop. Nowadays the shop

> had changed beyond all recognition since the days when she had loved it, those early days of infancy and grace, those childish days when the apple trees had borne fruit, and the counter in the shop had been a scrubbed wooden slab, and bacon had been kept in a muslin cloth, and cheese in a cold cheese safe, when tea had been measured out of large oval enamelled tins, and crackers kept in large boxes and sold by the ounce, when an indescribable smell of coffee and ham and bacon and sugar had hung over all. It was all gone now. (*RG*, 143)

Janet does not fully realize that, more than the smells and textures, the human contacts she so fears now but once enjoyed have gone too. It is these she vaguely attempts to restore when obeying 'some primitive edict of some long disrupted kinship network . . . she boarded the bus with her baby and folding pram' (*RG*, 279) to visit Constance. Lacking the courage to penetrate through the undergrowth of Mays Cottage itself, she leaves her chocolates as a 'bribe,' feeling that she 'had placated an ancient spirit, a spirit of blood' (*RG*, 282). Constance's death brings Janet into contact with Frances who, after initial coldness, reassures her by providing a family community at Mays Cottage, even though Janet does not fit in too comfortably.

As the French brother and sister David meets while sailing across the Mediterreanean point out, 'Death brings us together' (*RG*, 220). Death, the central and inescapable fact of human existence, death which paradoxically bestows and yet mocks the significance of human action, brings the Ollerenshaw family together literally and symbolically. Frances meet Janet and David and establishes her relationship with Karel on a firmer understanding. More than the literal re-establishment of family relationships, death brings Frances a wholeness which enables her to pull together her many facets around one informing and cohering center. Death has given her a moment of insight into the relationship of individuals and family in terms of pasts, presents, and futures. Just as Adra needs both its tin mines for the future and its Carthaginian roots in the past to be a whole, healthy, and vital country, Frances must be able to look back on where she and her family have come from to see where it is she and it are going.

Insight in Drabble's novels is ambivalent and subtle. There are no major moments of revelations as there are in nineteenth century novels. One sees, but one does not see much. Years later, Frances, we are told 'had never really understood her Phoenicians: nor had she been able to understand how Stephen could take the child's life as well as his own. . . Whatever had the Phoenicians believed? She did not want to know, she did not want to understand, she turned away' (*RG*, 350) – but not all the way. Frances has seen that 'if one can salvage one moment from the sentence of death let us do so, let us catch it, for we owe it to the dead, to the others, and it is all the living and the lucky can do for the dead, all they can do, given the chance, is to rejoice' (*RG*, 350). Nevertheless, at the end of the novel, Frances is healthy and happy – two qualities noticeably absent from her life ten months earlier. She has recognized her incompleteness and attempted to make herself whole, first, by redefining herself in terms of the past, especially the Ollerenshaw past. She has accepted the fact that a family cannot be all intellectual sweetness and light like the over-achieving Chadwicks, but must number Ollerenshaws 'running drug rings, murdering their mistresses, decrying nuclear reactors, entering monasteries, painting masterpieces' (*RG*, 270-1), and that the family split has ruined her own personality immediately in terms of her intellect and her darkness, her present and her past.

This provides the necessary framework for a final evaluation of Constance Ollerenshaw's symbolic function in the novel. A parallel must be drawn between the octopus at the beginning of the novel and Constance's history at the end of the novel. Both have fulfilled their biological role in life and have withdrawn to a closed box — a den and Mays Cottage — to die. They are, for Frances, potentialities that she wishes to avoid yet by being a mother she cannot fully avoid.

The opening paragraph of the novel, by concentrating on the octopus, violates perspective and in so doing establishes the octopus as a key symbol in the novel. Quickly the text draws a comparison between the octopus in its box and Frances in her hotel room. Frances herself senses the parallel:

> It wasn't presumably possible that an individual mother octopus could refuse to die. They always make the same decision, even when tempted from their deathbeds by choice morsels. Their role accomplished, they preferred death. She often wondered what she herself was programmed for. (*RG*, 6)

Mays Cottage, 'secretive, alluring' (*RG*, 295) in its isolation and 'terrible purity' (*RG*, 296), is the box to which Constance withdrew following the death of her illegitimate baby and the suicide of her lover. Constance seems to have done little with her subsequent life except exist, growing more and more eccentric, becoming a 'witch' (*RG*, 273) in the eyes of the neighbourhood, cutting herself off entirely from her family, arguing vehemently with the few farmers who lived nearby, and burdening herself with guilt. After all, she demands in her will to be buried in unconsecrated ground.

When she visits Mays Cottage for the first time, Frances feels 'curiously at home, and private' (*RG*, 303), because Constance has preserved her freedom and individuality although spending the ties, but this scene is followed immediately by her visit with the Barnards. In their home, Frances thinks, 'this is what life ought to be like. . . . She shivered on the edge of perfectly enjoying a perfectly ordinary experience, a perfectly ordinary encounter, an event so rare. . . . Everything was all right, how could anything be wrong?' (*RG*, 308). The Barnards reaffirm the family unity, as strongly as Constance had affirmed individuality, and 'engendered in her a social mood, which she needed to satisfy' (*RG*, 311). While recuperating following breast surgery some months earlier, Frances 'felt that she would like to know where she began and the family ended' (*RG*, 97). The novel's conclusion offers no precise answers, but it does affirm the necessity of both, while blurring the distinction between the two. At the end of the novel, Frances has become a matriarch within the family and has, almost by her express will, created not only a nuclear family unit but also an extended family unit embracing Janet and David as well as her children, Karel's children, and their grandchildren. Frances, an individual in the present, would be cut off from the family and the past without such a context. She now had both present and past. She and Karel find in Mays Cottage 'a terrifying, a safe, a giddy, a precarious, a secure and all-excluding secluding cohersion' (*RG*, 352) and an addition to the extended unit.

Frances' lover, Karel Schmidt, her complement in many ways, constantly affirms the necessity of wholeness. Frances cannot find wholeness in her own life until she begins to turn to Karel. In Frances' view, he wastes his life on 'past obligations' (*RG*, 74) and a string of 'boring fools, silly students, mad entrepreneurs, con men, thieves, and liars of every kind' (*RG*, 74), but Karel sees himself as spending love. He hopes that his most trying students 'would at last be made whole' (*RG*, 91). He distrusts the 'imbalance of [Frances'] nature' (*RG*, 94), and wishes to restore her to health. Ironically, he falls ill at the end of the novel and is cured by Frances — first in her caring for him, and secondly in his visit to Prague where he, too, reknots old ties.

II John Fowles: *Daniel Martin,* 'this re-entry into the past'

1977 saw the publication of three ambitious novels – John Fowles' *Daniel Martin,* Margaret Drabble's *The Ice Age,* and Angus Wilson's *As If By Magic.* These novels were particularly ambitious in their geographical, cultural, and thematic sweep, and *Daniel Martin* is perhaps the most ambitious of the three in its scope, integrity, and direction of social criticism for it attempts to encompass within one novel a searching study of a unique yet typical personality, an almost Tolstoyean view of a society during a time of crisis, and an international sweep which takes its protagonist to four continents in search of his lost self. Reviewing the novel for *Newsweek,* Richard Boeth commented that Fowles 'has given us here what seems to be everything he knew of life'.[1] John Gardner credited it with 'the power, range, knowledge, and wisdom' of a Tolstoy or James, but Roberta Rubenstein perhaps described its ambitiousness most accurately in her comment that 'what adds another facet to these sociological asides is the novel's implications that Daniel represents England itself – a nation in search of its idealized past, whose central social myth is that of history',[2] for, without a doubt, Daniel Martin, like Andrew Sinclair's Gog, is a man estranged from his own past and his culture's traditions but finding both a regenerating experience and an appropriate symbol for the state of his soul. Perhaps no contemporary English novel so daringly locates the ruins of a man's life symbolically in the ruins of a culture than Fowles' novel.

To many readers, *Daniel Martin* is yet one more novel in a chain of novels and films treating the male mid-life crisis, and there is some truth to this perception. Daniel Martin, the eponymous protagonist, is a once-playwright, now film script writer, caught in the turmoils of a mid-life crisis in his forties. He could easily stand as yet one more case

study in Gail Sheehey's *Passages*. Indeed, the Antonio Gramsci epigraph
to the novel pinpoints the concept of crisis and needful transition in the
best tradition of abstracting or generalizing epigraphs: 'The crisis consists
precisely in the fact that the old is dying and the new cannot be born;
in this interregnum a great variety of morbid symptoms appear.'[3] The
first half of the novel concentrates on the 'morbid symptoms', detailing
fully, within the boundaries of a host of juxtaposed opposites
(rural–urban, mythic–personal, whole–fragmented, English–American,
age–youth, male–female, past–present, freedom–determinism, *ka–ba*,
critic–creator, film–novel, summer–winter, etc.), Dan's growing awareness of failure, his dissatisfaction with the life he has created for himself,
and his emerging discontent with his profession. Charles Smithson, the
protagonist of *The French Lieutenant's Woman*, faced a similar moment of
crisis played out in terms of conflicting dualities, but in *Daniel Martin*,
the context has become denser and more complex in that the crisis has
become personal and cultural and the novel explores, with considerable
amplitude, whether the juxtaposed forces may or may not be reconciled.

Daniel Martin's difficulties are captured by images of rootlessness and
exile. He is a man in transit 'like a good leather suitcase in an airport
lounge, neatly locked, waiting to be taken somewhere else, with a
destination label you can't quite read' (*DM*, 33), or 'an old split parcel,
done up with fifty thousand clumsy knots' (*DM*, 34), and he perceives
himself as 'a suitcase with illegible labels safe for as long as I was locked'
(*DM*, 99). Dan is a 'cis-atlantic personality' constantly in transit between
America and England – like some Henry James character benefiting
from jet-age speed – but no longer at home in either world, being now
'totally in exile from what I ought to have been' (*DM*, 14). Jenny, a
young actress and his current lover, thinks he is 'terribly dated' (*DM*,
31), but more frequently he trails in his wake such phrases as 'in transit',
'Alone and lost', 'belonging nowhere', flying 'into an empty space',
'wilderness', and 'running away'. He harshly judges his failure to be a
playwright as a willingness to settle for the safe, the lucrative, rather
than pushing on into artistic maturity and fulfillment:

> But the distinction between the craftsman and the true artist is
> precisely between knowing what one can do and not
> knowing – which is why one occupation is safe, and the other always
> incipiently dangerous. I had only to glance back over my work to
> know which category I belonged to in the overwhelming bulk of it:
> it reeked of safety, mainly because it had been written out of what I
> (and my studio masters) knew the world wanted to hear, and less

and less out of my whole knowledge of reality, both personal and public. My most dismaying substitute retreat had been from the awareness of that. That was the horror of landing that drove the bird endlessly on: the risk of the real ground. (*DM*, 293)

A feeling of waste torments Dan, personal waste of his talents, his love, his entire being. He tells Jenny, 'If you want to know what the shored fragments are worth, ask the ruin' (*DM*, 13), and feels he inhabits a world in which 'grasped-for apples turned to wax, dreams becomes ashes' (*DM*, 108). He senses he has trapped himself with no hope of return.

Of course, any number of things could purge Dan's melancholy. Significantly, however, Fowles forces his character to confront his past in all its fullness, richness, and shortcomings, and to confront his resignations and fears by visiting four major ruins on four continents. These confrontations develop in the context of exploring the differences between film and fiction and weighing the different concepts of personality currently afoot in English fiction, concepts often obscured by discussions which focus on the sociological and political implications of literary characters.[4]

Is personality continuous or discontinuous? That is, does personality exist as something continuous, constantly acted upon and responding to external stimuli but in essence something growing and maturing like any other organism, or is personality fragmented into multiple shards, states unrelated to one another? Friedrich Nietzsche voiced the first concept quite emphatically when he outlined the duties of the biographers: 'However forcefully a man develops and seems to leap from one contradiction to the next, close observation will reveal the *dovetailing*, where the new building grows out of the old. This is the task of the biographer: he must think about the life in question on the principle that nature never jumps: the principle of continuity of the self.'[5] Some years later, Jean-Paul Sartre enunciated the opposite principle: 'What I was is not the foundation of what I am, any more than what I am is the foundation of what I shall be.'[6] Although these two principles have gone fairly unnoticed in the Anglo-French theoretical quarrels concerning character, the principles of the continuous and the discontinuous personalities are uniquely English in their origins. For John Locke, there was no doubt: personality was continuous. In the famous puzzle cases in *Essay Concerning Human Understanding*, Locke argued, 'Had I the same consciousness that I saw the ark and Noah's flood, as that I saw an overflowing of the Thames last winter, I could no more doubt that I who write this now, that saw the Thames overflowed last winter, and that viewed the flood at the general deluge, was the same *self* . . . than that I who write this am the same *myself* now whilst I write . . . that I was Yesterday.'[7] In *Treatise of Human Nature*, however, David Hume rejoined that because the self constitutes a character of shifting impressions, ideas, and perceptions, such personal identity within the same subject is impossible.[8] The paradox posed by change and identity within the same subject has exercised philosophers at length with the question of memory and its role often being the key to the riddle.

In twentieth-century fiction, English novels have grouped themselves loosely around these two poles. Stephan Dedalus, for instance, argues with Cranly near the conclusion of *A Portrait of the Artist as a Young Man*, that 'I was someone else then. . . . I mean . . . that I was not myself as I am now, as I had to become', an idea incipient in the famous passage in Joyce's earlier 'A Portrait of the Artist' essay commissioned for *Dana*: 'yet the past assuredly implies a fluid succession of presents, the development of an entity of which our actual present is a phase only'.[9] D. H. Lawrence's comments about the breakdown of the old stable ego, and Virginia Woolf's remarks concerning 'shredded character' suggest the extent to which modernist concepts of personality manifest the discontinuous principle, and Aldous Huxley's *Eyeless in Gaza*, whose very form embodies the principles of discontinuity, returns again and again to such statements as 'I would wish my day to be separated each from each by unnatural impiety,' an obvious parody of the Wordsworthian wish — and 'to himself and to others he was just a succession of more or less incongruous states' or 'Man, according to Blake (and, after him, according to Proust, according to Lawrence), is simply a succession of states', or 'One's free as a succession of unconditioned, uncommitted states without past or future, except in so far as one can't voluntarily get rid of one's memories and anticipations'.[10]

More recent authors have voiced similar use of the principle of the discontinuous personality. In Rayner Heppenstall's *The Connecting Door*, perhaps the finest anti-novel in English, one personality tells an earlier self, 'You were doing nothing . . . because I didn't think about you. In the past seventeen years, you've lived in occasional flickers, when I had you in mind. You forget, or, rather, you haven't quite realised, that without me you don't exist'.[11] Sammy Mountjoy in William Golding's *Free Fall*, driven by his experiences in the German prison camp to determine at what point he lost his freedom, thinks: 'I am not a man who was a boy looking at a tree. I am a man who remembers being a boy looking at a tree. . . . I can love the child in the garden, on the airfield, in Rotten Row, the tough little boy at school because he is not I. *He is another person*'.[12] And, even more recently, Brian Moore told an interviewer, 'I feel that gap between the different selves we are at different times of our life very strongly because I have been such a wanderer myself'; he then embodied this idea in *I Am Mary Dunne* where the title character finally concludes: 'I am no longer Mary Dunne, or Mary Phelan, or Mary Bell, or even Mary Lavery. I am a changeling who has changed too often and there are moments when I cannot find my way back'.[13] The voices for continuity of personality — Margaret Drabble, Angus Wilson, and others, especially the loosely knit Oxford group of W. J. Harvey, John Bayley, and Iris Murdoch have responded indirectly with their personally expressed admiration for the nineteenth century novels of character and their dependence on metaphors of organic continuity.[14] Always, though, the crux of the arguments centers on memory.

John Fowles' novel stands at the cross roads, dispassionately looking both ways before deciding to accept or to reject either principle. Three passages in particular raise the question of discontinuous self. In each, Dan is thinking about the past, the self he has become, and the conditions of his own generation. In the first, he perceives the problem in general terms affecting his entire generation:

> And then what we once were is now severed in a very special way from the present — reduced to an object, an artifice, an antique, a flashback... something discontinuous and disconnected from present being. . . . all pasts shall be coeval, a back-world uniformily not present, relegated to the status of so many family snapshots. The mode of recollection usurps the reality of the recalled. (*DM*, 89–90)

His second comment is a pointed exchange with his former brother-in-law, Anthony, as Anthony lies dying from cancer.[15] Dan tells Anthony, 'don't worry about the past', and Anthony responds: 'As long as you'll agree that the only remedies do lie in us. *As we are. Not were*' (*DM*, 194 italics added). Dan's third perception comes as he looks down from his bedroom window on a policeman and a tramp, a scene reminiscent of the narrator–madman–protagonist scene in *The French Lieutenant's Woman*. On the street below, Dan sees:

> the loneliness of each, the bedrock of the human condition. I am what I am. What is, is. Dan imagined that he was looking at his lost

real self down there, in that shadowy figure a thing living on the
edge of existence in a night street of his psyche; beyond conversation
and invitation, eternally separate. (*DM*, 244)

Simultaneously, parallel passages assert the continuity of self, maintaining that *was, is,* and *will be* are vitally linked in a pattern. Dan feels
that he cannot resist the emergence of an older self and senses that

Such changes in a person's character, and in the character of a
relationship, don't announce themselves dramatically; they steal
slowly over months, masking themselves behind reconciliations,
periods of happiness, new resolves. (*DM*, 149)

and he senses at one point that 'in method, habit, routine' are the
'prerequisites of continuity' I*DM*, 336). At least twice, norm figures
painfully spell out for Dan the insight he must grow into if the
mid-life crisis is not to plunge him deeper into depression or even into
self-destruction. Anthony reminds him, only hours before he himself
commits suicide: 'If only we learn that it must be in ourselves. In a true
history of our own lives. Instead of putting the blame on everything else
under the sun' (*DM*, 194). Later, as Dan waits for Jane, he thumbs
through *Selections from the Prision Notebooks of Antonio Gramsci*, a volume
Jane is reading and one in which she has left pencilled notes and
markings. In a scene, reminiscent in many ways of Maggie Tulliver's
reading marked passages in *The Imitation of Christ* in *The Mill on the
Floss*, Dan reads a passage Jane has heavily marked 'with double vertical
lines': '*For each individual is the synthesis not only of existing relations, but of
the history of these relations*' (*DM*, 207).

Far from being one of the many topics loosely related in this large
and sometimes rambling novel, the concern with the principles of the
continuous and the discontinuous selves is the key for relating many of
the other topics and for pulling these into focus. For example, Dan's
comments about film and fiction extend the topics of continuity and
discontinuity in unexpected ways, and Dan's interest mirrors Fowles'
own involvement in both worlds. Fowles has written at least one film
script and has concerned himself emphatically with the filming of *The
French Lieutenant's Woman. Daniel Martin* judges film somewhat harshly
in contrasting the two arts. Dan tells Jenny that a film autobiography
provides none of the satisfaction, consolation, or necessities of print:

What I was trying to tell Jenny in Hollywood was that I would
murder my past if I tried to evoke it on camera; and it is precisely

because I can't really evoke it in words, can only hope to awaken some analogous experience in other memories and sensitivities, that it must be written. (*DM*, 90)

This general, somewhat unfocused, complaint quickly becomes a reflection of the conflict between two concepts of personality, for Dan concludes that film is 'safe' because it 'excludes all but now; permits no glances away to past and future; is therefore the safest dream' (*DM*, 165). Film presents only the present; it allows no opportunity for interweaving past and present. In other words, it traffics in the discontinuous self, a point stressed by Susan Sontag's perceptive *On Photography*, in which she concludes that 'The photograph is a thin slice of space as well as time. . . . Through photographs, the world becomes a series of unrelated, freestanding particles; and history, past and present, a set of anecdotes and *fait divers*.'[16] In one of his earliest statements concerning his art, his creativity, and his interests, Fowles commented that 'writing a novel in 1964 is being neurotically aware of trespassing, especially on the domain of the cinema',[17] but during his own involvement with the filming of *The Magus*, his attitude began to shift sharply in the direction of Dan's. In 'Notes on an Unfinished Novel', he recalls that after completing the script for *The Magus*,

> The two producers have had their say, and the director; and a number of non-human factors, such as the budget, the nature of the locations, and the casting of the main roles, have had theirs. Most of the time I feel like a skeleton at the feast; this isn't what I had imagined, either in the book or in the script.[18]

Characteristically, Fowles saw the individual being bound more and more tightly by forces over which he had no control, whereas the novel offered freedom: 'unlike the play or the filmscript, it has no limits other than those of the language'.[19] Ironically, the sentence forecasts the artistic peregrinations of Daniel Martin. Although *Daniel Martin* does not echo Fowles' own peculiar experiences with film, it reflects his attitudes.[20]

This conflict between concepts of personality poses two problems for Dan, a practical one in that it is the conflict he faces as he plans a film on Lord Kitchener, and a very personal one in that it is the conflict surrounding him as he attempts to relate his present *now* with his past *then*. The solution to the one is the solution to the other, because the structure he evolves for treating Kitchener's life on film closely resembles the structure Fowles uses in the novel. Dan decides that 'he wanted to

catch Kitchener somewhere in mid-career and at some central focus
geographically: and then sally from that point in flashback and
flash-forward to the rest of his life' (*DM*, 297). More abstractly, Dan
sees 'a chance to use a flashback inside a flashback, and possibly a
flashback inside that as well; a Chinese-box gimmick; but with possibili-
ties' (*DM*, 443).

The novel resolves the conflict between the discontinuous and the
continuous personalities by allowing Dan to opt for fiction over film,
by forcing Dan to retrace his own past in order to emerge a newly wise
and much saner being, and by giving him a woman from his past — his
first truly serious love — as a wife at the end of the novel. The novel
bluntly affirms that the human self is continuous and that the identity
the self creates comes from the past with the sense of change. Alfred
North Whitehead called this integration a 'becoming of continuity' and
glossed the essential continuity of self in his *Modes of Thought*:

> I find myself as essentially a unity of emotions, enjoyments, hopes,
> fears, regrets, valuations of alternatives, decisions — all of them
> subjective reaction to the environment as active in my nature. My
> unity — which is Descartes' "I am" — is my process of shaping this
> welter of material into a consistent pattern of feelings, the individual
> enjoyment is what I am in my role of a natural activity, as I shape
> the activities of the environment into a new creation, which is myself
> at this moment; and yet, as being myself, it is a continuation of the
> antecedent world.[21]

Most contemporary studies of the mid-life crisis also reconcile continuity
and discontinuity. Gail Sheehy turned to a metaphor which combined
images of an inner continuity and an outer discontinuity to explain the
essential existence of something through various stages:

> We are not unlike a particularly hardy crustacean. The lobster grows
> by developing and shedding a series of hard, protective shells. Each
> time it expands from within, the confining shell must be sloughed
> off. It is left exposed and vulnerable until, in time, a new covering
> grows to replace the old.[22]

Daniel Martin depicts the process of sloughing off a shell which has
become confining, restrictive, and perhaps even deformed, and the
resulting vulnerability as a more capacious covering grows to replace
the old. What triggers the molting in the novel, however, is no biological
clock, but rather the clock of memory.

Whatever its inadequacy in philosophical terms in defining identity, memory is the key to Daniel Martin's identity crisis, for according to the George Seferis epigraph to Chapter 8, Dan must learn 'to remember correctly' (*MD*, 77). In Bergsonian terms, so long as the past as memory has a role in the present, identity is assured. Bergson turned to analogy to explain his point, arguing that just as a rolling snowball in its present state contains all its earlier states so a man in the present still contains his earlier conditions in the form of memory.[23] The point is crucial to the novel because Daniel Martin moves from belief in discontinuity to belief in continuity, accepting as he does the significance to his own past and its role, defined by memory, for his future. Throughout its first third, the novel stresses Dan's essential pastlessness. His daughter Caro tells him that Jane 'said you seemed to have cut yourself from your past more than anyone else. Even when you were all still at university' (*DM*, 282). Dan recalls this conversation near the end of the novel in more telling terms, recalling for Jane: 'Caro told me something you'd said about me recently. About my being someone in permanent flight from his past. From all enduring relationship' (*DM*, 630). Dan fears his past. He feels that 'this flinching from the I inherent in any honest recapitulation of his life was no more than a fear of judgement' (*DM*, 63–4) and senses that many of his colleagues 'grew so scared of their pasts and their social class' that they fled their talents in art to become 'journalists, critics, media men, producers and directors' (*DM*, 104). Perhaps he is justified; after all, when Anthony attempts 'an honest evaluation of [his] own life' (*DM*, 182) in terms of his past, present, and future, he opts for suicide. Dan feels that his evasion of the past is generational. He tells Jenny:

> We [his generation] had all our values wrong. We expected too much. Trusted too much. There's a great chasm in twentieth-century history. A frontier. Whether you were born before nineteen thirty-nine or not. The world, time... it slipped. Jumped forward three decades in one. We antediluvians have been left permanently out of gear...
> (*DM*, 50–1)

Jenny retorts with some truth that the 'chasm' is no more than 'a deliberate barricade' (*DM*, 51) he has personally erected, a barricade the reader sees Dan erect for the first time on 21 August 1942, in the opening chapter, when he carves his initials in a beech tree after the harvest scene and thus asserts his ego outside nature. The narrating voice of the older Dan senses this was a crucial moment in his life. Before the act, the younger Dan was 'without past or future, purged of tenses;

collecting this day, pregnant with being. Unharvested, yet one with the land,' but as he carves, the narrator bids 'Adieu, my boyhood and my dream' (*DM*, 10). Once expelled into a world of tenses, Dan rapidly becomes a ruin.

In rough outline, Dan's story resembles those of the protagonists of *Room at the Top* and *Stop the World, I Want to Get off*, in that he too has sold out his talents, his ideals, and his dreams for worldly success. A talented dramatist, Dan was enticed by the glamor and dollars of film to desert the theatre for the cinema. According to the imagery of the novel, temptation is not too strong a word. Dan is trapped in a destructive snare: 'Dan did a second draft, was drawn into the first fringes of the celluloid world — like a foolish shrimp into a sea anemone' (*DM*, 142). He is imaged as Ulysses enticed by Circe (*DM*, 144), 145) and knows that Nell, his wife, thinks he 'had sold out . . . was on the grab for quick success and cheap limelight' (*DM*, 150). Later, he experiences nausea from his action, but again finds some excuse in sheer numbers:

> So many other students he had known at Oxford had been sucked down into this world, with all the illusions of instant power; were in politics now, in television, on Fleet Street; had become cogs in the communications machine, stifled all ancient conviction for the sake of career, some press-lord's salary. (*DM*, 275)

Little wonder, then, that he sees only ruins in himself and 'the overweening narcissism of all their generation' (*DM*, 634). Jenny knows he is 'in ruins somewhere' (*DM*, 13) and has labelled his whole life a mistake, forcing him 'to wear a mask and invent a character...once more to write [himself] . . . belonging nowhere' (*DM*, 73). Dan concludes that 'faced with ruins, we must turn architects, not archaeologists' (*DM*, 90) at the very moment the novel calls out for him to remember and to remember correctly.

Ruins figure more prominently in *Daniel Martin* than perhaps any other contemporary English novel. Tarquinia, Tsankawi, Bandelier, Grimston Down, various Iron Age tumuli, Palmyra, and a dozen or so ancient Egyptian sites pass before the reader, at times giving the novel the feel and tone of travel literature. The ruins become a metaphor, what Edmund Burke called a 'philosophical analogy', for the state of soul Daniel Martin uncovers and retrieves from his own past, for his past is as multi-layered and as multifarious as the ruins he visits. No simplistic equation exists in the novel, however, for Dan clearly is moved by certain ruins, yet repelled by others. The Etruscan ruins of Tarquinia, for instance, provide one of the 'very few religious moments' (*DM*, 116) of his life: 'It was a moment that had both an infinity and an evanescence — an intense closeness, yet no more durable than the tiny shimmering organisms in the water around us' (*DM*, 116). But the Temple of Karnak oppresses him. Responding to 'the first full frontal assault of ancient megalomania', he thinks: 'The place was graceless, obsessed by the monumental,by exactly that same sort of grandiose and bloated vulgarity some more recent dictators had favoured in their architecture' (*DM*, 507). Gradually, Dan turns the cultures of the past into symbols, sorting them finally into opposing cricket teams:

> His opponents were here, in Rome, in modern America and Russia, in Kitchener's Britain; and his own team ran through the Minoans and Etruscans and the Renaissance to . . . well, not quite England as she is, but at least England as she sometimes still was; his England. (*DM*, 537)

This passage sophisticates Fowles' earlier description in *The Aristos* of 'male' and 'female' dominated societies, also expressed in a game metaphor:

> There are means orientated societies, for whom the game is the game; and ends-orientated societies, for whom the game is winning. In the first, if one is happy, then one is successful; in the second, one cannot be happy unless one is successful. The whole tendency of evolution and history suggests that man must become means-orientated if he is to survive.[24]

In the novel, Dan's 'team' appears prominently in the scenes at Tarquinia and Tsankawi, and to some extent at Palmyra. For the reverberations the scene has throughout the novel, the Tarquinia chapter — Chapter 11 — is surprisingly brief. During the summer of 1951, Dan and Nell, Anthony and Jane enjoy 'one golden period' (*DM*, 109) of vacation in Italy. Jane is pregnant; Anthony teaching successfully at Worcester; Dan has just signed the contract for *The Empty Church*, his first play and 'the first essential step toward being a professional dramatist' (*DM*, 113). Guided by D. H. Lawrence's *Sea and Sardinia*, they desert Rome as 'vulgar beyond belief' to 'play pagan' (*DM*, 114) in Tarquinia, the ancient Etruscan city in the Tuscan hills some sixty miles north of Rome, famous historically as a leader of the Etruscan league with cultural and commercial ties with classical Greece and famous archaeologically for its astonishing and beautiful tomb paintings. Virtually nothing is said in the chapter concerning the site itself; rather, the focus concentrates on Dan's response. We are told only that 'the climax and epitome of these blue-and-ocher weeks took place at Tarquinia' (*DM*, 114), and that after an unexpected visit to the tombs — still closed at the time to the public — that Dan senses:

> Some kind of avatar of so many things I had derived from the Devon countryside as a boy. . . . I think it was also the first time I had a clear sense of the futility of the notion of progress in art; nothing could be better or lovelier than this, till the end of time. It was sad, but in a noble, haunting, fertile way. (*DM*, 114)

Later, the same day, Dan grows 'unaccountably happy' (*DM*, 116) as the four of them swim naked in the phosphorescent sea, and he experiences 'a mysterious union, and strangely unearned' (*DM*, 115) during 'a moment that had both an infinity and an evanescence' (*DM*, 116).

Two decades later, he re-experiences this moment while visiting Tsankawi with Jenny. They fly from Los Angeles to Albuquerque and then drive to Santa Fe, which, Dan tells us, obtains in its landscape 'the pure balance, the classical perfection and nobility, almost the Greekness' (*DM*, 343), and he introduces Jenny to the Indian pueblos and mesa sites with their 'atmosphere . . . paradoxically very European — to be precise, Etruscan and Minoan . . . that is, they are haunted by loss and mystery, by a sense of some magical relationship . . . between man and nature' (*DM*, 344). His second moment of piercing insight comes at Tsankawi, the site perhaps least known to Fowles' readers outside America, as a feeling of personal loss, whereas the moment at Tarquinia anticipated. Forty-six miles northwest of Santa Fe, in Frijoles Canyon, Dan and Jenny first visit Bandelier National Monument, a quiet, wooded canyon with a small clear creek running through it and leaping twice over spectacular waterfalls. Along the canyon walls are two miles of cliff ruins or talus villages, dating back to the twelfth century, a tyonii ruin, ceremonial cave, and a shrine. Eleven miles north of the canyon is Tsankawi, a large unexcavated ruin high on a mesa top, providing unimpeded vistas of the mountains to the east and to the west. The Tsankawi pueblo contained some 350 rooms atop a seven-thousand-foot high mesa, occupied from around 1200 until about 1600. The guidebook to the area asks the visitors to contemplate the ruins thoughtfully:

The prehistoric inhabitants of Tsankawi were totally dependent upon their environment. Everything they owned — their homes, clothing, and tools; all of their food; everything came directly from their "mother Earth." Then, after many years of occupancy they suddenly vanished. Why? Archeologists tell us perhaps they ceased to live in harmony with their environment.

Are we today with all our technical advances any less dependent on our environment for survival? What will be our history if we live without regard for the laws of nature?[25]

Standing atop the mesa, thinking along such lines himself, Dan once again experiences a sense of 'perfect balance' (*DM*, 349):

In some way, the mesa transcended all place and frontier; it had the haunting and mysterious personal familiarity I mentioned just now, but a simpler human familiarity as well, belonging not just to some obscure and forgotten Indian tribe, but to all similar moments of supreme harmony in human culture; to certain buildings, paintings, musics, passages of great poetry. It validated, that was it; it was enough to explain all the rest, the blindness of evolution, its appalling wastage, indifference, cruelty, futility. There was a sense in which it was a secret place, a literal retreat, an analogue of what had always obsessed my mind . . . Tsankawi defeated time, all deaths. Its deserted silence was like a sustained high note, unconquerable. (*DM*, 346)

Other ruins, however, bring no such Arnoldian moments of tranquil harmony, but only repulsion, especially the Egyptian ruins visited by Jane and Dan as Dan checks location sites for the Kitchener film. The temples at Luxor, Karnak, Abybos, Esra, Edfa, Kom Ombo, and Abu Simbel affect him less favorably than does the Nile itself. At Abu Simbel, Dan sees only 'the megalomania of Ramses II' (*DM*, 592); Karnak becomes 'rather ludicrous; the way each succeeding pharaoh seemed to have spent most of his life ripping out his predecessor's stone bellows and trumpetings for the attention of posterity' (*CM*, 507–8). The Egyptian ruins become symbolic of a bent of mind through history producing art and monuments

based on conspicious consumption and status; the pharaohs and their gods were the first smug bourgeois of the world — the birth of fire-brigade art. . . . It reeked from calculated pressure, the formal, statuesque coolness of their paintings and sculptures. They had somehow banned personal sensibility, affection for life, all impulsive exuberance, all spontaneous exaggeration and abstraction . . . already Stalin and Zhdanov came. (*DM*, 537)

Dan's tastes are Fowles' own in these matters. In *The Enigma of Stonehenge*, Fowles contrasts the impact Stonehenge's openness has on most visitors, including himself, and his own personal revulsion from the temple of Edfu near Aswan; 'Edfu still stinks a mile off of the dark priesthood who once lived closeted behind its unbroken fortress walls — indeed, of an ancient lunatic, or at least highly self-involved, fringe'.[26] How different from the harmonies of Tarquinia and Tsankawi, of Thorncombe and Kitchener's Island. Lawrence himself had experienced the same attractions and repulsions and summarized his feelings in *Etruscan Places*:

> Myself, I like to think of the little wooden temples of the early Greeks and of the Etruscans: small, dainty, fragile, and evanescent as flowers. We have reached the stage when we are weary of huge stone erections, and we begin to realise that it is better to keep life fluid and changing than to try to hold it fast down in heavy monuments. Burdens on the face of the earth are man's ponderous erections.[27]

Contemplating the inner divisions within the individual through metaphoric use of famous ruins culminates a general centripedal inclusiveness which has marked Fowles' works from his very first published novel, which allowed us to see in the relationship of the neurotic Ferdinand and his captive Miranda as many levels of allegorical meaning as in the polysemous writings of Dante. In *The French Lieutenant's Woman*, the inner conflicts of Charles Smithson were projected outwards onto the women in his life, the architecture, and the topography, Interestingly, *Daniel Martin* began with a broadly conceived metaphor. Unlike Fowles' other novels which began from simple and single images, *Daniel Martin* actually began in 1964 as an essay, 'On Being English but Not British', in which Fowles defined the essential differences between Englishness and Britishness by using Robin Hood and the Sheriff of Nottingham as symbols of the two perspectives — the 'split in the English mind between the Green England and the Red-white-and-blue Britain'. 'What Robin Hood was, or who he was, in the dim underwoods of history, is unimportant', Fowles writes, 'it is what folk history has made that matters. He is the man who always, when faced with taking to the forest or accepting injustice, runs for the trees'.[28] This essay echoes throughout the novel (see especially *DM*, 166–7, 287–8) as Dan voices his conclusions that the 'whole nineteenth-century was a disease, a delusion called Britain. The true England was freedom to be self, to drift like a spore, to stay unattached to anything, except transiently, but the drifting freedom' (*DM*, 451). Similarly, Fowles seized a central metaphoric relationship between attitudes towards the world in *Islands* and *The Tree* which also relate to *Daniel Martin*.[29] In *Daniel Martin*, 'Green England' manifests itself not only in Tarquinia and Tsankawi, but also in Thorncombe, Dan's Devon home, Rabelais, and Kitchener's Island. Dan uses these and Restif de la Bretonne's *Monsieur Nicolas* as his 'own favorite Quarlesian emblem' (*DM*, 290).

Within these three conceptual frameworks operates an essentially simple journey plot. Daniel receives a call while in Hollywood with Jenny, asking him to return to England because of the wishes of the dying Anthony. On the flight to London, as the door on his past opens, Dan begins to review his past.[30] Only after the brief scenes in Oxford with Jane and Anthony does the review intensify. Charged the evening of Anthony's suicide 'to help disinter the person Jane might have been from beneath the person she now is' (*DM*, 188), Dan invites Jane to accompany him on a trip to Egypt while he checks potential locations for the Kitchener film. As the present action proceeds, Dan gives us reminiscences of his childhood in Devon (chapters 1 and 8), his adolescent love affair with Nancy Reed (chapter 30), his student days at Oxford (chapters 3 and 6), and his years immediately after Oxford as he struggled to become a playwright (chapters 11, 14, 16, and 22). Thus, the physical journey parallels and encloses a psychological journey, loosely structured, at times, with allusions to Orpheus's journey undertaken to rescue Eurydice, for as Dan 'disinters' the Jane he once loved, and his own past we see Dan recalling the moments when the unexpected death of his mother, his own first assertions of ego, his burgeoning sexuality, and a lover's suicide have exiled him from edenic realms.

Mere immersion in the past, however, is not salvation in and of itself. Indeed, that would be the way of 'Red-white-and-blue Britain'. The novel contains two foils to Dan – Barney Dillon and Andrew Randall – who stand as warning signposts. Barney Dillon, a television-show host and columnist, disgusts Dan, because he has discarded all for success and power. To Dan he typifies one 'who takes no real risks' (*DM*, 104) and his affair with Dan's daughter, Caro, helps Dan see and understand his own affair with Jenny. Andrew Randall, a classmate from Oxford and now the husband of Dan's ex-wife, has taken the opposite route. Whereas Barney fled from the past, Andrew, a likable sort in his way, has 'turned his back on the future' (*DM*, 328) as he convincingly plays squire on his very *Country Life* estate. Dan, though, finds something to admire in Andrew who apparently has seen through the falsities hedging his position and has adopted a role. 'I guessed', Dan thinks, 'that he had somehow made a choice of which traditions and rituals were worth keeping and which could be dismissed: live like a squire, work like a farmer, think like a free man . . . and make out you are only the first'(*DM*, 233). The much desired freedom is available to Andrew, but not to Barney, because Andrew's values, at the very least, have come to terms with the past.

In *The Aristos*, Fowles commented: 'I prove I exist by using my acceptance of past and bad actions as a source of energy for the improvement of my future actions or attitudes inside that reality', reminding one of the similar lines in Sartre's *Being and Nothingness*, 'the character often is what the for-itself tries to recover in order to become the in-itself-for-itself which it projects being'.[31] A review of and dialogue with his past frees and energizes Dan. They enable Dan to emerge with an ironic sense of freedom and responsibility he accepts more maturely and more knowingly than the earlier Charles Smithson was able to do. After meeting Jane and Anthony in Oxford, Dan realizes 'that he no longer wished he had never come to Oxford proved this re-entry into the past had answered some previously unseen lack' (*DM*, 220), and Dan knows that much of the appeal of Thorncombe, like Tsankawi and Tarquinia, comes from the feeling that 'at them one's past seems in some mysterious way to meet one's future, one was somehow always to be there as well as being there in reality' (*DM*, 345–6). Freedom comes from facing up 'to the evidence of one's own past' (*DM*, 577): 'that existential bit about using the past to build the present' (*DM*, 575), he tells Jane. His keen understanding of his dilemma comes precisely as this 'existential bit' though. Standing on the banks of the Nile — the journey up which is a journey back in time itself — Dan sees that: 'For days now he had been split, internally if not outwardly, between a known past and an unknown future. That was where his disturbing feeling of not being his own master, of being a character in someone else's play, came from. The past wrote him; and hatred of change, of burning boats' (*DM*, 579). When he actually does 'burn boats', however, it is neither the past nor the future he evades; it is the present he has made for himself that he rejects. As his review of his past begins to function as a catalyst, 'a release from the mire' (*DM*, 221), and he faintly begins to see 'the ghost of a central character' (*DM*, 286), Dan comes to 'the most important decision of his life' (*DM*, 431), a decision which involves rejection in order that he may grow:

To hell with cultural fashion; to hell with elitist guilt; to hell with existentialist nausea; and above all, to hell with the imagined that does not say, not only in, but behind the image, the real. (*DM*, 432)

With the ground thus cleared, both by rejection of the present self and excavation and re-evaluation of the past self, Dan is ready to begin to shape his future self. At this point, the novel flags for many readers. All of Fowles' novels to date involve a relationship between a bound man and a free woman, electric in its intensity, crackling with implications, sparking complex ideas and mysteries. To many readers, Jane simply is not as successfully realized as were Sarah Woodruff and Miranda Grey. Jane is Dan's past as well as his future. She is the woman he once loved, but because of bad faith on both sides, they married others even though they knew they should not. Anthony's dying request is for Dan to restore Jane and, though he does not say so, his suicide removes the major impediment separating the two. Long before Dan experiences his key recognition that

She was also some kind of emblem of a redemption from a life devoted to heterogamy and adultery, the modern errant ploughman's final reward; and Dan saw, or felt, abruptly, for the first time in his life, the true difference between Eros and Agape. (*DM*, 600)

Jane has been transformed into a symbolic presence. Early in the novel, Dan senses that he 'had to rediscover her' (*DM*, 164), and when once again with her, the old love beginning to re-emerge, he knows 'something in Jane's presence satisfied some deep need in me of recurrent structure in both real and imagined events; indeed, married the real and imagined; justified both' (*DM*, 421–2). Rescuing Jane becomes symbolic of rescuing that essential self or part of self eclipsed in Dan in his present life and restoring this self to wholeness, once again an echo of the Orpheus and Eurydice myth.

But the reconciliation almost fails. After Egypt, Dan and Jane fly to Lebanon and then drive to Syria to visit Palmyra, some 140 miles northeast of Damascus, an ancient city purportedly founded in the tenth century by Solomon. The ruins, 'the place where sybaritic Rome married the languorous Orient' (*DM*, 637), could easily have stood as a statement concerning synthesis, but Fowles presents instead an almost surrealistic landscape of fog, snow, and desolation. As they approach Homs, the landscape changes 'to look more like the edge of a limbo nearest to a hell' (*DM*, 621); once in Palmyra, 'an endless vista of ruins and isolated heaps of rubble, like a city stricken in some ancient nuclear holocaust and half buried again in sand . . . so chilling, so hopeless, so static, so vast' (*DM*, 645) chills them, and love among the ruins that night seems to threaten them. 'They stood', the narrator tells us, 'at the opposite poles of humanity, eternally irreconcilable' (*DM*, 649), but while in the ruins, Dan is able to confess to Jane that he has betrayed his talents for handling words and his ability to love 'one single other human being wholly' (*DM*, 631).

The novel's final chapter, 'Future Past' (an oxymoron fusing the paradoxes of the time themes), presents Dan as a free and reconciled being, and the George Serferis epigraph to the chapter pointedly underlines the source of his newly-found well being: 'you must find the man who then and now, from the very beginning, ruled your body' (*DM*, 658). Meeting Jenny in Hampstead to break off their relationship, Dan finally leaves her and walks on across the Heath to Kenwood House, unexpectedly to experience one final moment of epiphany as he contemplates the Rembrant self-portrait which figures so crucially in Fowles' fictional collection of art works. In *The Aristos*, Fowles first mentioned the painting: 'if I am adequately to explain in words the sadness of this Rembrandt self-portrait, I must study his entire work and his biography' — though one cannot be certain that he alludes to the Kenwood House painting here.[32] As Dan stands before the painting, we realize that the exile has come home, the fragmented being has been restored to wholeness, the man cut off from the past has forged new and vital links with and a new understanding of the past. 'Standing there before the Rembrandt', Dan experiences

> a kind of vertigo; the distances he had to return. It seemed frightening to him, this last of the coincidences that had dogged his recent life; to have encountered, so punctually after a farewell to many more things than one face, one choice, one future, this formidable sentinel guarding the way back. (*DM*, 672)

Although one may entertain doubts as to the total success of *Daniel Martin*, one must admire Fowles for the risks he takes. He hold nothing back, but rather offers his entire talent in technical, structural, and thematic risks which, if successful, invigorate his novel and echo outwards into life. Indeed, Fowles' willingness to confront the complexities of a man and a culture mediating the uses of their past grants *Daniel Martin* a daring profundity and establishes it as a key work in any consideration of the English novel's engagement with the past.

Notes and References

PART I: FUTURE PASTS
Chapter 1: One Curious and Significant Melody

1. *Auto-da-Fé*, trans. C. V. Wedgewood (New York: Continuum, 1947) p. 159. This novel of the 1981 Nobel Laureate was first published in Germany under the title *Die Blendug*.
2. The Henry Ford comment is discussed by E. R. Chamberlain in *Preserving the Past* (London: J. M. Dent 1979) pp. 166–7, and Monroe K. Spears, *Dionysus and the City* (New York: Oxford University Press, 1970) p. 234. The Marinetti citations are to *Selected Writings*, ed. R. W. Flint, trans. R. W. Flint and Arthur A. Coppotelli (New York: Straus & Giroux, 1972) p. 67.
3. Quoted in Hayden White, 'The Burden of History', *Tropics of Discourse* (Baltimore: Johns Hopkins University Press, 1978) pp. 32, 36. White's essay brilliantly surveys the decline of the historical consciousness in the twentieth century and the hostility expressed towards it in modernist fiction; however, White fails to distinguish the qualitative differences in attitude between modernist and contemporary fiction. The treatment of history in Angus Wilson's *Anglo-Saxon Attitudes*, for example, differs significantly from that in André Gide's *The Immoralist*.
4. See *Ulysses* (New York: Random House, 1961) p. 34; *Brave New World* (New York: Harper, 1932) ch. three; and *1984*, ed. Irving Howe, 2nd edn (New York: Harcourt, Brace, Jovanovich, 1982) pp. 103, 28, 51.
5. 'Mr. Bennett and Mrs. Brown', *The Captain's Death Bed and Other Essays* (New York: Harcourt, Brace, Jovanovich, 1950) p. 96. Woolf read this essay at a meeting of The Heretics, Cambridge University, 18 May 1924.
6. Michael Hudson and Vincent Coppola, 'Back to the Iron Age', *Newsweek*, 91 (13 March 1978) 78.
7. Timothy Green, 'Modern Britains Try the Iron Age, Find They Like It', *Smithsonian*, 9:3 (June 1978) 81.

8. Hudson and Coppola report the trend towards matriarchy, p. 78; Rockcliff is quoted in 'Reliving the Iron Age in Britain', *Time*, 111 (13 March 1978) 68.

9. Quoted in Green, p. 86, and Hudson and Coppola, p. 78.

10. Quoted in Green, p. 86.

11. *Tess of the d'Urbervilles*, ed. Scott Elledge, 2nd edn (New York: Norton, 1979) p. 105; hereafter abbreviated *TD*.

12. *Lord Jim*, ed. Thomas C. Moser (New York: Norton, 1968) p. 119.

13. *Under Western Eyes* (London: Methuen, 1911) p. 151. An interchange between the novel's narrator and Peter Ivanovitch in the manuscript voices the hostility towards the past most pointedly: 'Have you ever reflected on the frightful encumbrance of dead ideas, dead through and through; dead to the core, dead in the uttermost branches. It is like an immense grey forest where the last drop of vivifying sap has ceased to run a long time ago. It is in this forest that our revolutionary parties are wandering round and round looking for some sort of fruit', MS, pp. 609–10, quoted with permission of the Joseph Conrad Estate and the Beinecke Rare Book and Manuscript Library, Yale University.

14. *The Remembrance of Things Past*, trans. C. K. Scott Moncrieff, Uniform Edition (London: Chatto & Windus, 1941) pp. x, 255. Proust, of course, is one of the major exceptions to modernist hostility towards the past.

15. See Spears, p. 34. Spear's interpretation of modernist discontinuity contrasts sharply with the interpretations advanced by Frank Kermode, *The Romantic Image* (London: Routledge & Kegan Paul, 1957) and Graham Hough, *Image and Experience* (London: Duckworth, 1960).

16. Summarized from Spears, p. 21.

17. White, pp. 31, 35, and 31.

18. *The Death of the Past* (Boston: Houghton Mifflin, 1970) p. 14.

19. *Memories, Dreams, Reflections*, quoted in Christopher Booker, *The Neophiliacs* (Boston: Gambit, 1970) p. 135.

20. The 1957 essay is quoted in Daniel Counihan, *Royal Progress: Britain's Changing Monarchy* (London: Cassell, 1977) p. 200.

21. *New Statesman and Nation*, 30 May 1953, p. 637. Also see Counihan, p. 4 for other examples, including the *Daily Express's* picture of such modern Elizabethans as T. S. Elliot, Margot Fonteyne, and figures with blank faces for readers to fill in. For a later assessment of this rhetoric, see ch. 27 of A. S. Byatt's *The Virgin in the Garden* (London: Chatto & Windus, 1978).

22. Quoted in Robert Lacey, *Majesty: Elizabeth II and the House of Windsor* (New York: Harcourt, Brace, Jovanovich, 1977) p. 11.

23. 'Throughout the Country', *New Statesman and Nation*, 43 (13 June 1953) 696.

24. *The Intellectual Part* (London: Barrie & Rockcliff, 1963) p. 141.

25. 'The Story of the Exhibition Tells', reprinted in *A Tonic to the Nation: The Festival of Britain 1951* (London: Thames & Hudson, 1976) p. 74.

26. 'Exhibition of Industrial Power, Glasgow', *A Tonic to the Nation*, p. 154.

27. 'A Monument to the Future', *A Tonic to the Nation*, p. 176 and 29 September 1979 interview with DLH.

28. 8 October 1979 interview with DLH.

29. In 1978, the editors of *New Review* surveyed eighty 'novelists and story writers' asking them 'How would you describe the development of fiction in English over the last ten years or so? Has it been a good or bad time for the novel? What developments would you hope for, or anticipate, over the next decase?' The fifty-six responses received(*New Review*, 5:1 [Summer 1979] 14–76) illustrate well the variety of styles, attitudes, assumptions, hopes, and fears. A. L. Barker, author of *Apology for a Hero and A Case Examined*, replied, 'Everytime is a good and a bad time for the novel, as for any form of life. And the novel is one of the major lively forms. Futile to try to predetermine what it ought or ought not to do, one can only express a preference' (p. 20). Other novelists, however, saw the genre losing its audience and importance for a variety of reasons – declining literacy, migration of talents to film and television, decreasing numbers of bookshops, small royalties, etc. Christine Brooke-Rose called attention very pointedly to the 'stifling of fiction by non-fiction on the part of the critical establishment and publishers' (p. 28), and Mervyn Jones saw the 'greatest threat' as the English novel's 'own lack of ambition' p. 47).

30. Richard B. Sale, 'An Interview in London with Brian Moore', *Studies in the Novel*, 1:1 (1969) 76.

31. Quoted in David A. Pailin, 'Theology', in *The Twentieth-Century Mind*, ed. C. B. Cox and A. E. Dyson (London: Oxford University Press, 1972) pp. 111, 116.

32. *Justine* (New York: E. P. Dutton, 1957); hereafter abbreviated *J*.

33. *A Word Child* (London: Chatto & Windus, 1975); hereafter abbreviated *WC*.

34. *The Novel Today*, ed. Malcolm Bradbury (Manchester University Press, 1977) p. 154, and 'The Use of Theory', in *For a New Novel: Essays on Fiction*, trans. Richard Howard (New York: Grove Press, 1965) p. 9.

35. In the 8 October 1979 interview, I asked Margaret Drabble if she still felt this way. She replied: 'No, I don't feel quite the same about that. I mean I see that the tradition is much more complex than I thought it was then, and that there is no way of writing a straight nineteenth century novel, nor should there be. . . . I hadn't read Virginia Woolf when I made that remark. I didn't read Woolf until quite late in life. And now I see that one can take, one can combine elements from all these people. that is not the question of committing yourself to rewriting to be like James Joyce. There is a sort of huge middle area where you are conscious of all these traditions, and with any luck you can find your own voice, which I think I am still committed to.'

36. 'Non-fiction Novelists,' *Atlantic*, 178 (1946) 129.

37. *As If By Magic* (New York: Penguin, 1976) pp. 202–3.

38. Quoted in Bernard Bergonzi, *The Situation of the Novel* University of Pittsburgh Press, 1970) p. 23.

39. 'Fable', *The Hot Gates and Other Occasional Pieces* (New York: Harcourt, Brace, World, 1965) p. 89. In the same essay, Golding notes that *The Coral Island* was published 'at the height of Victorian smugness, ignorance, and prosperity' (p. 88).

40. See Joe David Bellamy, *The New Fiction: Interviews with Innovative American Writers* (Urbana: University of Illinois Press, 1974) p. 128.

41. Quoted in Bergonzi, p. 78.

42. 'England's Greatest Tourist and Tourist Attractions: Andrew Sinclair's *Gog, Magog*', in Morris, p. 152.

43. Quoted in Bergonzi, p. 76.

44. Quoted in Bergonzi, p. 77.

45. See *Contemporary Novelists*, ed. James Vinson, 2nd edn (New York: St. Martin's Press, 1976) p. 1245.

46. *Gog* (London: Weidenfeld & Nicolson, 1976); hereafter abbreviated *G*.

47. Quoted in Booker, p. 45.

48. Hermann Hesse, *The Glass Bead Game*, trans. Richard and Clara Winston (New York: Holt, Rinehart, Winston, 1969) p. 15. The glass bead game led by Joseph Knecht is one of the most searching

looks at uses of the past within a culture: see pp. 33, 40, 119, 197, and 317.
49. Chamberlain, p. ix.

PART II: WAVES OF MEMORY

1. Rosamund Bernier, 'The Painter Miro, this month 87, is as lively as ever', *Smithsonian*, 11:1 (April 1980) 107.
2. Bernier, p. 107.
3. V. S. Pritchett, *Midnight Oil* (New York: Random House, 1972) pp. 3‒4.
4. *Free Fall* (New York: Harcourt, Brace, World, 1959) p. 46.
5. Quoted in Georg Lukacs, 'The Ideology of Modernism', in *Perspectives in Contemporary Criticism*, ed. Sheldon Norman Grebstein (New York: Harper & Row, 1968) p. 214.
6. Quoted in Susan Sontag, *On Photography* (New York: Dell, 1977) p. 166. Sontag's book contains many insights into the ties created between past and present by photographs; see, for example, her comment 'The photograph is a thin slice of space as well as time. . . . Photography reinforces a nominalist view of social reality as consisting of small units of an apparently infinite number ‒ as the number of photographs that could be taken of anything is unlimited. Through photographs, the world becomes a series of unrelated, freestanding particles; and history, past and present, a set of anecdotes and *faits divers*' (pp. 22‒3).
7. *Christopher and His Kind* (New York: Avon, 1977) pp. 39‒40.
8. Quoted in Vinson, p. 705.
9. Quoted in Bradbury, *The Twentieth Century Mind*, pp. 111, 116.

Chapter 2: L. P. Hartley, *The Go-Between*

1. 'Introduction', *The Go-Between* (London: Heinemann, 1963) p. 1.
2. 'Three Wars', *Promise of Greatness: The War of 1914–1918*, ed. George A. Panichas (New York: John Day, 1968) p. 251.
3. *The Go-Between* (New York: Avon, 1968) p. 11; hereafter abbreviated *GB*.

4. See *The Complete Poems of Emily Jane Brontë:*, ed. C. W. Hatfiel(
   (New York: Columbia University Press, 1941) pp. 39–40; the poem
   was written in July, 1837.

5. Samuel Taylor Coleridge, *The Selected Poetry and Prose*, ed. Donal(
   A. Stauffer (New York: Random House, 1951) p. 419; the passag(
   appears in *Biographia Literaria*, ch. xxiv.

6. For discussions of the novel's tight and accurate time scheme anc
   the theoretical implications of retrospective structure, see my *Tim(
   and English Fiction* (London: Macmillan, 1977) pp. 45–50. Othe(
   critical essays on Hartley's novel include Peter Bien, *L. P. Hartle(*
   (University Park: Pennsylvania State University Press, 1963) pp
   167–83; Margaret A. Moan, 'Setting and Structure: an Approach
   to Hartley's *The Go-Between*', *Critique*, 15:2 (1973) 27–35; Anne
   Mulkeen, *Wild Thyme, Winter Lightning: the Symbolic Novels of L. P.
   Hartley* (Detroit: Wayne State University Press, 1974) pp. 97–112:
   M. B. Willmott. '"What Leo Knew': The Childhood World of L.
   P. Hartley', *English*, 24 (9175) 3–10; and, most recently, Edward
   T. Jones, *L. P. Hartley* (Boston: Twayne, 1978) pp. 100–13.

7. *My Sister's Keeper* (London: Hamish Hamilton, 1970) p. 104.

8. 'Introduction', p. 5.

9. 'Three Wars', pp. 254–5.

10. *Eustace and Hilda* (London: Putnam, 1958) p. 452. In the title essay
    of *the Novelist's Responsibility* (London: Hamish Hamilton, 1967),
    Hartley commented: 'The influence of Dostoevsky has been enor-
    mous, and it has been reinforced by the influence of two writers
    of whom he would probably not have approved — Marx and
    Freud. Different as they are, the doctrines of Marx and Freud
    have combined to undermine the individual's sense of personal
    responsibility. Marx held that our actions are conditioned by the
    class of society to which we belong; and Freud held that our actions
    are subject to influences — pre-natal and juvenile — over which
    we have no control. Marx (I imagine) thought that the evil in
    man's nature could be cured by political acion; Freud thought
    that when a man had been properly psycho-analysed, properly
    integrated, and adjusted to his surroundings, he would
    automatically lose his anti-social tendencies.

    So far neither of these doctrines has been proved right. The
    countries ruled by the Soviet are not morally impeccable, while
    in countries where modern methods of psychiatry are having a
    good trial the figures for delinquency go up and up' (p. 10). In
    the essay, 'The Novelist and His Material', Hartley returned to

the motif: 'If the novelist of today finds himself in a difficult position, it is not so much his fault as the fault of his human material. Perhaps I should not say fault in either case. For one thing, with the weakening of our belief in free-will, the word "fault" like the word "ought" has lost much of its strength and meaning: some defect of character or conduct which would once have unhesitatingly been called "our fault" is now ascribed to causes over which we have no control, or very little' (p. 184).

11. *The Interpretation of Dreams*, trans. James Strachey (New York: Basic Books, 1955) p. 262.

12. 'Introduction', p. 4.

13. For an insightful discussion of the film's adaptation, see Michael Riley and James Palmer, 'Time and the Stucture of Memory in *The Go-Between*', *College Literature*, 5 (1978), 219–27.

14. 'Introduction', pp. 6–7.

15. R. D. Laing, *The Politics of Experience* (New York: Ballantine, 1967) p. 55.

16. *A Perfect Woman* (New York: Knopf, 1956) p. 271.

Chapter 3: Angus Wilson, *Late Call*

1. See John Fowles, 'Notes on an Unfinished Novel', *Afterwords*, ed. Thomas McCormack (New York: Harper & Row, 1969) p. 161, and 'William Faulkner', *Writers at Work*, First Series, ed. Malcolm Cowley (New York: Penguin, 1977) p. 130. An interesting study of this interplay between the male novelist, the female image, and the offspring novel remains to be done.

2. Lawrence Poston, III, 'A Conversation with Angus Wilson', *Books Abroad*, 44 (Winter 1966) 30.

3. *Late Call* (New York: Viking Press, 1964). All subsequent quotations are from this text.

4. *Britain 1978: an Official Handbook* (London; Her Majesty's Stationery Office, 1978) p. 161. The 'first jewel' comment appears in Gordon E. Cherry, *The Evolution of British Town Planning: a History of Town Planning in the United Kingdom During the Twentieth Century and of the Royal Town Planning Institute, 1914–1978* (Leighton Buzzard: Leonard Hill Books, 1974) p. 140.

5. *Britain 1978*, p. 162.

6. 'New Towns Versus Old Towns', in *Perspectives on New Town Development*, ed. Ray Thomas (Milton Keynes: The Open University, 1976) p. 9.
7. Poston, p. 31.
8. Horst W. Drecher, 'Angus Wilson – An Interview', *Die Neueren Sprachen*, 17 (1968) 355.
9. Daniel Curley, 'The Virtues of Service', *New Leader*, 48 (15 February 1965) 22, and William B. Hill, S. J., 'Angus Wilson, *Late Call*', *Best Sellers*, 24 (15 February 1965) 446, respectively
10. Drescher, p. 350.
11. *Emile Zola* (New York: William Morrow, 1952) p. 1. Wilson repeats the idea several times during the study: 'His sense of personal humiliation in childhood and adolescence gave him a hatred for all sections of society, though for the poorest he retained an emotional compassion as great as his physical disgust' (p. 37), and 'The events, the circumstances of a great writer's youth must claim the attention of the literary critic who attempts to unravel the tight ball of emotional strands from which the finished works receive their pattern' (p. 69). Also see note 39 below.
12. *The Wild Garden* (Berkeley and Los Angeles: University of California Press, 1963) p. 11.
13. 'Angus Wilson: the Territory Behind', *Contemporary British Novelists*, ed. Charles Shapiro (Carbondale and Edwardsville: Southern Illinois University Press, 1965) p. 149.
14. *No Laughing Matter* (New York: Viking Press, 1967) p. 104.

Chapter 4: Rayner Heppenstall, *The Woodshed*

1. Sylvere Monod, 'Rayner Heppenstall and the Nouveau Roman', in *Imagined Worlds*, ed. Maynard Mack and Ian Gregor (London: Methuen, 1968) p. 461. Monod's is one of the few essays on Heppenstall.
2. *The Intellectual Part* (London: Barrie & Rockliff, 1963) p. 87; hereafter abbreviated *IP*.
3. *The Connecting Door* (London: Barrie & Rockliff, 1962) p. 1, and *The Woodshed* (London: Barrie & Rockliff, 1962); hereafter abbreviated *CD* and *N*.
4. *Repetition: an Essay in Experimental Psychology*, trans. Walter Lowrie (New York: Harper & Row, 1941). In the 4 October 1979

interview with DLH, Heppenstall commented: 'And, but you mentioned Kierkegaard, I think; I don't know whether you mentioned anyone else, but anyway, you take Kierkegaard. I would say he was a very big influence indeed, on *The Connecting Door*, and in particular a book of his called *Repetition*, which is set within the framework of him going back to Berlin and as much as me, if you like, going back to Strasbourg. I have been, I was at one time, more involved with Kierkegaard, than with Freud, and the one thing that I thought at the time, with first reading it which was while I was still in the army towards the end of the second World War, was that this book *Repetition* of Kierkegaard's, a philosophical work perhaps in many ways, was nevertheless an important picture. I thought *Repetition* as a great step in the history of the novel, and . . .'.

5. *IP*, p. 21.

6. See Gregor Malantschuk, *Kierkegaard's Thought*, ed. and trans. Howard V. and Edna H. Hong (Princeton University Press, 1971) pp. 12–13.

7. See the 'Prefatory Aphorisms' in *The Living Thoughts of Kierkegaard*, ed. W. H. Auden (New York: David McKay, 1952) p. 25.

8. Quoted in John W. Elrod, *Being and Existence in Kierkegaard's Works* (Princeton University Press, 1975), p. 70.

9. *A Kierkegaard Anthology*, ed. Robert Bretall (Princeton University Press, 1946) p. 28.

10. *Blaze of Noon* (London: Secker & Warburg, 1939) p. 178.

11. *The Fourfold Tradition* (Norfolk, Connecticut: New Directions, 1961) p. 180.

12. Interview with DLH, 4 October 1979

13. See *Raymond Roussel: A Critical Study* (Berkeley and Los Angeles: University of California Press, 1967). For an authoritative discussion of the anit-novel, see Vivian Mercier, *The New Novel from Quenueau to Pinget* (New York: Farrar, Straus & Giroux, 1971) esp. pp. 3–42.

14. Monod, p. 472.

15. Monod, p. 463.

Chapter 5: Brian Moore, *I Am Mary Dunne*

1. *Fergus* (New York: Penguin, 1970) p. 34.

2. Quoted in Granville Hicks, 'Mary and Her Mad Twin', *Saturday Review*, 51 (15 June 1968) 24.

3. Hallvard Dahlie, 'Brian Moore: an Interview', *Tamarack Review*, 46 (Winter 1968) 25–6.

4. Richard B. Sale, 'An Interview in London with Brian Moore', *Studies in the Novel*, 1:1 (1969) 71.

5. In the 'Preface' to *The Ambassadors*, Henry James dismissed first person as 'a form foredoomed to looseness'; see this and other comments on the use of first person in *Novelists on the Novel*, ed. Miriam Allott (New York: Columbia University Press, 1959) pp. 256–74.

6. *I Am Mary Dune* (New York: Penguin, 1973); hereafter abbreviated *MD*. The phrase *memento ergo sum* which figures so importantly in the novel should be *memini ergo sum*.

7. *The Rhetoric of Fiction* (Univeristy of Chicago Press, 1961) p. 300; the entire discussion of impersonal narrative (pp. 271–398) bears on the consideration of unreliable narrators.

8. John Graham, 'Brian Moore', *The Writer's Voice: Conversations with Contemporary Writers*, ed. George Garrett (New York: William Morrow, 1973) p. 64.

9. '*I Am Mary Dunne*', *Commonweal*, 88 (27 September 1968) 662, and '*I Am Mary Dunne*', *Harper's*, 237 (July 1968) 105.

10. Graham p. 59.

11. For Erik Erikson's theory of the stages of psychosocial development, see his *Dimensions of a New Identity* (New York: W. W. Norton, 1974) pp. 85–111; *Toys and Reasons: Stages in the Ritualization of Experience* (New York: W. W. Norton, 1977) pp. 67–118; and 'Reflections on Dr. Borg's Life Cycle', in *Adulthood*, ed. Erik H. Erikson (New York: W. W. Norton, 1978) pp. 1–31.

12. The comment concerning alienation comes from an interview in *Publisher's Weekly*, 193:22 (27 May 1968), 16; information about the working title appears in Dahlie, p. 21 where Moore comments: 'My current book — *A Woman of No Identity* is its working title — is about a woman who is successful, quite good-looking, and fairly intelligent — a Canadian woman who has been married three times, and has lived in various places in Canada and the States. She has reached a point in her life at which she begins to wonder who she really was, who she really is, and who she is going to be.'

13. Dahlie, p. 21.

14. Graham, p. 60.

15. Sale, p. 78.

16. Sale, p. 71.

17. Sale, p. 73.

18. Dahlie, p. 18.

19. '*I Am Mary Dunne*', *America*, 119 (6 July 1968) 18 and 'Mary's Day', *New Statesman*, 76 (25 October 1968) 550.

20. 'Day of Squalls', *Time*, 91 (21 June 1968) 88; 'News from the Novel', *New Republic*, 159 (17 August 1968) 29; and 'Moore's Poor Bitches', *Tamarack Review*, 68 (Autumn 1968) 64.

21. 'Moore's New Perspective', *Canadian Literature*, no. 38 (Autumn 1968) 83; and John Wilson Foster, *Forces and Themes in Ulster Fiction* (Dublin: Gill & Macmillan, 1974) p. 177.

22. Jeanne Flood, *Brian Moore* (Lewisburg: Bucknell University Press, 1974) p. 80. Flood's reading of the novel is heavily Freudian, see pp. 71–80.

23. Dahlie, p. 29.

PART III: CHALLENGED COMPARISONS

1. *The Ebony Tower* (New York: New American Library, 1974) p. 17.

2. *The Ebony Tower*, p. 102.

3. Northrop Frye, *Anatomy of Criticism* (Princeton University Press, 1957) p. 97; also see Harold Bloom, *The Anxiety of Influence: A Theory of Poetry* (New York: Oxford University Press, 1973) p. 99.

4. For informative histories of forgery in the various arts, see Frank Arnau, *The Art of the Faker*, trans. J. Maxwell Brownjohn (Boston: Little, Brown, 1961) and Richard D. Altick, *The Scholar Adventures* (New York: Free Press, 1966), especially chs II and VI. Arnau comments that 'the forger of real distinction stands head and shoulders above the commercial hacks of the international antiques racket. Intellectually and technically, he is a genuine artist – nor does he find himself in bad company. Michelangelo was not averse to dubious artifices. Rubens "treated" other artists' paintings and executed copies to order. Andrea del Sarto was commissioned to paint a Raffaello Santi, now known as Raphael' (p. 10).

5. Quoted in Joe David Bellamy, *The New Fiction: Interviews with Innovative American Writers* (Urbana: University of Illinois Press, 1974) p. 128.

6. Bellamy, pp. 22, 82–3, and 103.

7. 'Tlön, Uqbar, Orbis Tertius', trans, Alastair Reid, *Ficciones* (New York: Grove Press, 1972) p. 29.

8. 'The Approach to Al-Mu'tasim', trans. Anthony Kerriga
   Ficciones, p. 42.
9. Fraser letter to DLH, 9 December 1980.
10. Bloom, p. 30.
11. Drabble interview with DLH.

Chapter 6: George MacDonald Fraser, *Royal Flash*

1. *Flashman* (New York: New American Library, 1970) p. vii; hereaft
   abbreviated *F*.
2. *Flashman's Lady* (New York: New American Library, 1979) p.
   hereafter abbreviated *FL*.
3. *Royal Flash* (New York: New American Library, 1971) explanato
   note; hereafter abbreviated *RF*.
4. *Flashman at the Charge* (New York: Alfred A. Knopf, 1973) explan
   tory note; hereafter abbreviated *FC*.
5. *Flashman in the Great Game* (New York: New American Librar
   1977) explanatory note; hereafter abbreviated *FGG*.
6. Quoted in Alden Whitman, 'Gen. Sir Harry Flashman and Ai
   Con the Experts', *New York Times*, 29 July 1969, p. 26.
7. *The Steel Bonnets* (New York: Alfred A. Knopf, 1971) p. 6; hereaft
   abbreviated *SB*.
8. *The Old School Tie: The Phenomenon of the English Public School* (Ne
   York: Viking Press, 1977) pp. 77–8.
9. *Fifty Works of English Literature We Could Do Without* (New Yor
   Stein and Day, 1968) p. 85.
10. Thomas Hughes, *Tom Brown's School Days* (New York: E.
    Dutton, 1972) pp. 160–1.
11. See A. E. W. Mason, *Sir George Alexander and the St. James Thea*
    (London: Macmillan, 1935) p. 103, and Sir Charles Mallet, *Antho*
    Hope and His Books (London: Hutchinson, 1935) p. 76.
12. Mallet, p. 76.
13. Mallet, p. 79. Also see Roger Lancelyn Green, 'Introduction', *T*
    Prisoner of Zenda [and] Rupert of Hentzau (London: Dent, 1966) p
    ix–x, and Anthony Hope, *Memories and Notes* (London: Hutchinso
    1927) in which Hope recalls: 'One day – it was the 28th
    November 1893 – I was walking back from the Westminst
    County Court (where I had won my case) to the Temple whe
    the idea of "Ruritania" came into my head. Arrived at n

chambers, I reviewed it over a pipe, and the next day I wrote the first chapter' (p. 119).

4. *The Prisoner of Zenda* (New York: Grosset & Dunlap, 1921) p. 305; hereafter abbreviated *PZ*.

5. Melvin Maddocks, 'Royal Flash', *Life*, 69:23 (4 December 1970) 10.

6. See *The Magnificent Montez: From Courtesan to Convert* (New York: Hillman-Curl, n.d.) pp. 49–59.

7. *The Uncrowned Queen* (New York: Harper & Row, 1970) pp. 126, 138.

8. Quoted in Wyndham, p. 53.

9. Bismarck recalled that Schleswig-Holstein affair was 'the diplomatic campaign of which [he] was most proud'. Quoted in Alan Palmer, *Bismarck* (London: Weidenfeld & Nicolson, 1976) p. 90. See pp. 90–105 for a succinct discussion of the entire affair.

hapter 7: **Jean Rhys,** *Wide Sargasso Sea*

1. Patrick O'Donovan, 'Britain's Stately Homes Lose Their Attraction', *Observer*, 23 September 1979, p. 3.

2. *Jane Eyre* has been adapted for film at least ten times: 1910 (Italian, Mario Caserini), 1910 (American, Edwin Thanhomer), 1914 (American, Whitman), 1915 (American), 1918 (American, Edward José, 1921 (American, Hugo Ballin), 1926 (German, Kurt Bernhardt), 1934 (American, Christy Cabanne), 1944 (American, Robert Stevenson), and 1970 (English, Delbert Man).

3. *Jane Eyre*, ed. Richard J. Dunn (New York: Norton, 1971) p. 257; hereafter abbreviated *JE*.

4. *Jane Eyre*, pp. 420–1. Elizabeth Gaskell recorded the first source for Bertha in *The Life of Charlotte Brontë*, ed. Alan Shelston (Harmondsworth: Penguin, 1975) pp. 159–60; also see Winifred Gerin, *Charlotte Brontë: The Evolution of Genius* (New York: Oxford University Press, 1967) p. 299.

5. *Hard Times*, ed. William W. Watt (New York: Holt, Rinehart, & Winston, 1958) p. 62; hereafter abbreviated *HT*.

6. 'Pornography and Obscenity', in *Phoenix: the Posthumous Papers of D. H. Lawrence*, ed. Edward D. McDonald (New York: Viking, 1936) pp. 174, 176.

7. *John Thomas and Lady Jane* (New York: Viking, 1972) p. 338; hereafter abbreviated *JTLJ*.

8. 'Memoir of D. H. Lawrence', in *D. H. Lawrence: Novelist, Poet, Prophet*, ed. Stephen Spender (New York: Harper & Row, 1973) p. 23.

9. *The Collected Letters of D. H. Lawrence*, ed. Harry T. Moore (New York: Viking, 1962) p. 34; letter of 4 November 1908.

10. *Lady Chatterley's Lover* (New York: Grove Press, 1962) p. 338. In 'Jane and the Other Mrs. Rochester: Excess and Restraint in *Jane Eyre*', *Novel*, 10 (1977) 145 – 57, Peter Grudin has perceptively discussed Bertha Mason as a symbolic character and concludes 'If, finally, Bertha can be seen as the hyperbolic emblem and ultimate stage of the adultress' progress, she is most effectively significant in her particular role, that of Jane's "secret sharer", a substitute self who realizes and suffers for all the dangerous potentials of the protagonist's character' (p. 157).

11. *Jane: a Story of Jamaica* (London: Methuen, 1914) p. 15.

12. *The White Witch of Rosehall* (London: Ernest Benn, 1929) pp. 266–7.

13. See Diana Athill, 'Jean Rhys, and the Writing of *Wide Sargasso Sea*', *Bookseller*, 20 August 1966, pp. 1378–9, 'Jean Rhys and Her Autobiography', in *Smile Please: an Unfinished Autobiography* (New York: Harper & Row, 1979) pp. 3–9, and the more general comments of John Hall, 'Jean Rhys', *Arts Guardian*, 10 January 1972, p. 8 and Hanna Carter, 'Fated To Be Sad', *Guardian*, 8 August 1968, p. 5.

14. Letter of 5 October 1957 to Selma Vaz Dias. This letter and the other letters quoted in the discussion are cited with permission of Francois Wyndham, Executor of the Jean Rhys Estate and the McFarlin Library, University to Tulsa which owns the letters. Rhys's hand is so shaky and unsteady and the punctuation at times so eccentric that the letters are extremely difficult to transcribe. The envelope for this particular letter carries the note 'Idea born in my kitchen when they came to dinner . . . 1957.'

15. Tulsa letter, 10 January 1959.

16. Tulsa letter, 5 February 1959.

17. Tulsa letter, 25 May 1959.

18. Interview with DLH, 11 October 1979. Athill also said that Rhys discarded scenes using Grace Poole because she wanted little overlap with Brontë's novel, that Rhys did not like *Jane Eyre*, and that Rhys always felt isolated in England. The final point was confirmed most tellingly when Rhys commented during the Carter interview: 'I was utterly wretched when I had come here [Cheriton]

... the people were horrid at first. They said I was a witch. Someone told me Cheriton used to be a great centre for witchcraft. After my husband died the rumours got worse. In the evenings, reinforced with wine, I used to shout defiance at them from the window ...' (p. 5).

19. Tulsa letter, 5 October 1957 and 17 November 1959.

20. Tulsa letter, 5 February 1959 and 9 April 1959.

21. Ten review clippings are filed with the Tulsa letters. The citations in the paragraph are to Collin MacInnes, 'Nightmare in Paradise', *Observer*, 30 October 1966, p. 28; Rivers Scott, 'Jane Eyre's Rival', *Sunday Telegraph*, 30 october 1966; 'A Fairy-Tale Neurotic', *TLS*, 17 November 1966, p. 1039, and Kay Dick, 'A Wife to Mr Rochester', *Times*, 30 October 1966.

22. Quoted in Michael Thorpe, '"The Other Side": *Wide Sargasso Sea* and Jane Eyre', *Ariel*, 8:3 (1977) 99.

23. Thorpe, p. 99.

24. Tulsa letter, 5 October 1957.

25. Tulsa letter, 9 April 1959.

26. *Wide Sargasso Sea* (New York: Popular Library, 1967), p. 17; hereafter abbreviated *WSS*.

27. For a photograph of the Geneva garden, the original of Coulibri, see *Smile Please*, illustration 11.

28. Add. MS. 57857. The 179 folios of this file compromise the following: fols 1–48 (typescript of almost all of Part One); 49–60 (Autograph manuscript in black ink in red notebook headed Part II Daniel Letter/Interview); 61–3 (Autograph manuscript headed 'Part II/Continuation of Chapter IV/to be inserted after "I Don't say nothing Master"'.); 64–9 (typescript of fols 61–3); 70–87 (autograph manuscript in black ink headed 'Part II/Chapter 7 (cont) *Christophine speaking*'); 88–101 (typescript of fols 70–87); 102–16 (autograph manuscript in red exercise notebook, apparently the early conclusion of Part II); 117–36 (autograph manuscript in red exercise notebook headed ('The Last Chapter of Part II'.); 137–40 (autograph manuscript in red exercise notebook headed 'End of chapter'.); 141–52 (typescript as fols 177–40); and 153–179 (revised proofs of pp. 17–60).

29. Tulsa letter, 17 November 1959.

30. 'Mr. Rochester's First Marriage: *Wide Sargasso Sea* by Jean Rhys', *World Literature Written in English*, 17:1 (April 1978) 351.

31. Walter Allen, 'Bertha the Doomed', *New York Times Book Review*, 18 June 1967, p. 5.

32. *Voyage in the Dark* (New York: Popular Library, n.d.) p.7.

Chapter 8: Brian Aldiss, *Frankenstein Unbound*

1. W. H. Lyles, *Mary Shelley: an Annotated Bibliography* (New York: Garland, 1975) pp. 219 – 37, lists twenty stage versions, thirty-eight film versions, and twelve television adaptations.

2. George Levine, 'The Ambiguous Heritage of *Frankenstein*', in *The Endurance of Frankenstein: Essays on Mary Shelley's Novel* ed. George Levine and U. C. Knoepflmacher (Berkeley and Los Angeles: University of California Press, 1979) pp. 3 and xiii. For further discussion of Frankenstein's 'hideous progeny', see Martin Tropp, *Mary Shelley's Monster* (Boston: Houghton Mifflin, 1976).

3. Mary Wollstonecraft Shelley, *Frankenstein, or the Modern Prometheus*, ed. James Rieger (Indianapolis: Bobbs-Merrill, 1974) p. 163.

4. 'Magic and Bare Boards', in *Hell's Cartographers: Some Personal Histories of Science Fiction Writers*, ed. Brian W. Aldiss and Harry Harrison (London: Weidenfeld & Nicolson, 1975) p. 189; italics added. In *Greybeard* (1964), Aldiss explores life on the dying Earth following 'The Accident', resulting from nuclear explosions in space.

5. *Billion Year Spree: the True History of Science Fiction* (Garden City, New York: Doubleday, 1973) p. 3. Aldiss's discussion of Shelley appears on pp. 7–39.

6. Aldiss interview with DLH, 29 September 1979.

7. *Last Orders and Other Stories* (London: Johnathan Cape, 1977) pp. 196 and 62.

8. *Billion Year Spree*, p. 3.

9. *Hell's Cartographers*, p. 195.

10. Aldiss interview.

11. Squire's book is mentioned in *Billion Year Spree* (p. 37), but in the interview, Aldiss discounted its influence on his own writing.

12. Aldiss interview.

13. In the Brian Aldiss flies at the Bodelian Library, Oxford, there are nine folders containing *Frankenstein Unbound* materials, as follows:

    No. 1 – 133 folios of typescript, 16 Random House proof pages, and 7 pages of responses to Random House editorial queries.
    No. 2 – A 238 page carbon typescript of the novel.
    No. 3 – A xerox copy of item 2.
    No. 4 – Dummy for Random House prepared from two disbound copies of the Jonathan Cape edition.
    No. 5 – A xerox copy of item 4 with Random House alterations.

No. 6 — Page proofs for the Random House edition.

No. 7 — Galley proofs for the Random House edition.

No. 8 — Page proofs of the Random House edition marked 'Dead Matter'.

No. 9 — Random House blue-line copy, dated 20 March 1974.

The phrase quoted is from Folder No. 1, p. 1 of the responses to the queries, cited with permission of Brian W. Aldiss and the Bodleian Library.

14. *Frankenstein Unbound* (New York: Random House, 1973) p. 3, hereafter abbreviated *FU*. Folder No. 1, mentioned in note 13, contains a full record of Aldiss's struggles with his unsympahtetic Random House editor, Jim Silberman. In the seven pages of closely typed responses to 121 queries about the text in which the American editor ultimately made 405 changes — 115 of them substantive, 290 of them accidentals — Aldiss often replied with an impatient, defensive edge: 'No, as indicated, it would have been out of character for Shelley to make obscene remarks. They make *lurid* remarks — melodramatically colourful, brimstoney. Follow text'; 'A quibble. Text okay, follow text'; 'I see no objection to the text as written'; 'Glistening means sparkling. If I had said 'the sparkling sound of water', you would surely have not challenged it. Isn't it pedantic to complain of 'glistening'?; and 'No, do not mean 21st century. Plenty of 20th yet to go.' Obviously, though, the editor objected to far more than the diction and phrasing in individual sentences, because Aldiss felt compelled to defend his close imitation of the form of Shelley's novel and his violations of realistic probabilities. Almost pained by the extent of the misunderstanding, Aldiss wrote: 'My novel modestly echoes the methods of Mary's novel, right down to concluding with the same phrase. The diversion of this letter is consistent with Mary's methods. In any case, it forms a complete chapter by itself, and is thus easily skipped by a hasty reader. As with the diaries and letters in *Frankenstein*, or the correspondence in Richardson's *Clarissa*, realism is hardly the effect aimed for. . . . Incidentally, I don't care for the comment that "these lectures" "bog down" the narrative; the debate about the role of science in life is the central one of the book.' Aldiss refused to tinker with the structure and themes of his novel but agreed to the requests for local revisions.

15. Helen Rogan, 'Future Imperatives', *Time*, 104:6 (5 August 1974) p. 88.

16. 'Symbols on his Sleeve,' *Spectator*, 231 (29 September 1973) p. 408, and 'Brian Aldiss, *Frankenstein Unbound*', *Books and Bookmen*. 19:4 (January 1974) 21–2.

17. *The Classical Tradition in Poetry* (New York: Vintage, 1957) p. 10.

18. *Billion Year Spree*, pp. 21–2.

19. Bodelian Folder No. 1.

20. Bram Stoker, *Dracula* (Harmondsworth: Penguin, 1979) p. 449.

21. *The Private Memoirs and Confessions of a Justified Sinner*, ed. John Carey (London: Oxford University Press, 1969) p. 240. For a brief discussion of the structural conventions of gothic fiction, see my 'Conrad's Book of Black Science': a Revisionist View of Conrad and the Gothic', *Journal of the Joseph Conrad Society (UK)*, 3:3 (1978) 1–11.

22. *Frankenstein*, p. 25.

23. See *FU*, p. 165.

24. H. G. Wells, *The Time Machine* (New York: Ballantine, 1957) p. 31. Aldiss is, of course, looking backwards largely in reaction against the usual direction of time travel.

25. See *FU*, p. 196 and the Aldiss interview. For a detailed catalogue of the exhibition, see William Vaughan, Helmut Börsch-Supan, and Hans Joachim Neidhardt, *Caspar David Friedrich, 1774–1840: Romantic Landscape Painting in Dresden* (London: Tate Gallery, 1972).

26. *The Time Machine*, p. 77.

27. *Hell's Cartographers*, p. 201.

28. *Hell's Cartographers*, p. 208.

29. See *Billion Year Spree*, pp. 23 and 26.

30. *Frankenstein*, p. 51.

31. 'A Defense of Poetry', in *The Selected Poetry and Prose of Percy Bysshe Shelley*, ed. Carlos Baker (New York: Random House, 1951) p. 516.

32. In the interview, Aldiss recalled this line from Kingsley Amis's *Daily Mail* review with considerable satisfaction.

33. *Nightmare Abbey* (New York: Norton, 1964) p. 61.

34. Probably the most thorough *roman à clef* reading of Shelley's novels is Elizabeth Nitchie, *Mary Shelley, Author of Frankenstein* (New Brunswick: Rutgers University Press, 1953).

35. Aldiss interview.

36. *Frankenstein*, p. 48.

37. 'Time is the spectre haunting the stage of most of my books: Time in its own right and in one of its nastier disguises, as Change. The

characters cope with this as best they can', wrote Aldiss for *Contemporary Novelists*, ed. James Vinson, second edition (New York: St, Martin's Press, 1976) p. 23; also Aldiss interview.

38. 'Science Fiction – A Personal View', in *Broca's Brain: Reflections on the Romance of Science* (New York: Random House, 1979) p. 149.

39. Quoted in *Newsweek*, 93 (4 June 1979) p. 149.

40. *Hell's Cartographers*, p. 208.

Part IV: RICH EVOCATIONS OF THE PAST

1. Stephen Haseler, *The Death of British Democracy* (Buffalo, New York: Prometheus Books, 1976) pp. 17–18, and Daniel Snowman, *Britain and America: An Interpretation of Their Culture 1945–1975* (New York University Press, 1977) p. 17.

2. Haseler, p. 205.

3. Snowman, p. 261.

4. Gail Sheehy, *Passages: Predictable Crises of Adult Life* (New York: Bantam Books, 1977) p. 19.

5. Drabble Interview with DLH, 8 October 1979.

6. *The Enigma of Stonehenge* (New York: Summit Books, 1980) p. 51.

7. *A Writer's Britain: Landscape in Literature* (New York: Alfred A. Knopf, 1979) p. 270.

8. *The Realms of Gold* (New York: Alfred A. Knopf, 1975) pp. 244, 352.

9. *Anglo-Saxon Attitude* (New York: Penguin, 1978) p. 229.

10. *Daniel Martin* (New York: New American Library, 1978) pp. 526, 13.

11. Heppenstall Interview with DLH, 9 October 1981.

12. Fraser letter to DLH, 12 September 1980; Adams Interview with DLH, 19 October 1979.

13. 'In Absentia: Some Books of the Year', *TLS*, 23 November 1979, p. 4.

14. Quoted in Richard Holmes, 'Once More Unto the Breach', *Harper's*, 225 (October 1977) 87.

Chapter 9: Angus Wilson, *Anglo-Saxon Attitudes*

1. Kendrick is so quoted in Charles Green, *Sutton Hoo: the Excavation of A Royal Ship-Burial* (London: Merlin Press, 1963) p. 17; Bruce-

Mitford's comment appears in his preface to Bernice Grohskopf, *The Treasure of Sutton Hoo: Ship-Burial for An Anglo-Saxon King* (New York: Atheneum, 1970) p. ix.

2. Ronald Millar, *The Piltdown Men* (New York: St Martin's Press, 1972) pp. 9, 10.

3. *Anglo-Saxon Attitudes* (New York: Penguin, 1958), see pages 9, 31, 144–5, 148, 255, 321, and the paratexts. Hereafter the text will be abbreviated *ASA*. Although similarities between the excavation and the action of Wilson's novel were noted by some reviewers, Jay Halio was the first to reveal that 'a remark overheard in the Museum canteen about the dating of the Sutton Hoo burial ship suggested the theme of professional responsibility in *Anglo-Saxon Attitudes*,' *Angus Wilson* (Edinburgh and London: Oliver and Boyd, 1964) p. 9. Wilson discussed the relationship between his novel and the two finds at length in his 22 May 1979 interview with DLH. Wilson has recently described the origins and composition of his novel in 'The Genesis of *Anglo-Saxon Attitudes*', *Books at Iowa* no. 34 (April 1981) 3–8.

4. Quoted in Millar, p. 126.

5. Quoted in Grohskopf, pp. 3–4.

6. See Millar, p. 212. Wilson's flair for pastiche is unmatched, as witness the skillful pastiches of Grillparzer in *Late Call*, De Sade's *One Hundred and Twenty Days of Sodom* in *As If By Magic*, and the variety of examples offered in *No Laughing Matter*.

7. Interview of 22 May 1979. Halio briefly discusses the historians Wilson studied, see pp. 5–7.

8. *Such Darling Dodos and Other Stories* (London: Secker & Warburg, 1954) p. 155.

9. Kingsley Amis, 'Dodos Less Darling', *New Republic*, 135 (15 October 1956) 27–8, 'A Carnival of Humbug', *Time* 68 (29 October 1956) 108, and Charles Rolo, 'Scandal in a Coffin', *Atlantic Monthly*, 198 (October 1956) 105–6.

10. Rupert Bruce-Mitford, *Aspects of Anglo-Saxon Archeology: Sutton Hoo and Other Discoveries* (London: Victor Gollancz, 1974) p. 137.

11. See Millar, ch. One, for discussion of the nationalistic fervour behind anthropological findings, theories, and hopes at the turn of the century.

12. Quoted in Millar, p. 217.

13. 'The Anglo-Saxon World', *New Statesman and Nation*, 51 (11 February 1956) 159–60.

14. Bruce-Mitford, p. 156; Brown's diary is printed in full.

15. Phillips' foreword to Grohskopf, p. xi.

16. *ASA*, pp. 337–47; also included are 'extracts' from books by Reginald Portway, Lionel Stokesay, and Rose Lorimer, a review by Arthur Clun, and a *Times* article.

17. *A History of the English Church and People*, trans. Leo Sherley-Price (Baltimore: Penguin, 1955) p. 128 (Book 2, ch. 15).

18. Joseph S. Weiner, *The Piltdown Forgery* (London: Oxford University Press, 1955). Also see note 2.

19. White, p. 31.

20. *The Immoralist*, trans. Richard Howard (New York: Alfred A. Knopf, 1970) pp. 49–50.

21. *The Wild Garden*, p. 32. In addition to his use of 'Thingummy' and 'Thingy' to connect Eorpwald and Ingeborg, Wilson uses the following echo phrases: 'mirror' (p. 16); 'heart sank' (p. 22); 'don't fuss' and 'don't get into a fuss' (p. 35); 'anyway Scandinavian' and 'Scandinavian anyway' (p. 28); 'the wider truth of the situation the country's in' (pp. 100, 102); 'the lesser has to be sacrificed to the greater' (pp. 103, 107, 126); 'the one thing that matters' (p. 118); and 'Am I the keeper of my brother's conscience' (p. 135).

22. 'Angus Wilson: The Territory Behind', in *Contemporary British Novelists*, ed. Charles Shapiro (Carbondale and Edwardsville: Southern Illinois University Press, 1965) p. 145.

23. *Writers at Work*, ed. Malcolm Cowley (New York: Penguin, 1977) p. 174; this First Series of the *Paris Review* interviews also contains an Angus Wilson interview in which Wilson indirectly responds to O'Connor: 'In a novel I also take a point in time, but feel every room for development backwards' (p. 257).

24. Amis, p. 27.

25. *The Middle Age of Mrs. Eliot* (New York: Viking Press, 1959) pp. 337–8.

26. Edelstein, p. 157.

27. *The Wild Garden*, p. 33.

28. *The Wild Garden*, p. 60.

29. *The Free Spirit: a Study of Liberal Humanism in the Novels of George Eliot, Henry James, E. M. Forster, Virginia Woolf, Angus Wilson* (London: Oxford University Press, 1963) p. 142. Cox comments: 'The image of the tunnel is conventional, and as a whole this scene lacks force. The use of reverie lacks dramatic power and it is not clear why at this moment Gerald should have made this decision. But his return to life is of crucial importance in the development of Wilson's conception of the humanist.'

30. In *Aspects of Anglo-Saxon Archaeology*, for example, Bruce-Mitford writes: 'We have now reached the crux of a difficult but fascinating problem. We have seen good reason to believe that the Sutton Hoo ship-burial is that of an East Anglian king, we have seen, from the study of the course of Christianity in East Anglia and from what we know of the dating evidence for the burial, that it must have taken place precisely in the phase of transition between paganism and Christianity. In and close to the "body space" in the burial chamber is a group of significant Christian objects. These would suggest that the burial is that of a Christian, for they seem to have been grouped and placed with deliberation. Yet it is against every historical probability and the known facts that the body of a Christian Wuffinga king should have been deposited in the pagan fashion in the old pagan burial place when the church was so insistent on the burial of kings in Christian precincts. There is no doubt that these facts suit very well the interpretation of the burial as that of Raedwald (624–5) to whose relapse and subsequent compromise between pagan and Christian practices we have referred, (p. 33).

Chapter 10: Margaret Drabble, *The Realms of Gold*

1. *A Summer Bird-Cage* (Harmondsworth: Penguin, 1967) p. 173, and *The Needle's Eye* (New York: Popular Library, 1977) p. 84.
2. Drabble interview with DLH, 8 October 1979. The past was apparently much on Drabble's mind in 1974. She wrote in *Spectator:* 'The same cannot be said for Peter Hall's *Akenfield* (LWT), shining like paradise with England's heavenly lanes of cow parsley, resplendent with corn fields. The interweaving of old and young Tom's stories, of past with present, and all the ambiguities of attitude of writers, directors and characters seemed both rich and lucid', 'Natural Hazards', *Spectator*, 89 (31 January 1975) 152–3.
3. 'Shabby, Golden Lives', *Saturday Review*, 3 (15 November 1975) 20.
4. 'Drabbling in the Mud', *New Worker*, 51 (12 January 1976) 89 and 88.
5. 'Margaret Drabble's England', *New York Times Book Review*, 16 November 1975, p. 5.
6. 'A Tangled Bank', *New Leader*, 59 (26 April 1976); 18. In discussing reviews in the interview with DLH, Drabble said 'the kind that I

like is the sort that isn't written from any particular angle, it just seems to respond to the book and I love criticisms that prove that I have read books that I haven't . . . there is a lot of that. And that is just a joke on them and a joke on me, too, because there are always books I ought to have read and didn't. Like *On the Origin of Species*. There was one wonderful, a very nice, review indeed, and I can't recall what it was published in, but it began saying, "The references to Darwin are rather too close an emphasis on this particular paragraph in *The Origin of Species*" . . . and I have never read it. I was shocked.'

7. 'Archaeology Begins at Home', *TLS*, 26 September 1975, p. 1077.

8. *The Poems of John Keats*, ed. Jack Stillinger (Cambridge: Harvard University Press, 1978) p, 64.

9. Aileen Ward, *John Keats: the Making of a Poet* (New York: Viking Press, 1963) p. 76.

10. Asked when she selected the title, Drabble replied, 'Oh, when I had practically finished it. I usually get the title when I am about three-quarters of the way through it. I may even have finished it; I can't remember, but I certainly didn't start out with it.' At the time, she had completed *The Middle Ground*, but had no idea what its title would be. Interview with DLH.

11. *The Realms of Gold* (New York: Alfred A. Knopf, 1975); hereafter abbreviated *RG*.

12. Early in Woolf's novel, Clarissa Dalloway experiences a moment's confrontation with her shadow, 'this brutal monster . . . in the depths of that leaf-encumbered forest, the soul', but sweeps it aside: 'Nonsense, nonsense! she cried to herself, pushing through the swing doors of Mulberry's the florists' *Mrs. Dalloway* (New York: Harcourt, Brace, World, 1925) p. 17. Drabble's novels are saturated with allusions to other literary works (see *RG*, 15, 47, 52, 153, 192, 247, and 333 for allusions to Virginia Woolf, William Shakespeare, John Milton, William Wordsworth, John Updike, Stendahl, and others), but Woolf has a peculiar importance to her canon. In *Virginia Woolf: a Personal Debt* (London: Aloe Editions, 1973), Drabble comments: 'The novels are haunting. They work in the mind long after they are back on the shelf' (p. 5). This short booklet, originally published in *Ms.*, details Drabble's story of her discovery of Woolf.

13. 'An Interview with Margaret Drabble', *Contemporary Literature*, 14 (1973) 288–9.

14. Interview with DLH.

15. 'Crossing the Alps' *Mademoiselle*, February 1971, pp. 154–5, 193–8.
     In the story, the protagonist thinks: 'And oddly enough, long after
     they had returned to England, years after, he had only to think
     of pine trees and Alpine landscapes to be reminded of something
     half realized, a revelation of comfort too dense to articulate, a
     revelation that had lost its words and its fine edges and its meaning,
     but not its images. He thought of pine trees, and he thought of
     her, and the memory (why should he not choose, even for himself,
     a word of some dignity?) – the memory sustained him' (p. 198).

16. 'Faithful Lovers', *Saturday Evening Post*, 6 April 1968, pp. 62, 64–5.

17. *Arnold Bennett* (New York: Alfred A. Knopf, 1974) p. 5; also see
     pp. 100, 109–10.

18. King James translation. For a discussion of biblical allusions in
     Drabble's novels, see Valerie Grosvenor Myer. *Margaret Drabble:
     Puritanism and Permissiveness* (London: Vision Press, 1974).

19. Drabble's thought seems remarkably close to that of George
     Steiner, who has written: 'Behind today's posture of doubt and
     self-castigation stands the presence, so pervasive as to pass largely
     unexamined, of a particular past, of a specific "golden time." Our
     experience of the present, the judgments, so often negative, that
     we make of our place in history, play continually against what I
     want to call the "myth of the nineteenth century" or the "imagined
     garden of liberal culture", in *Bluebeard's Castle: Some Notes Towards
     the Redefinition of Culture* (New Haven: Yale University Press, 1971)
     p. 4.

20. Interview with DLH.

21. For a photograph of the Hotel du Lac, see Mike Edwards, 'Tunisia:
     Sea, Sand, Success,' *National Geographic*, 157:2 (1980) 196–7.

22. These comments come from *'Realms of Gold'*, *Publisher's Weekly*, 208
     (6 October 1975) 79; Oates, p. 20; and Jane Miller, 'New Novels',
     New Review, 2 (October 1975) 66.

23. 'Ivory Bower', *New Statesman*, 90 (26 September 1975) 375–6, and
     'Fretting about the Novel Form', *New York Times*, 125 (31 October
     1975) 31.

24. Interview with DLH.

25. *The Waterfall* (New York: Popular Library, 1977) p. 47.

26. In one of his few theoretical comments concerning structure,
     Charles Dickens wrote: 'It is the custom on the stage, in all good
     murderous melodramas, to present the tragic and the comic scenes
     in as regular alternation as the layers of red and white in a side

of streaky bacon', *Oliver Twist* (New York: New American Library, 1961) p. 157 (ch. xvii). For a sophisticated discussion of the multiple plotting in Victorian novels, see Peter K. Garrett, 'Double Plots and Dialogical Form in Victorian Fiction', *NCF*, 32 (1977) 1–17.

27. *The Golden Notebook* (New York: Bantam, 1973) p. vii.
28. Interview with DLH.
29. Both Tess and Jude express strong wishes not to mature and ultimately not to be, reflecting similar wishes in Hardy's autobiography. Drabble has written on Hardy and also edited a collection of essays, *The Genius of Thomas Hardy* (New York: Alfred A. Knopf, 1976).
30. Interview with DLH.
31. Oates, p. 22 and Johnson, pp. 375–6.

Chapter 11: John Fowles, *Daniel Martin*

1. 'Soul Search', *Newsweek*, 90 (19 September 1977) 110.
2. 'In Defense of the Real', *Saturday Review*, 5 (1 October 1977) 22; and 'Lives in Crisis', *Progressive*, 41 (November 1977) 55.
3. *Daniel Martin* (New York: New American Library, 1978); all subseqeunt citations are from this text and will be abbreviated *DM*.
4. An excellent overview of the current discussions of character appear in Bernard Bergonzi, *The Situation of the Novel* (University of Pittsburgh Press, 1970) pp. 35–55. For a more theoretical approach to the problem, see Joel Weinsheimer, 'Theory of Character: *Emma*', *Poetics Today*, 1 (Autumn 1979) 185–211 and Robert Scholes and Robert Kellogg, *The Nature of Narrative* (New York: Oxford University Oress, 1966) pp. 160–206.
5. Quoted in Ronald Hayman, *Nietzsche: a Critical Life* (New York: Oxford University Press, 1980) p. vii. The passage is from Nietzsche's 'Human, All Too Human — The Wanderer and His Shadow', Section 198.
6. Quoted in Frank Kermode, *The Sense of an Ending* (New York: Oxford University Press, 1967) p. 139.
7. *An Essay Concerning Human Understanding*, ed. Alexander Campbell Fraser (New York: Dover Publications, 1959) p. 458. ch. 27 (pp. 439–70) contains an excellent discussion of continuity of identity.

8. *Treatise on Human Nature*, Book I, Part IV, Section 6, see Terence Penelhum, 'Personal Identity,' *Encyclopedia of Philosophy*, ed. Paul Edwards (New York: Macmillan, 1967) 6:95–107.

9. *A Portrait of the Artist as a Young Man*, ed. Chester G. Anderson (New York: Viking, 1968) pp. 240, 257–8.

10. *Eyeless in Gaza*, Perennial edition (New York: Harper & Row, 1974) pp. 6, 100, 98, and 250. Woolf's comment concerning shredded character appears in the 19 June 1923 entry in *A Writer's Diary*, ed. Leonard Woolf (New York: New American Library, 1968) p. 63.

11. *The Connecting Door*, p. 121.

12. *Free Fall*, p. 46; italics added.

13. Hallvard Dahlie, 'Brian Moore: an Interview', *Tamarack Review*, 46 (Winter 1968), 21 and *I Am Mary Dunne* (New York: Penguin, 1973) p. 27.

14. See especially, W. J. Harvey, *Character and the Novel* (Ithaca: Cornell University Press, 1965) and John Bayley, *The Characters of Love: a Study in the Literature of Personality* (New York: Basic Books, 1960).

15. See Susan Sontag, *Illness as Metaphor* (New York: Farrar, Straus & Giroux, 1978), which contains an excellent discussion of cancer as 'the' twentieth-century disease in literature as tuberculosis was 'the' nineteenth-century disease, with cancer 'now imagined to be the wages of repression' (p. 21).

16. *On Photography* (New York: Dell, 1977) pp. 22–3.

17. 'I Write Therefore I Am'. *Evergreen Review*, 33 (August–September 1964) 16.

18. 'Notes on an Unfinished Novel', in *Afterwords*, ed. Thomas McCormack (New York: Harper & Row, 1969) p. 169; hereafter abbreviated *NUN*. The notes, appearing first in *Harper's* in July 1968, have been reprinted several times, most recently in *The Novel Today: Contemporary Writers on Modern Fiction*, ed. Malcolm Bradbury (Manchester University Press, 1977) pp. 136–50.

19. 'NUN', p. 170; also see David Halpern, 'A Sort of Exile in Lyme Regis', *London Magazine*, 10 (March 1971), where Fowles comments: 'I don't like either of them [the films of *The Collector* and *The Magus*]. suppose *The Collector* was just passable. It ought to have been made as we originally intended to make it. That is, as a small cheap-budget, black-and-white movie. In fact, the man I would have liked to make it was the French director, Bresson. He would have done it marvellously. Unfortunately it got into the hands of Hollywood, and that was that. The second film, *The Magus*, was terrible. *Justine* and *The Magus* were the two worst films of the Sixties' (p. 44).

John Fowles letter to DLH, 18 December 1979.
Modes of Thought (New York, 1928) p. 228.
Passages: Predictable Crises of Adult Life (New York: Bantam, 1977) p. 29.
See William L. Reese, *Dictionary of Philosophy and Religion* (Atlantic Highlands, New Jersey: Humanities Press, 1980) p. 55.
The Aristos, Revised edition (New York: New American Library, 1970) p. 159.
The Trail to Tsankawi (Globe, Arizona: Southwest Parks and Monuments Association, n. d.) p. 1.
The Enigma of Stonehenge (New York: Summit Books, 1980) p. 51.
Twilight in Italy, Sea and Sardinia, Etruscan Places (New York: Viking, 1972) Part 3, p. 25.
'On Being English but Not British', *Texas Quarterly*, 7 (1964) 155, 158.
In *Islands* (London: Jonathan Cape, 1978), Fowles wrote: 'It is this aspect of islands that particularly interests me: how deeply they can haunt and form the personal as well as the public imaginaton. This power comes primarily, I believe from a vague yet immediate sense of identity. In terms of consciousness, and self-consciousness, every individual human *is* an island, in spite of Donne's famous preaching to the contrary. It is the boundedness of the smaller island, encompassable in a glance, walkable in one day, that relates it to the human body closer than any other geographical conformation of land' (p. 12). Fowles later remarks the 'I have always thought of my own novels as islands, or as islanded' (p. 30). Recently in *The Tree* (Boston: Little Brown, 1979), Fowles contrasted Essex gardens and Devonshire villages and woods, 'where all my secret yearnings were to be indulged beyond my wildest dreams. I happily forgot his [Fowles' father] little collection of crimped and cramped fruit trees in my own new world, my America of endless natural ones in Devon. I will come to what mine meant, and mean, to me, but I must first try to convey what I now suspect his meant to him; and why they did. As I grow older I see that the outwardly profound difference in our attitudes to nature — especially in the form of the tree — had a strange identity of purpose, a kind of joint root-system, an interlacing, a paradoxical pattern' (v3–v4). In *The Tree*, Fowles notes the originals of several scenes in *Daniel Martin:* the memories of apples (v1), the village in Devon (v14), the collecting of orchids (v34), and the personality and presence of the author (v50).

30. In *The Enigma of Stonehenge*, Fowles indirectly explains the import-
    ance of the door images in *Daniel Martin:* 'And Stonehenge is a
    ring not merely of doors, but of open doors. It invites entry, it
    does not rebuff the outsider, like the Pyramids and so many other
    monuments to an elite caste or an elite knowledge. In some way
    it it porous, fenestrated like a huge stone sponge, and I believe
    this has a great deal to do with its power over us. Aesthetically, it
    is its greatest attraction. The door ajar is the oldest trick in all art,
    from the folk-tale to the most avant-garde cinema, and especially
    when mystery and eventual treasure beckon through the gap'
    (p. 52).

31. *The Aristos*, p. 163; and *The Philosophy of Jean-Paul Sartre*, ed. Robert
    Denoon Cumming (New York: Random House, 1965) p. 277; also
    see pp. 271 and 272.

32. *The Aristos*, p. 205.

Index